THE POLITICS OF INTERNATIONAL AVIATION

The Politics of International Aviation

Eugene Sochor

MACMILLAN

First published 1991

Published by
MACMILLAN PRESS LTD
Houndmills, Basingstoke, Hampshire RG21 2XS
and London
Companies and representatives
throughout the world

Phototypeset by Input Typesetting Ltd, London

Printed in Great Britain by Billing & Sons Ltd, Worcester

British Library Cataloguing and Publication Data
Sochor, Eugene
The Politics of International Aviation.
1. Aeronautics, Commercial—Political Aspects—History
2. United Nations–Specialised Agencies–ICAO
I. Title
387.74
ISBN 0–333–51864–0

For Assad Kotaite and Yves Lambert
who piloted ICAO during
its most turbulent years

Contents

List of Abbreviations and Acronyms

ACC	Area Control Centre
ANC	Air Navigation Commission (ICAO)
ATC	Air Transport Committee (ICAO)
ATC	Air Traffic Control
ATS	Air Traffic Services
CAA	Civil Aviation Authority (UK)
CAB	Civil Aeronautics Board (US)
CEAC	Committee for European Airspace Coordination (NATO)
CIA	Central Intelligence Agency (US)
CRS	Computerised Reservation Systems
DOT	Department of Transport (in the US and the UK)
EC	European Communities (usually referred to as European Community)
EEC	European Economic Community
ECAC	European Civil Aviation Conference
ECOSOC	Economic and Social Council (UN)
EUROCONTROL	European Organisation for the Safety of Air Navigation
FAA	Federal Aviation Administration (US)
FANS	Future Air Navigation Systems
FIR	Flight Information Region
GATT	General Agreement on Tariffs and Trade
GLONASS	Global Orbiting Navigation Satellite System (USSR)
GPS	Global Positioning System (US)
IATA	International Air Transport Association
ICAO	International Civil Aviation Organisation
IFALPA	International Federation of Air Line Pilots' Associations
ILS	Instrument Landing System
INMARSAT	International Maritime Satellite Organisation
ITA	Institute of Air Transport (Paris)
KAL	Korean Air Lines (now Korean Air)

MLS	Microwave Landing System
NATO	North Atlantic Treaty Organisation
NOTAM	Notice to Airmen
OECD	Organisation for Economic Cooperation and Development
SAA	South African Airways
SARPs	Standards and Recommended Practices
UIC	Unlawful Interference Committee (ICAO)
UN	United Nations
UNDP	United Nations Development Programme
UNCTAD	United Nations Conference on Trade and Development
VOR/DME	VHF Omni Directional Radio Range/Distance Measuring Equipment

Acknowledgements

This book started as a journey into academia; the original flight plan was an outline for a doctoral thesis. Even before take-off, it became clear that this would not be a routine flight along well-travelled routes but more likely a pioneering flight without recourse to familiar maps and navigational aids.

One could not undertake such a solo flight without careful preparation and assistance. I am particularly grateful to all my former colleagues at ICAO who shared their expertise and experience. I cannot possibly thank all of them but want to name those who took the time to go over portions of the draft and provide thoughtful comments: Ronald Bickley, Vladimir Zubkov, J.R. Chesen, Duane Freer, Dr William Fromme, Paul Sheppard, Charles LaFond, and John Gunther who also guided me through the intricacies of GATT. I owe a special word of thanks to Dr Michael Milde, the Director of the Legal Bureau at ICAO and Director of the Institute of Air and Space Law at McGill University for his scholarly insights and encouragement. Richard Smithies was most helpful with his personal files. Several other persons have assisted me: David Kydd, Terry Denny and Dr R. R. Shaw at IATA, Ed Smart at IFALPA, N. Argyris and F. Sorensen of the EC Commission and Professor Yonah Alexander, Director of Studies on International Terrorism at the State University of New York. I am solely responsible for any errors and oversights and for the opinions and judgements expressed in this book which in no way can be attributed to ICAO or its Secretariat.

Parts of this book have appeared in various scholarly journals. I am grateful to the anonymous readers who reviewed the original articles and to the editors for their permission to rework them in this book. The journals are listed in the bibliography.

Assisting me beyond the call of duty at ICAO were Susan Beliveau; Jacqueline Tousignant in the Public Information Office; Mary Manzone in the Aviation Security Office and Mrs M.C. Tuduri de Miranda, Ghislaine Giroux and Jose D'Anna in the Library. Michael Ballantyne, the senior editor at Reader's Digest, was of invaluable help in reading and editing the complete manuscript with consummate skill and intelligence. Belinda Dutton handled the final stages of publication at Macmillan.

Last, but not least, I owe much to my wife Noreen, who came aboard this adventure as an innocent passenger, but once aloft, became a trusted co-pilot and resourceful mechanic.

A la première appréhension, le passé est cette masse de menus faits, les uns éclatants, les autres obscurs et indéfiniment répétés . . . mais cette masse ne constitue pas toute la réalité, toute l'épaisseur de l'histoire.

Fernand Braudel, *Ecrits sur l'Histoire*

(On the surface, the past is a mass of small events, some striking, others obscure . . . but this mass does not constitute the total reality, the total texture of history.)

Introduction

Half a century in human terms is but a brief episode. In the life of the International Civil Aviation Organisation (ICAO), this time span testifies to the stupendous growth of international aviation from the short-range DC–3 flying trans-border hops to the prospect of a hypersonic passenger aircraft flying around the world in just two hours.

Created in 1944 when delegates from 52 nations gathered in Chicago to sign the Convention on International Civil Aviation, ICAO has been responsible for the rules and regulations which made possible the orderly development of civil aviation. Air transport today encompasses some 16 000 airports linked into a gigantic cobweb of routes used by about 950 commercial carriers operating 12 billion flights every year.

It is a moot point whether ICAO's founders had a vision of this dense network of services. What matters is that they drafted a convention which still today governs all aspects of international air travel. They also gave ICAO an administrative structure unique among international agencies. The system which resulted from the Chicago Convention has served the world well in spite of the conflicting interests of states, armed conflicts, fuel crises, inflation and world recessions. No crystal ball, however, would have been large enough in 1944 to predict the political developments which shaped ICAO, such as rivalries between major aeronautical powers, the expectations of Third World countries, conflicting national interests in the current deregulated market and the scourge of hijackings and criminal attacks against passengers.

While ICAO's founding fathers did not conceive of commercial aviation as an area of international life much subject to the vagaries of international politics and regional conflicts, political issues have in fact encroached on its activities from the very first day the Organisation became a full-fledged member of the United Nations system. If ICAO was spared much of the acrimony that reverberated through the work and debates of the General Assembly and the Security Council, several confrontations and other incidents have nevertheless forced its governing body to deal with issues which often lay beyond the technical mandate and the competence of the Organisation.

In a broader context, political conflicts in aviation are inherent in an industry geared to sovereign states eager to show their flag around the world. In law, the inviolable principle of sovereignty confers a dubious sense of equality but in civil aviation it is primarily the economics of air transport which governs relations between countries.

Over the years, commercial aviation has had to serve the political and economic interests of states. But economics and politics themselves are interlinked with military and strategic considerations. The aircraft has also been part of the global defence posture of states. For the political scientist, international civil aviation is therefore a pertinent, yet a neglected field of inquiry. The development of international aviation has actively contributed to the trend toward 'interdependence' highlighted in various studies of the changing international system. In addition to being linked to important economic interests and other issue areas such as environment protection (that is, airport curfews and noise control) international civil aviation differs from other industries in that it is also closely linked to national security and military interests as well as to the sovereignty and prestige of almost all countries of the world.

To quote A.F. Lowenfeld: 'international aviation is not just another problem in a changing economic system, though it is that; international civil aviation is a serious problem in international relations, affecting the way governments view one another, the way individual citizens view their own and foreign countries, and in a variety of direct and indirect connections the security arrangements by which we live.'[1]

Civil aviation by its very nature made ICAO different from any other international agency. It was created in an atmosphere of political wrangling about its mandate and the echo of the debates at Chicago can still be heard today. The issues which were left unsettled at the time continue to influence the course of civil aviation.

Perhaps what distinguishes ICAO most from other technical agencies is that it incorporates two unrelated systems.[2] ICAO is part of the United Nations where international politics is played in a variety of relationship patterns of a universal nature. The Organisation is also the central element in a regulatory system in which transnational actors, that is the airlines, play a dominant role. The cleavage between the two systems is felt particularly by the Third World countries. Their putative political clout in the United Nations carries little weight in the other system dominated by the large aeronautical states.

Conflicts and cooperation are two sides of the same coin and must be studied together, the more so in an agency where conflicts between states appear to be technical in nature but are in fact part of broader political issues. Any illusion that ICAO could deal with these technical problems on their own merit was quickly dispelled when accidental shootdowns of civil aircraft and a growing number of brutal hijackings and criminal attacks against civil aviation came to dominate the agenda of the ICAO Council and its subordinate bodies.

Although ICAO has been in existence for more than four decades, the political aspects of its activities have received little attention.[3] Most of the literature on the Organisation has been written by economists and jurists who have emphasised their own concerns. Political scientists, to the extent that they have shown any interest in ICAO at all, have lumped it in with the other technical agencies of the United Nations system. This omission may be due to a large extent to the lack of readily available first-hand documentation and also to the perception that ICAO, like other 'functional' agencies regulating mail and communications, was insulated from politics and less worthy of attention.

Much of the material in this book is drawn from primary sources, mostly official documents and notes gathered in the course of my long association with ICAO and from interviews with those actively involved in the events under study. While some of the front-page events like the shootdowns of KAL Flight 007 and the Iranian Airbus or the Air India and Pan Am explosions have been well documented, there are nonetheless related political issues which have received less attention.

In this respect, while an insider has the advantage of being close to the scene and the players, he must also come to grips with the 'bewildering and indigestible amount of theoretical literature' to use John Garnett's apt description.[4] It would be easy enough to dismiss theoretical ruminations and let the facts speak for themselves. However, one cannot make sense of what goes on in the social world without resorting to an organising process. I have therefore relied on the literature to illuminate certain facts and clarify certain issues without attempting to fit the facts within a particular conceptual framework.

This book is not a general history of ICAO. It relates and analyses developments which have marked ICAO's evolution as a political body, focusing more on those aspects of its activities which have been overlooked and less on structural analyses which abound in the literature but contribute little to the understanding of an organisation. This writer agrees with Inis Claude that 'one can learn something about an automobile by studying the blueprints, and something more by peering under the hood and at its parts, but real understanding comes with checking its behavior in traffic.'[5]

The timing of this book has influenced the content and approach. I have kept in mind two important dates on the horizon. First 1992 which will see the final implementation of the single market in Europe with all that it entails for air transport. The other date is 1994 marking the 50th anniversary of the Chicago Convention – a propitious time to reflect on the changes in civil aviation and on the role of ICAO.

Chapter 1 places ICAO in its historical context. It points out how the international aviation system has evolved from the conflicting interests of aeronautical states. It also takes a fresh look at major issues to show that in spite of the critical assessment at the time, the Chicago Conference left a lasting legacy.

Chapter 2 analyses the technical and economic factors in the development of international aviation and looks at the constraints imposed on ICAO in providing lasting solutions to crowded airports and congested airways.

Chapter 3 is concerned with ICAO's role as a 'functional agency' in the United Nations context. It shows that ICAO's decision to join the UN system was itself a highly-loaded political decision which resulted in the Organisation taking positions not necessarily in accord with the requirements of air transport.

Chapter 4 focuses on the Organisation's decision-making mechanisms and the allocation of power in favour of large aeronautical states. It also examines the role and effective power of the decision-making bodies and policy makers.

Chapter 5 shows how the developing countries have been short-changed in a system dominated by large aeronautical powers and major airlines. As a result, multilateral aid to developing countries to modernise their fleets and aviation infrastructure have fallen short of expectations.

Chapter 6 analyses the links between civil and military aviation as they affect the use of airspace, security needs, the misuse of civil aircraft and the application of military technology in civil aviation.

These issues leave little doubt that we are still a long way from achieving close cooperation between civil and military authorities and a common strategy for a more rational use of the airspace.

Chapter 7 focuses on past and current conflicts in international aviation and assesses conflict management mechanisms to ensure the safety of international routes and continued operations of international flights in regions of the world torn by hostilities.

Chapter 8 is concerned with aerial intrusions and attacks against straying aircraft, more particularly with the destruction of KAL Flight 007 by Soviet fighters in 1983 and the 1988 attack on the Iranian Airbus by the US Navy. Debates in the ICAO Council on these and related issues show that a majority of states consider civil aviation as part of international politics with technical questions being inseparable from the political context.

Chapter 9 reviews ICAO's security programme in light of the long string of attacks against civil aviation. It analyses the problems of implementing international standards in a world of sovereign states in which each country is expected to enforce the rules.

Chapter 10 identifies the political problems of hijackings and terrorist attacks with respect to ICAO conventions. It assesses the shortcomings of legal instruments without enforcement mechanisms.

Chapter 11 deals with the changing aeropolitical map of Europe as the result of liberalisation policies in air transport, the congested airspace and the creation of the single market. These changes are analysed in respect of the political integration process, the organisation of civil aviation and the management of the airspace.

Chapter 12 analyses the dysfunctions in the international regulatory system brought about by conflicting policies and the strategies of airlines and new entrepreneurs in air transport. This chapter raises questions about reforms in the system and about the role of ICAO.

The final chapter projects a future course of action in international aviation based on the global nature of air transport and new forms of international cooperation that go beyond the traditional concepts of sovereignty.

1 The Chicago Conference Revisited: The Record and Legacy

It is our desire, as is it yours, to reconcile the greatest possible freedom of air commerce with a broad justice to all nations, large and small.

Prime Minister Churchill to President Roosevelt, 6 December 1944

THE HISTORICAL CONTEXT

In one sense the International Civil Aviation Conference which produced the Chicago Convention in 1944 had its origins in the first attempts at regulating international travel by air. If the need for some regulation became evident when the first balloons began crossing international frontiers in the second half of the last century, concerns became more pressing with the first heavier-than-air flights. The first diplomatic conference to draft a convention on air navigation was convened in Paris by the French Government in 1910. There were conflicting legal notions on the rights and privileges of flying. On the one hand, there were those who wanted complete freedom modelled on Hugo Grotius' *mare liberum* doctrine to be applied *ad coelum* to the entire airspace above a national territory while others wanted this freedom restricted. At Paris, the German and French delegations headed by lawyers, argued in favour of extensive freedom. The British, headed by an admiral, spoke out for complete state sovereignty. The first international conference which ran aground on this issue was to show that civil aviation could never be divorced from its political implications. The Paris Conference, however, was not a complete failure. At the centrepiece of the debate was a draft of a multilateral convention which identified many key terms, concepts and technical provisions that appear in subsequent international instruments.[1]

While jurists continued to debate theories of freedom of the air, the politicians acted to safeguard national sovereignty. The British Aerial Navigation Act, passed by Parliament in 1911 and amended in 1913, gave the Home Secretary full powers to regulate the entry

1

of foreign aircraft and to close its airspace. Thus, most of the
channel coast of Britain became a prohibited zone. France and
Germany and other European countries followed suit in the political
climate prior to World War I when military considerations were of
uppermost concern.

At the end of hostilities, when an extraordinary number of pioneering long-distance flights opened a new chapter in the history of
aviation, the Peace Conference assembled in the winter of 1918–19
faced two aviation problems. It had to decide what to do about
military and civil aviation in Germany and other defeated states as
well as how to regulate air transport. An aeronautical commission
composed of military and naval officers quickly agreed on the need
to demilitarise Germany in the air but faced initial disagreements
on what to do with German civil aviation. The least restrictive
American view prevailed and Germany was allowed to develop its
civil aviation, but only inside its own frontiers. On the broader
question of regulating international aviation, the Commission
drafted the so-called Paris Convention of 1919 which was adopted
by the Paris Conference. In its first article this convention proclaimed that each state has 'complete and exclusive sovereignty
over the airspace above its territory'. This has since become a
fundamental principle of international law in matters of civil aviation.

The Paris Convention had serious shortcomings which limited the
development of air transport in the period between the two wars.
It placed states which had been on the losing side in a permanent
condition of inequality and gave, in theory at least, control of
international aviation to the erstwhile victors. In any event, this
convention was destined to remain a regional accord without the
participation of the United States and Russia. While the United
States took an active part in drafting the document, the Senate in
its post war isolationist mood rejected it along with the rest of
President Woodrow Wilson's peace package.

For all its defects, however, the Paris Convention was a living
document which remained in effect until it was superseded by the
Chicago Convention of 1944. Its most noteworthy feature was a
permanent Paris-based International Commission on Air Navigation
(ICAN) with a full-time secretariat staff linked to the League of
Nations but which in practice acted as an independent body. On
the other side of the Atlantic, a pan-American convention was
signed in Havana in 1928 which was ultimately ratified by the US

and eleven Latin American countries. Unlike the Paris Convention, it anticipated the concept of 'freedom of the air' which the US was to advocate in Chicago. The two conventions governed air transport until the close of World War II.

Given the importance of aviation as an instrument of economic, military and foreign policy, it was not surprising that civil aviation developed under extensive government control through restrictive national regulations and the outright ownership or control of the airlines. The privately-owned US carriers were the only exception. Yet they too depended on the government for subsidies and political support. The heavy participation of governments in international aviation ushered in a period of intensive bilateral bargaining for air rights, including transit and stopovers, based on reciprocity and privileges which sometimes had nothing to do with aviation.[2] Transatlantic services provided a good illustration of the ways in which the governments operated. By 1935, the United States had the capacity, but not the right, to fly across the Atlantic. After long negotiations, Pan American received the right to land in Newfoundland and Bermuda, conditional on the simultaneous initiation of transatlantic operations by Imperial Airways.[3] Because of technical reasons, the British were unable to start such services until the summer of 1939. By then, Portugal had granted the United States and Britain landing rights in the Azores, but insisted that Lisbon be the first or last stop of any transatlantic flight using the Azores. The outbreak of the war put an abrupt end to this type of barter.

PREPARING THE GROUNDWORK

In the midst of the war, as they were elaborating their strategy for a world at peace, leaders on both sides of the Atlantic decided that aviation was to be an important element of post-war reconstruction. The notion of freedom of the air was seen by many politicians as part of the general pursuit of freedom and security. Vice-president Henry Wallace proposed nothing less than a network of globe-girdling airways and international airports under the control of the proposed United Nations. At the same time, Wendell Willkie, Roosevelt's rival for the presidency in 1940, proclaimed his own grandiloquent version of 'one world'. He saw the modern aircraft as creating a new geographical dimension and declared: 'the American people must grasp these new realities if they are to play their essential part in winning the war and building a world of peace and freedom.'[4]

Such fuzzy notions about the freedom of the air were easily debunked by hard-headed airline executives like Juan Trippe and by politicians like Clare Boothe Luce who in her maiden speech to Congress in February 1943 attacked Wallace's rhetoric as 'globaloney'. During the heated controversy that followed the speech, she soon felt obliged to retreat from her original position and expressed the hope that fair agreements might be signed with Britain and other nations to share foreign air services after the war. There were others, however, who looked at problems and needs in more practical terms. Edward Warner, the vice-chairman of the Civil Aeronautics Board, who was to become a leading figure in international aviation as the first Council President of ICAO, anticipated that air navigation agreements would henceforth be drawn which would take into account the needs of all countries to share in the benefits of civil aviation and that in planning air routes 'there shall be no return to the evil days when air transport was regarded with caution and suspicion'.[5]

Roosevelt's own policies for civil aviation were influenced by Adolf Berle, the one-time law professor who had been a dominant fixture in the Roosevelt entourage as a member of his 'Brain Trust'. Although appointed Assistant Secretary of State in 1938, his position only brought out the best in him when he became responsible for aviation in the State Department under Cordell Hull. In this assignment, he could formulate his ideas in the service of a grand purpose, doing for aviation what Grotius had done in the seventeenth century for the sea in his '*mare liberum*'. He set himself the task of preventing the world from building up air trading companies which, like the old seafaring British, Dutch and Portuguese trading companies, 'were fruitful sources of imperialist wars'.[6]

As Anthony Sampson has pointed out, from this viewpoint Berle was determined to confront both Trippe's Pan American empire and the British Empire. Yet he was too much of a realist to ignore the fundamental elements of a strong air policy. As he told Hull: 'aviation will have a greater influence on American foreign policy than any other non-political considerations.'[7] As early as 1943 Berle was worried that the British were way ahead in their postwar plan for aviation while 'the dunderheads' in the State Department were helpless. He persuaded Hull to set up an interdepartmental committee to plan US policies. This committee in its initial report (in April

1943) called for the start of negotiations towards an international agreement on technical matters and rates and it recommended apportioning US foreign operations among several carriers, in effect clipping the wings of Pan American.

With Roosevelt and Churchill due to meet in Quebec in August 1943, Berle sent a memorandum to Hull suggesting that if a proposal for an international conference came up, the United States should express interest and leave open the question as to whether negotiations on the post war commercial rights should be held bilaterally between the US and Great Britain or in wider context involving the Dominions and other allied nations. Until then, Berle pointedly suggested that both countries should renounce 'their policy of competitive grab', which, he noted, suited British interests because they were probably in a better position to obtain exclusive rights throughout Africa, the Commonwealth and Europe.[8]

Since the main purpose of the first Quebec summit meeting was to prepare for Overlord, the cross-channel invasion, and to discuss other pressing military matters and since no records were kept of private conversations, it is not clear to what extent Churchill and Roosevelt discussed postwar aviation matters. According to Berle, the President told a group of advisers that he had considered the need for a United Nations conference on aviation and probably a United Nations organisation to handle such matters as safety standards and other technical matters as well as economic problems such as competitive subsidies and rates.[9] Thus, even as it was first proposed, the Chicago Conference contained the seeds of future discord.

Before going home, Churchill confirmed his intention to hold a preliminary Commonwealth meeting on aviation matters. He also took note of Roosevelt's views that air transport should be in private ownership, that key points should be available for international use on a reciprocal basis, that there should be no cabotage (foreign carriage of domestic traffic) and finally that government support might be necessary for non-profitable international routes.[10] Interestingly, these early proposals survived practically intact in the bilateral regime which evolved from the Chicago Conference.

In preparation for the forthcoming conference, the United States had also opened bilateral discussions with the Dominions, as well as with the Chinese and the Soviet Union. Before leaving for London, Berle had called in Andrei Gromyko, the Soviet Ambassador, who reported back two weeks later that Moscow was indeed interested and that the Soviet Government would be glad to start conversations with the United States in respect to postwar civil aviation.[11]

As in other matters, the wartime leaders expected that cooperation with the Soviet Union would extend to postwar aviation. When the Soviets in 1944 put forward a proposal for an international air force, Churchill regarded the prospect as 'an event of the utmost importance'.[12] But the Soviets had other ideas about international civil aviation and made it clear to Berle that they must carry all traffic inside their country, in their own aircraft, with their own pilots, connecting up with foreign planes at fixed points. Berle was not unduly concerned about what amounted to a 'closed Soviet system' for 'as long as all the other countries got together, it would be possible to make a reasonably satisfactory world aviation system with the Soviet Union left out', he wrote in his diary.[13]

Meanwhile the British were trying hard to shape a common front at the Dominion and Empire Conference held under Lord Beaverbrook's chairmanship in October 1943 but sharp differences emerged when the participants failed to agree on granting reciprocal rights. In May of 1944, the Dominion ministers met again in Montreal to determine which routes needed to be protected and under what conditions they would be operated. Shortly after, Britain made known its plans in a White Paper without consulting the United States. This publication came as a surprise because it called for an international regulatory body with broad powers to decide on such matters as routes, frequencies and fares.[14] Nothing was said about the way this agency would function and make decisions, an omission which caused uneasiness in the British press. The plan was obviously unacceptable to Washington.

It was clear by then that the Chicago Conference was shaping up as a classic power struggle. The United States was capitalising on its overwhelming position as the leading aircraft producer to secure for itself a near monopoly on long-haul traffic. The British in the meantime had been encouraged to build only fighter bombers, leaving them dependent on the Americans for their transport planes once the war was over. Britain's extensive overseas connecting points in the colonies and the Commonwealth gave it the only edge over the US whose main weakness was the need for landing bases strategically located along trunk routes. As the leading aviation publication put it at the time: 'never before in history has a nation manoeuvred itself into a position of such overwhelming advantage for the propagation of its overseas trade'.[15]

THE CHICAGO CONFERENCE IN ACTION

On 1 November 1944 – after Bretton Woods but before San Francisco – representatives of fifty-four states were convened in Chicago by the US Government to discuss 'the principle to be followed in setting up a permanent international aeronautical body and a multilateral convention dealing with the field of air transport, air navigation and aviation technical subjects'. In the expectation that agreement would be difficult to achieve, the United States had scheduled the conference after the 1944 presidential elections when it would have greater freedom of action. Invitations were restricted to the 'United Nations' meaning the countries allied or associated in the war effort and the neutral states. Enemy states and their sympathisers were specifically excluded. Thus Argentina was left out, while strangely enough Franco's Spain made it and so did the Irish Republic which had not participated in the Dominion meetings because of its alleged pro-German sympathies.

Of the fifty-five countries invited, only Saudi Arabia declined to come. The Soviet position has remained a mystery. While it accepted the invitation in principle and actually sent a delegation to the Conference, Soviet authorities must have had second thoughts and left their seat vacant. Two days before the official opening, the news agency TASS issued a statement declaring that in view of the presence in Chicago of 'countries like Switzerland, Portugal and Spain which for many years have conducted a pro-Fascist policy hostile to the Soviet Union, representatives of the Soviet Union will not take part in this Conference'. Ambassador Andrei Gromyko officially notified Washington of the Soviet position and said he had nothing to add to his instructions.[16] The absence of Soviet representatives led to various interpretations. They would have been under pressure to grant overflight rights which they were not about to concede or perhaps they were not in a bargaining mood. Thus, as one scholar put it, 'the conference opened with all persons present conscious of the fact that any achievements were predestined to have a political shadow cast upon them'.[17]

The opening message from Roosevelt, as read by Berle and most probably drafted by him, was an eloquent call to open up the sky for world travel and an admonition 'not to dally with the thought of creating great blocs of closed air, thereby tracing in the sky the conditions of future war. Let us rather', Roosevelt said, 'work together in order that the skies of the world can be exploited by man for all mankind'. Berle, who was elected chairman of the Conference, outlined the American position as head of the US delegation that 'nations have a natural right to communicate and trade with each other in times of peace and friendly nations do not have a right to burden or prevent this intercourse by discriminatory measures'.[18]

The prevailing mood at the opening session was one of uncertainty. Several delegations representing countries still under German occupation had more immediate concerns than postwar travel. Most delegates used to tight government control over air transport simply did not know what to make of the American plan. American leaders may have considered their requests for fewer restrictions on civil aviation as morally justified but the details tended to obscure the basic points of contention. US commercial aviation, if granted complete access to all areas without discrimination, would dominate postwar civil aviation, driving British carriers out of routes they had previously had or wanted. Even the usually pro-American *Economist* of London had some bitter words for the US position: 'This would seem to be another instance in which the fine moral principles proclaimed in Washington turn out to have very special definitions, tailored to self interest'.[19]

As the conference opened, participants found on their tables the texts of draft conventions submitted by Australia and New Zealand jointly, Canada, Great Britain and the United States. The American proposal for unrestricted rights with market forces determining frequencies and rates attracted few supporters. Britain's proposal to have a world regulatory body distribute routes and determine frequencies fared no better because no other government was willing to surrender its sovereignty to an organisation likely to be controlled by the major powers. In a move designed to show its bargaining strength, Britain publicised the possibility of developing an all-Commonwealth airline to be called the 'All-Red' line, the colour designation deriving from the cartographic practice of showing Britain, the Commonwealth and British territories in red on the map. The 'All-Red' line would fly round the world, landing only on British-controlled territories to which it would have exclusive rights.

This far-fetched proposal never materialised, but it served to underscore Britain's strength in landing rights.[20]

Australia and New Zealand proposed an even more radical concept; international ownership and management of all long-range international services. This idea was also rejected. Canada offered a compromise between the American and British positions, calling for some competition on limited operations and a multilateral body to allocate routes, review rates and determine additional frequencies. The Canadians also proposed a list of principles which would define air traffic arrangements between nations. These principles termed 'freedoms' defined important new principles of air law and underscored much of the debate on the extent nations should apply limitations to international operations. Basically, the first two freedoms covered the right of innocent transit and technical stops for refuelling, while the third and fourth freedoms were commercial agreements to carry traffic to and from another country. The fifth freedom, by far the most controversial, would allow for the pickup and discharge of traffic between two points or to points beyond and thus necessarily involved the rights of third parties.

The four draft proposals were referred to Committee I, leaving the other three committees to deal with less controversial technical matters, provisional routes and the creation of an Interim Council. While the delegates in the technical committees were helped by precedents set in previous conventions, this was not the case for the first Committee which soon became the focus of attention. Behind the rhetoric much of the Chicago Conference turned on the question of whether nations would allow each other some or all of the 'freedoms'. As the discussions proceeded, the British agreed in principle to collaborate and exchange landing rights as far as possible. Conscious of their own shortage of aircraft and anxious to protect their own industry, they came out for a system of quotas to prevent the American airlines from flooding their routes and argued for an 'escalation' formula to regulate flights according to the numbers of passengers. The Americans would not accept it.

Midway through the conference, as the technical committees were completing their work, it seemed hopelessly deadlocked on economic issues. In his diary on 18 November, Berle jotted down the basic American position of what he called his 'open sky' charter. There should be no quotas or limitations leading to cartels or national combinations but instead freedom of shippers and passengers to choose the airlines they wished. The international authority should be restricted to setting the rules of the air with enforcement left to individual states.[21]

Berle, however, was unable to understand clearly what the British position was at this point. He was now more than ever convinced that Lord Swinton who had replaced Lord Beaverbrook as the chief British negotiator in aviation matters, was 'ill-prepared' and inflexible and could make no changes in his instructions. He believed that the other European delegates were in despair about it 'while publicly the relations were on a basis of complete and almost exaggerated courtesy and cooperation'.[22] At one point, Berle thought he had reached an agreement with Swinton only to find out that the British, while retreating on the question of 'escalation', remained adamant on their position on fifth freedom rights so as to restrict American operations in Europe.[23]

Berle, who believed that the switch was done on orders from London, appealed to Roosevelt for support. The President sent a cable to Churchill stating that limitations of fifth-freedom rights would be tantamount to 'a form of strangulation' and 'violated a cardinal principle in American policy throughout that the ultimate judge should be the passenger and the shippers'.[24] Churchill replied that Britain would stand by what Swinton had already agreed but would not yield further.[25] The impasse led the two parties to turn up the pressure at the highest level. The ensuing exchange of correspondence between Churchill and Roosevelt on the technicalities of air transport might seem surprising in view of the still difficult military situation, were it not that both leaders were fully aware of what was at stake in Chicago.

Churchill's stubbornness placed Roosevelt's advisers in a predicament. A message was prepared for the President's signature but it was not sent because it was felt that it was too technical for the usual President–Prime Minister messages. Instead Ambassador John G. Winant was instructed to inform Churchill that the US went as far as it could in reaching a satisfactory agreement and to let the naked threat of a termination of a lend-lease agreement end the discussion.[26]

Churchill's response on 28 November was a measured outline of the British position. A tentative agreement had been reached in Chicago between Berle and Swinton, Churchill wrote, 'but your side of the table put forward an entirely new set of ideas and arguments which, in our judgment, took away with one hand what had been given with the other.' Unless complete agreement could be reached, Churchill suggested a temporary adjournment. He had hoped that the lend-lease issue would not be raised but he would not take a decision contrary to British interests.[27]

Meanwhile Canada, Britain and the United States could not find a common ground between the divergent views. Mumblings of discontent with the slow progress of the conference and the exclusion of other countries from the closed discussions were getting louder. Berle found it necessary on several occasions to reassure participants that all interests were being considered and that all would have an equal voice in the final resolution. There was no way to avoid a general debate in plenary on the unresolved issues. In the tensest debate of the conference, Swinton urged the necessity of protecting small nations from competition while Berle reiterated the United States position on competition without cartels or limitations except on setting rates.[28]

As other countries entered the fray some, like the South American bloc, supported the US position. Other countries were unhappy with the British restrictions, but were nevertheless not prepared to support the United States. Canada in the meantime was still working on a compromise. Swinton then asked Berle to join him in a motion to send the unsettled issues to the proposed Interim Council for further study. Berle agreed, since at this point he felt that 'the game was over' in view of Churchill's reply of 28 November. But Roosevelt, at Berle's instigation, was still keeping up the pressure. 'The smaller states have spoken and, if I may say so, our position seemed to have by far the greatest support', he told Churchill. If the conference failed, the reason would be all too clear. Roosevelt then made a last plea for a compromise based on the Canadian formula.[29] That same day, 30 November, the *Chicago Daily News* headlined: 'Parley to End with Air Pact Row Unresolved'. It expected that the conference would rush to a unsatisfactory conclusion within two or three days. On the following day, the newspaper followed up by calling the conference 'a complete flop'. London newspapers were just as pessimistic: *The Times* under a headline 'Conference a Failure' referred to an offer by Berle to supply thousands of surplus war planes to other countries and accused the US of using 'a big stick' in an attempt to force acceptance of its position.[30]

The custodians of power in Washington and London had great difficulty keeping up with the situation in Chicago. By the time

Churchill had communicated with Swinton to examine the prospects of an agreement based on the Canadian plan, he was told that the conference had already decided to approve all the technical decisions and to refer the unfinished business to the Interim Council.[31] The game was not yet over. Swinton's motion, which Berle seconded, was deferred on a motion from the floor as the conference apparently still felt that an overall agreement could be reached. Berle who wanted to salvage as much as possible convinced Roosevelt to send one more message to Churchill urging a final agreement.[32]

It was finally the Netherlands which broke the deadlock at the 1 December plenary after Swinton suggested that the British might join in an agreement on the first two freedoms. The Netherlands immediately moved to guarantee the right of transit and technical stop-over as part of a multilateral agreement. The session adjourned on this hopeful note. The following day, the British stated that they were prepared to accept the proposal on the two freedoms, much to the surprise of Berle 'because Swinton had steadily and bitterly opposed any such agreement throughout the Conference'.[33] The other freedoms were to become part of a separate agreement for those countries wishing to exchange them on a reciprocal basis.

The conference moved to a close with a decisive evening plenary on 5 December during which the delegates gave final approval to a flood of key decisions.[34] On 7 December at 12.02 p.m., after five weeks of hectic deliberations, Berle pounded his gavel for the last time and the International Civil Aviation Conference adjourned. He wrote in his diary: 'it took two hundred years of squabbling and several major wars to get this result on the sea.'[35]

Berle reported to the President that as far as US interests were concerned, the combination of bilateral agreements and the general acceptance of the rights of transit and technical stops had vastly enlarged the possibilities available to American carriers. The full benefits would have to await the negotiations on commercial rights. On the international side, 'great issues of air transport had been faced and met with an international organisation capable of administering the agreements'. This is more than had been expected when the US entered the negotiations.[36]

The conference produced six important documents, five of which still govern the way air transport operates today. On that score alone, the conference was a success. The first and foremost document is the Convention on International Civil Aviation, or Chicago

Convention, which spells out the rights and obligations of states in international aviation. The convention came into force on 4 April 1947 after it was ratified by 26 states. An Interim Agreement on International Civil Aviation established the framework of the new international agency. A provisional International Civil Aviation Organisation (PICAO) was created and functioned remarkably well until the permanent agency came into being in 1947. In the absence of a multilateral agreement on air rights the first two freedoms were adopted as part of an international agreement acceptable to all participants. They remain in force today as the International Air Services Transit Agreement which has been ratified by some 100 countries. The so-called 'five freedoms' or International Air Transport Agreement was also opened for signature. Eventually, 19 states came to accept the granting of full reciprocal rights but nine, including the United States, subsequently denounced it so that this agreement never gained acceptance. Finally, a standard form of Bilateral Agreement for the Exchange of Routes and Services was adopted as part of the Final Act. The text proved to be of great help in drafting future bilateral agreements.

Perhaps those who had the most to gain from the outcome were the airline executives who attended the conference as government delegates or advisers. They quickly foresaw that failure to resolve the issues of fares would give a vastly expanding role to their trade association. So eager were they to fill the regulatory vacuum that they were told to wait until the end of the conference to meet lest it would appear that their gathering was associated with the intergovernmental sessions.[37] The airlines executives met in Chicago on 6 December and within a week launched a new International Air Transport Association and convened a meeting of airlines in Havana in April 1945.

Although all the attention in Chicago was focused on economic matters, it was in the technical field that the conference achieved the most immediate impact. The subcommittee on technical standards and procedures prepared drafts for twelve technical annexes to the Convention to serve as a guide pending the coming into force of the Convention and their formal adoption by the Council of ICAO.

The fact that the conference was unable to come up with a multilateral answer to economic issues and left these for bilateral negotiations was viewed by some as proof of failure. Most participants, however, accepted the documents as an interim solution pending renewed efforts to reach an overall agreement.

Reflecting on the events, Churchill admitted to Roosevelt that the aviation discussions were 'perhaps premature' and that both might have been spared 'too heavy a burden on our minds at a time when so many anxieties of war weigh down upon us'. As for the agreement reached, 'we are not satisfied', he wrote, 'that the projects which have succeeded one another in such profusion during intricate discussions at Chicago represent the final contribution of human ingenuity towards a solution'.[38]

Given the circumstances of 1944, it is difficult to imagine how the Chicago Conference could have produced any other outcome than to secure air travel through a flexible system combining bilateral and multilateral features. As R.L. Thornton sees it, 'the important lesson to be learned from the conference, in a tactical, bilateral sense, was the extreme importance of controlling the access to markets. No strength in technical matters, no amount of operating know-how or superiority in quality can overcome an inability to reach the market. Thus, so long as Britain controlled one end of such a large number of international journeys, the United States operating strength was sharply constrained'.[39] As for other countries, they would not likely have entered into multilateral arrangements unless the resulting situation was more satisfactory than the bilateral alternative.

Looking back, one may well question the US commitment to an 'open sky' policy since it is hard to recognise any such idealistic stand in the bilateral bargaining which followed the conference. There was bound to be scepticism about the aims pursued by the US based on a continuing commanding lead. For all practical purposes, the US abandoned its 'open sky' policy when it renounced the International Air Transport Agreement in 1946 rather than face the prospects of granting fifth freedom rights to foreign carriers at the expense of its own airlines. As one author put it: 'by renouncing its dream of an open sky, the US has had to adjust to the fact that there could be no stable commercial activity without some kind of reciprocity'.[40]

For all their rivalries, the two major players at Chicago had more in common than they suspected at the time. They could only assume that the political map would remain the same and that the same colonial powers would continue to control the valuable landing rights in Africa and Asia. The Chicago Convention was shaped to meet the needs and interests of the major aeronautical powers as perceived at the time. To the extent that the Convention was based on the principle of complete and exclusive sovereignty of states, it could be argued that it could accommodate the needs of the newly-independent states but this sovereignty proved of little help in their bilateral dealings with the major players. The Chicago Conference left the door open for future talks on a multilateral system, but after ten years of futile efforts, the multilateral option was definitely buried.

Even before the conference was over and it became doubtful that full agreement could be reached on a multilateral system, the United States entered into preliminary discussions with a number of countries, including Portugal, Spain, Belgium, Iceland, Greece, Turkey, Sweden, Czechoslovakia, Poland, Lebanon, Iraq and Canada. By early 1945, Washington had reached an agreement with Eire for the precious stopping place at Shannon. Churchill, who was still harbouring resentment at the Irish, expressed his astonishment to Roosevelt only to be told that this was 'a postwar matter' and that bilaterals were the direct result of the failure of the Chicago Conference to reach a global settlement.[41]

By far the most important bilateral agreement was signed with Britain. This so-called Bermuda Agreement of 1946 between the two major powers was to serve as the model for all future bilateral air treaties. Unfortunately, Britain had to bargain from a position of weakness since it was at the same time negotiating to obtain a $3.75 billion loan from Washington. The most important feature in the Bermuda Agreement was the formula of granting reciprocal rights to designated carriers with capacity and frequency levels left to the operators subject to vague guidelines and review by the governments. The US was able to obtain from bilateral agreements what it had expected from a multilateral system, giving little in return because its partners were not ready to take advantage of reciprocal rights.

The lasting significance of the Chicago Conference goes well beyond the bilateral tugs of war. It resulted in a regulatory triangle comprising the technical, legal and operational functions of the inter-governmental International Civil Aviation Organisation, a bilateral regime for the exchange of commercial rights and routes and a multilateral mechanism which allowed airlines to set their own rates subject to government approval. By 1947 the post-war aviation system based on the general principles proclaimed in

Chicago was firmly in place. Over a hundred bilateral agreements had been signed and the IATA tariff-setting mechanism was officially recognised, first in the Bermuda accord and in the other agreements which followed in quick succession.

THE CONFERENCE LEGACY

As indicated previously, attempts to find multilateral arrangements for the transport of passengers and cargo proved futile since states viewed commercial rights as too valuable to be exchanged any other way than through bilateral negotiations. The multilateral approach could not meld the widely different policies towards regulation and competition among airlines. It also aroused the fears of some countries that their national traffic would be dominated by powerful foreign carriers moving in and out of international markets without having to make substantial investments or commitments.

Bilateral regulation stems from the sovereignty principle enshrined in Article 1 of the Chicago Convention under which authorisation must be sought to operate flights over or into the territory of another state. This regime in air transport is in sharp contrast with most other forms of international economic activity. Bilateral agreements regulate market access and routes, the number of seats and the frequency of flights and tariffs. In practice, bilateral negotiators seek a balance of economic opportunities or benefits which means that competition may be limited in terms of market entry (traffic rights and designation), supply (the provision of capacity) and pricing (tariffs). As William O'Connor observes, the most important feature of bilateralism is what the US Government calls 'an equitable exchange of economic benefits' which is a polite way of saying 'horse trading'.[42]

After the Chicago Conference, the states with well-established aviation industries and those enjoying an advantage in terms of major traffic sought to maximise the benefits for their carriers. They succeeded in negotiating agreements that incorporated relatively liberal provisions on traffic rights, designation and capacity. By and large, however, the early era in post-war international aviation was one in which air services were closely regulated and controlled. In one important respect, that is tariff establishment, states in their bilateral agreements have traditionally delegated a large measure of responsibility to the carriers, primarily through the IATA tariff conferences.

There were intermittent attempts within ICAO to question IATA's role in setting tariffs but no serious effort was made until 1957. The Council of ICAO then included the subject of air transport rates in its work programme for 1957–59 to be carried out 'as resources permitted'.[43] However, this item was dropped by the Council. The question came up again in 1963 before the Air Transport Committee under the modest title: 'The possibility and desirability of action by ICAO in the field of airline tariffs'. According to one author 'at the outset the possibility and desirability of even a discussion on the issue itself appeared to be so enigmatic to some members that they pleaded for closed discussion'.[44]

The opponents repeatedly argued that ICAO stay clear of tariffs because these matters were competently handled by the airlines. Some argued that ICAO's intervention would undermine the harmony between the Organisation and IATA and that by taking over IATA's tasks, ICAO would discharge governments from their responsibility, something that could not be done without amending the Chicago Convention.[45]

A minority thought that the IATA system was at fault because as one member explained: 'the so-called participation of and supervision by states in the system was illusory and elusive'. Some members felt that ICAO's intervention would strengthen the enforcement of tariffs and that ICAO's refusal to recognise the problem was a 'self-delusion'. The Air Transport Committee wound up the debate in less than six hours and concluded by a vote of 16 to 8 that 'at present, there is no justification for ICAO to undertake specific studies and other economic work on the subject of airline tariffs'.[46]

The official policy of ICAO is still that 'multilateralism in commercial rights to the greatest possible extent continues to be an objective of the Organisation' although this policy is no longer debated and the relevant Assembly resolutions hardly ever cited.[47] In its advisory role, ICAO seeks to harmonise policies on a wide range of issues and provides guidance material to states to help them in their bilateral negotiations. It has, for instance, drafted model clauses for bilateral agreements and has provided guidance for states in their regulation of non-scheduled services. In recent years, ICAO has offered a forum through the Air Transport Conference to permit a worldwide examination of important issues, a task which is possible only to a limited extent in ICAO's triennial assemblies. The three air transport conferences held so far considered a number of recommendations to states and the ICAO Council. It cannot be said, however, that the Organisation is involved in these economic issues in a substantive way.[48]

On the other hand, the wide range of trade activities combined with the fare-setting conferences have long given IATA a dominant voice in economic matters. IATA holds a privileged position within ICAO because it is able to participate and table documents in all committees and panels. The same status is not reciprocated since ICAO participates in only a few of the IATA forums.[49]

As the result of deregulation policies, IATA has undergone such drastic changes, that it is difficult to imagine the power ascribed to it when the association was branded 'a strong and effective cartel . . . to mutually control conditions of sale and minimise competition in their business'.[50] For Besty Gidwitz IATA could only have been 'an imperfect cartel' since scheduled services were regulated by bilateral agreements and tariff conferences were open to all scheduled airlines whose governments were members of ICAO.[51]

IATA officials have always maintained that tariff conferences account for a small part of the association's activities and that no government has ever advocated doing away with tariff 'coordination' and other cooperative practices to pro-rate tariffs, facilitate interlining of passengers and cargo and standardise airline documentation and procedures. These arrangements were justified by the industry and are accepted by most governments as necessary for the integration of the worldwide network of services. Thus in the years following the Chicago Conference, an extensive pattern of cooperation between airlines was superimposed upon the regulatory framework, usually in preference to a more competitive environment. This cooperative approach sanctioned by most governments provided a structured and predictable environment for the development of their international aviation links. It also made possible a reasonably stable period of growth and expansion of the international air transport system in the 1950s and 1960s despite the strains on the industry such as the competition from charter carriers and periodic cycles of overcapacity.[52]

Beginning in the 1970s, but increasingly in the 1980s, the regulatory environment experienced significant changes and adjustments as the result of the vast expansion of the leisure market. The basic framework of bilateralism has not been an issue to any great extent.

Instead, national regulatory policies have been re-evaluated. In the aftermath, airline arrangements and practices have become a matter of public debate. The effects of deregulation policies have been most noticeable in IATA which went through a complete reorganisation and made participation in tariff conferences optional. The association has even dropped its tariff enforcement programme. According to one writer, 'tariff coordination still exists but it provides more an opportunity for carriers to meet than to set fares that actually will be charged in the market place'.[53]

After all these years, the Chicago Convention remains a remarkable and relevant document. Continual changes in the regulatory environment have not altered that fact. The general principles have never been called in doubt even if states are not always too scrupulous about their applications. First, it is the law of the state over which an aircraft is flown which regulates the admission and departure from its territory and such matters as clearance, sanitation, customs, air traffic and air navigation services. States also ensure that their regulations are in conformity with international provisions. The second principle applies to non-discrimination with respect to overflights, rules of the air, the use of airports and services and the imposition of taxes. Finally, states are bound to seek the highest practicable degree of uniformity in the rules and regulations relating to personnel, airways and services.

To avoid legal hassles, the drafters of the Chicago Convention kept definitions to a minimum. One such definition found wanting is that of 'state aircraft' used for military, customs or police tasks which are specifically excluded from the Convention. As will be shown in Chapter 6, there have been instances in which such aircraft were fired upon while carrying civil passengers. The broad definition in the final Article 96 of the Convention of such terms as 'air service' and 'airline' were bound to cause problems. The difficulty of defining various types of air services caused endless debates beginning in the Second ICAO Assembly in 1948 and later on in the Air Transport Conferences as the result of the vastly-expanding use of charters in air travel.

On the whole, the Convention was flexible enough so as to permit ICAO to undertake activities not specifically foreseen in Chicago. One such field not expressly mandated is the vast body of legal work, in particular the codification and development of international air law, leading to the adoption of fourteen international instruments in the form of conventions and protocols.

The drafters of the Chicago Convention avoided legal questions such as compensation and liability which remain among the most contentious issues in the codification of air law. These questions come under the Warsaw Convention which sets limits for death or personal injury. When drafted in 1929, this Convention was aimed at protecting fledgeling airlines from the possibility that suits filed after a single crash could put them out of business. The damage limit was initially set at $8300. To make claims more uniform and stable, gold was used as the common standard based on the value of the French franc.

Over the years, ICAO has spent much time trying to find a common ground among the divergent interests, the more so after the US threatened to pull out of the Warsaw Convention if limits were not increased. Judging by the various protocols which have been adopted to revise the Warsaw Convention limits, it has never been an easy task to evaluate the cost of a human life. The opponents were the Third World countries which insisted that liability on international flights should not follow the trend set by US courts for internal flights. They argued that their carriers could be wiped out if saddled with intolerable insurance costs. A first compromise arrived at in the Hague in 1955 was never ratified by the US Senate. As a result the world's major airlines in what is known as the Montreal Agreement voluntarily increased liability limits to $74 000 per person on flights travelling to, from or through the United States.

The most recent attempt to increase liability even further resulted in the Montreal Protocols of 1975 (not to be confused with the Montreal Agreement) which would increase the liability ceiling to around $320 000 regardless of fault. Liability limits would be expressed in terms of the special drawing rights of the International Monetary Fund instead of the long-abandoned French gold franc. Nonetheless, the Montreal Protocols lost in the US Senate in 1983 leaving a liability muddle which has yet to be sorted out.

In spite of the omissions and loopholes, or perhaps because of them, the drafting of the Chicago Convention showed farsighted imagination. The Convention has survived as its drafters intended with only a few substantive amendments. The very first amendment was also the first political test for the new Organisation. When adopted by the First ICAO Assembly in 1947, it embodied a new provision to expel a member state.[54] This was followed by a series of amendments of an administrative nature as to the frequency of

Assembly meetings and the composition of the Council and Air Navigation Commission. The only important amendment (Article 83 *bis*) reflecting the changing economic environment was adopted in 1980 to recognise legal problems posed by the use of lease, charter or interchange of aircraft. The latest substantive amendment is the new Article 3 *bis*, adopted at the 25th session of the ICAO Assembly in 1984, banning the use of weapons against civil aircraft. (Neither amendment has yet come into force.)

The Chicago Convention has passed the test of time. In the words of the director of ICAO's Legal Bureau, 'all its provisions have proved capable of providing a suitable legal framework for the accomplishments of the main aims and objectives of ICAO to promote the development of all aspects of international aviation'.[55] One notable exception is the settlement of disputes by the Council. The half-hearted efforts of states to use the judicial process as provided by the Convention have placed a heavy political burden on the Organisation.[56]

The international system which evolved from the Chicago Convention has remained in place through years of economic turbulence, not to mention political stresses. The major challenges, however, lie ahead as the system faces a completely new environment brought about by the globalisation of the industry.

2 From the DC-3 to Hypersonic Flight: The Changing Environment

The progress of technology is not a natural process, like the growth of a tree. It is not automatic. Air transport makes technical progress only because man or a group of men does something.

Edward Warner, *Technical Development and its Effect on Air Transportation* (1938)

As civil aviation is poised to enter the twenty-first century, it will choke on its own success unless it can develop innovative approaches to increasingly complex problems that evolve more quickly than the body politic can absorb. These problems concern technological developments, consumer demands, constraints on the infrastructure, and deregulation policies that have buffeted the industry. The challenges are not new and apply to other industries as well in the global market, but they affect airlines on an unprecedented scale. These challenges are forcing both the international airlines and their governments to rethink such fundamental issues as their role in controlling a traditionally well-protected industry. The effects of these developments on the international system are still far from clear, but they are felt by all those who have a part in managing the system: governments, airlines, and their international counterparts, the International Civil Aviation Organisation (ICAO) and the International Air Transport Association (IATA).

TECHNOLOGICAL DEVELOPMENTS

The international carriage of passengers and cargo by air is a complicated procedure based on a complex technology which requires the cooperation and goodwill of all nations. Since ICAO came into existence in 1944, the number of passengers carried on the world scheduled airlines has increased more than a hundredfold – from nine million to over one billion in 1989. Looked at in another way, the number of passengers carried on scheduled domestic and international routes in a single year represents more than the combined populations of North and South America. Air freight which did not exist 45 years ago has become an essential component of world trade.

From the start, ICAO's major task has been to set the basic international standards contained in the 18 annexes to the Chicago Convention. These regulations have been constantly updated to meet successive generations of aircraft and advances in technology as they affect flight operations, airworthiness, rules of the air, the transport of dangerous goods, personnel licensing, airports, aeronautical communications and environmental protection. In their foresight, the drafters of the Convention provided that these rules be separated from the body of the Convention so that they could be adopted by the Council and come into effect without a cumbersome ratification process. By contrast, amendments to the Convention must be adopted by a two-thirds vote of the Assembly and must be ratified by no less than two-thirds of all contracting states.

Another key to the growth of civil aviation is the vast work undertaken under the regional plans which list the services and facilities in the nine regions of ICAO. To give an idea of this undertaking, more than 60 000 such services have been listed, these being the nuts and bolts of the global infrastructure.[1]

ICAO's heyday of regulatory activity was the first decade of its existence when the Organisation adopted more annexe material than in the following 35 years. The first and foremost priority was the assignment of responsibilities for the provision of services and facilities for international civil aviation within each portion of the global airspace. Such formal allocations, encompassing all recognised international air routes, caused occasional problems in the domestic portions of the airspace. In many cases, there were also sensitive and complex issues involving portions of the international airspace over the high seas.

One of ICAO's most ambitious accomplishments was the establishment of weather stations and rescue teams in the North Atlantic financed jointly by the airlines using these facilities. The Organisation was thus not only laying the ground rules but was also breaking new ground in international cooperation. It also mounted a network of radio beacons to guide aircraft. To a large extent this was done by national authorities under the supervision of ICAO. But here too there were some international ventures. ICAO helped establish a set of long-range radio aids to navigation (LORAN), together with meteorological stations in Iceland, Greenland and the Faeroe Islands for use along transatlantic routes. These services were again financed jointly by the users. This cooperative scheme developed extensively over the years to become the central element of safe and efficient travel over the North Atlantic.[2]

In setting world-wide standards, ICAO has had to keep pace with the rapidly-growing technology from the DC–3 to the supersonic aircraft. It had to focus not only on the aircraft, but on the flight environment. Technological innovations in air transport have far outstripped that of any other mode of transport except perhaps for supertankers and the development of high speed trains. Dr R.R. Shaw, who directed IATA's technical activities for 20 years, recalled the extraordinary willingness of the airlines in the 1960s to pursue 'an aggressive program of far-sighted activities' dealing not only with immediate day-to-day concerns but also with long-term needs.[3]

This emphasis on long-term objectives developed out of the challenges of the jet age. The emergence of the turbojet engine, for example, had a two-fold impact. In the early 1960s, the turbojet led to a dramatic increase in speed while the size of the aircraft remained fairly constant. In the late 1960s and 1970s, speed remained constant since it was already approaching the sound barrier, but aircraft grew in size.[4] The advent of the jet age brought about a change of all ICAO regional plans and practically all the annexes and related documents since these were tailored for a far different flight profile of speed, altitude and passenger seating.

Because adjustments to technological changes brought about by new aircraft is an expensive and long process, the Organisation has steered a cautious line in formulating plans. From 1960, it had a panel looking into the problems likely to be created by the advent of the supersonic aircraft, only to be overtaken by the much larger problems of the jumbo jets which arrived on the scene first.[5] At present, in view of the considerable doubts as to the viability of the hypersonic aircraft and notwithstanding the glowing forecasts of its promoters, the Organisation is remaining on the sideline.

Over the years, ICAO has had to make momentous choices in selecting new communications and navigation systems for worldwide use. New equipment inevitably creates new types of problems because it takes years for a new system to be fully implemented. In the meantime, the new must coexist with the old. For example, in 1949 ICAO laid down requirements for the Instrument Landing System (ILS) which is still used as the standard precision landing aid. Ten years later, after an exhaustive consideration of alternative short-range navigational aids, ICAO settled upon the VOR/DME as the basic international air navigation system aid. By the early 1970s, the aviation community had concluded that an improved landing aid was needed to meet the growing requirements of a jet era[6] and that in order to assure the safety and efficiency of air transport the ILS would have to be replaced on a global basis. After a long and protracted decision-making process in which various states championed their own equipment, ICAO chose a new system – the Microwave Landing System (MLS).

The Organisation has been faulted for being too slow in responding to technical developments and for being overtaken by events. To the extent that this is true, it is due to the nature of the complex technology and to the fact that the Organisation is ill-equipped to make decisions that involve the high stakes of avionics. The Organisation does not have a think tank, nor does it have the expertise to deal with every complex issue. The Air Navigation Commission (ANC), ICAO's technical arm, relies on the advice of specialised panels. These panels, depending on the issue, are themselves heavily dependent on the recommendations of the airlines and the aeronautical industry.

After a specialised panel submits its report, a long development stage begins with an analysis of the proposals by the ICAO Secretariat. The Secretariat then submits its findings, together with its own recommendations, to the ANC. The ANC decides on the best means of tackling the problem, and on whether there is a need for the Council to adopt new or amended SARPs (standards and recommended practices). A proposed change in the annexes can be a laborious process, requiring consultation with member states and possible consideration at either a worldwide conference or one of the divisional meetings that ICAO convenes to discuss specific technical problems. Much to ICAO's credit, there has never been a case where a final action by the Council has been rejected by either a member state or by the aviation community.

One might argue that the role of ICAO is to advance technology, but in practical terms, there is no way this can be done without the support of the international aviation community and more particularly that of the airlines. Unlike earlier years, the carriers have been remarkably cautious in supporting technical innovations for fear that they would have to bear the brunt of the cost. They now leave it to the aircraft and the avionics industries to promote advanced concepts and theories that may have useful applications to civil aviation. All segments of the industry including the airlines are part of a task force on future air navigation systems (FANS) to implement new concepts, including satellite technology, for global communications, navigation and surveillance services.

Considering that we are already in the space age, it seems incongruous that satellite technology is not fully used to relieve airspace congestion. As early as 1968, ICAO had been alert to the potential of satellites for air navigation when it set up an international mechanism (AEROSAT) to plan a satellite for the exclusive use of civil aviation. A consortium of states comprising the United States, Canada and the nine members of the European Space Research Organisation, was scheduled to launch an experimental satellite in 1979–80, when the whole programme had to be shelved because of the concern of the airline industry over the long-term financial implications.[7] To be sure, the airlines at the time were suffering heavy financial losses.

When the aviation industry belatedly woke up to the missed opportunities, the best that could be done was to share services for mobile communications with the maritime users and to make sure that the next generation of satellites launched by INMARSAT (the International Maritime Satellite Agency) includes specifications for aviation use as set by ICAO.[8] Beyond immediate communications needs, the aviation community looks towards a highly accurate, multi-purpose satellite system.

There is no doubt that such a system will come to be. The central question is what ICAO's role will be in managing this global enterprise. Fortunately, ICAO was spared a political clash on the choice of a system from among those under development when the United States and the USSR announced in April 1989 that they would offer their systems for joint use by the aviation community. It was significant that the surprise announcement was made at the last meeting of the FANS Committee, thereby ensuring a prime role for ICAO in planning the political, financial and institutional aspects of the new system.[9] The ICAO Council lost no time in appointing a new group to carry on the tasks of the FANS panel and develop the technical requirements for the use and management of the global system expected to be in operation by the mid-1990s. The effectiveness of the system will ultimately depend on these detailed specifications.

CROWDED AIRSPACE AND REGULATORY CONSTRAINTS

By far the most pressing problems facing the air transport industry concern the congested airspace and airport gridlock that affects the busiest air routes in North America, Europe and the Asia/Pacific region. One FAA study shows that 18 major airports in the United States each experiences more than 20 000 hours of delay annually.[10] Airport construction is nearly at a standstill. The last major airport built in the United States was Dallas/Forth Worth International which opened in 1974. Moreover, construction of a new airport for Denver has been delayed by bitter wranglings over noise and cost.

The picture is just as grim in Europe. What used to be known as 'summer peak' congestion in Europe is now prevalent from early spring to late autumn, resulting in heavy and costly delays for the airlines and passengers.[11] The only major airport being built is in Munich and it is already expected to be operating over capacity when it opens in 1991. The problem is all the more acute in a continent where large areas of the airspace are reserved for military use and where frequent labour problems with air traffic controllers cause havoc with flight operations.

The largest traffic growth is in the Asia/Pacific region with annual increases averaging about nine per cent annually, well above the world's average. ICAO expects this growth to continue to the point that the region will account for 39 per cent of the world's passenger traffic by the year 2000, compared to 19 per cent in 1986.[12] Looking at the region as a whole, the problem is not so much lack of facilities as the need for a more efficient route structure to accommodate the longer-range aircraft – mostly the Boeing 747s – which have revolutionised trans-Pacific air travel in recent years.

Worldwide, if one assumes a continuing average annual traffic growth of some five to six per cent, the number of scheduled passenger journeys can be expected to double to two billion by the year 2000. The number of aircraft is expected to double to more than 11 000 with a resulting increase in volume of aircraft movements.[13] These dire predictions are a matter of concern to the aviation community because the supporting infrastructure cannot keep pace with the demand. The continued development of civil aviation faces its most acute test on the ground where national interests are tied to a host of policy and environmental issues at the federal, state or provincial, and local level.

Decisions on airport and traffic control at the national level are often thwarted or slowed by local and state officials who must contend with their own constituents. Even the FAA does not have the political clout to get its own way when it comes to deciding on the use of its airport construction grants. Throughout Europe and in Japan, environmental groups have mounted fierce, sometimes fatal opposition, to increasing existing airport facilities. In November 1987, two policemen were shot during a protest outside Frankfurt airport, the first police officers to be gunned down in postwar Germany. Tokyo's international airport at Narita has long been a battleground between police and local residents.

With runways, terminals and air traffic control stretched to capacity on both sides of the Atlantic, hardly a week goes by without a statement by an airline executive, an editorial or a report warning of an impending crisis if coordinated action is not taken soon. A recent report of the London-based Aviation Industry Strategy Group concludes: 'Governments must bite the bullet of expansion of runways, air traffic control and infrastructure if their current aviation industries are to survive'.[14]

Solutions to the air traffic gridlock require as urgent action in the sky as on the ground. One of ICAO's priorities is to convince states that they must provide more airspace for civil traffic to allow a more direct and more efficient route structure. In preparation for the introduction of the new, long-haul Boeing 747–400, certain routes have already been redrawn so that it may be used to best advantage in the Far East and the Pacific.[15] The Soviet Union may at long last be ready to open its trans-Siberian route between Europe and the Far East hitherto reserved for East bloc countries and a few privileged Western carriers.[16]

Technical solutions can provide short-term relief by increasing the flow of traffic and the capacity of airports. Studies on congested airways are under way in several countries to reduce separation minima in flight. Horizontal separation between adjacent aircraft has been redefined several times thanks to improved radar surveillance and foolproof navigation systems. Improving the height-keeping accuracy to reduce vertical spacing is more difficult. It is, however, technically feasible to reduce by half the 2000-foot vertical separation in the upper airspace and increase capacity without more than a modest investment in air-data systems.[17]

New separation rules will improve the flow of traffic but will not address the problem of congestion in terminal areas. Possible solutions to terminal congestion include an increase in the number of runway exits, and a reduction in both the three-mile separation between landing aircraft and the space between parallel runways. The gradual introduction of the MLS promises further improvements in the use of existing airport facilities. Noise curfews at airports may also be eased as older aircraft are being replaced by new and quieter jets. Finally global navigation systems can further reduce minimum separation distances between aircraft and provide precision approaches to runways, thus greatly expanding the number and safety of flight operations.

The safety risks inherent in drafting new separation specifications must be assessed constantly. The International Federation of Airline Pilots Associations (IFALPA) has steadfastly opposed reducing separation rules before they are demonstrated to be safe.[18] Another regulatory development to enhance safety and reduce the number of near-misses is causing concern in the aviation community. It stems from the United States decision to require that all aircraft of more than thirty seats flying in United States airspace be equipped with an anticollision device known as Traffic Alert and Collision Avoidance System (TCAS-II). The rule requiring TCAS-II installation no later than 30 December 1991, is equally applicable to foreign carriers. It has resulted in protests that the United States is acting unilaterally by imposing its own requirements ahead of ICAO standards which have yet to be decided. There also have been negative reactions as to the usefulness and effectiveness of such an airborne collision avoidance system.[19]

The problems of congested airspace are not easily solved and extend beyond regulatory issues. ICAO can look at global needs, but the detailed requirements are set forth in the regional air navigation plans and implemented by the countries concerned with due regard to their own priorities. An acute need exists for additional resources practically everywhere, in developed as well as developing countries.[20]

ICAO has had great difficulty over the years translating its paper norms into practical realities. Setting standards and procedures for air navigation services does not mean they will be applied in practice. The same holds true for the regional air navigation plans. ICAO's regional offices, in following up on the implementation of regional plans, hear constant laments over lack of money, trained technicians and equipment. Unlike IATA and the airlines, which have been known to put pressure on governments to correct deficiencies, ICAO stays clear of national policies. ICAO, however, may intervene in an extraordinary situation, such as when Nigeria lacked navigational aids and the airlines threatened to suspend operations, the Council President discussed the matter with officials and arranged for a technical assistance mission.[21]

As planners have been overtaken by their own predictions, governments are coming under increasing pressure to resolve congestion problems, especially those involving air traffic control. As one trade publication noted, 'the whole subject is a political mine-field [since] nobody wants airports next door and spending on ATC [air traffic control] is often a lower priority than housing or health services. It is also a longer-term problem than most politicians are interested in'.[22]

The first test of the political will of states to provide long-range solutions will come in Europe. The twin pressures of liberalisation policies and overcrowded facilities have already led to a public outcry that has compelled governments to begin talking about supra-national solutions to deal with continent-wide problems. The first step has been a decision by the 23-member European Civil Aviation Conference to establish two central and interlinked flow control centres in Europe by 1994, one in Brussels to handle all the traffic in Western Europe and the other in Moscow to coordinate flights in Eastern Europe.[23] Flow control, however, is not a means by itself. It can help relieve congestion but it cannot eliminate shortcomings in the system and increase its capacity to absorb traffic growth.

The global nature of aviation, which transcends sovereign borders, poses problems in management that go beyond existing mechanisms and requires global solutions. In legal terms, the Chicago Convention gives states considerable scope for organising air transport on a regional basis (Articles 77–9). In a modest way, ICAO is prompting European states to think about multinational facilities and services. It is developing guidance material to show that certain services can be provided more effectively and at a lower cost by a single entity operated by one or several states. To achieve this, technical planning groups need to apply a different approach and focus on the broader financial and managerial questions rather than on the strict implementation of the regional plans.

The provision of air navigation facilities and services is the responsibility of each state as spelled out in Article 28 of the Chicago Convention, but nothing prevents states from delegating these functions to a public or private entity. This is already the case in Africa and Central America where individual countries cannot provide services on their own. Within ICAO's own institutional framework, the joint financing agreements for air navigation services over the North Atlantic have given the Organisation considerable experience in managing services on an international scale.

THE SHAPE OF FUTURE TECHNOLOGY

The past 35 years have brought significant changes in the international airline industry starting with the ill-fated de Havilland Comet[24] through successive generations of turbojets. During this period, technical advances in aircraft and engine designs have revolutionised commercial air transport. As significant as these developments have been, they will pale in comparison with the changes travellers can expect in the future. As the President of the ICAO Council (Assad Kotaite) put it:

A technical revolution is sweeping through the world air transport industry. It has already been experienced by passengers, to a limited extent, in such new airliners as the Boeing 757 and 767 twin-engined aircraft. The extent of the technological revolution brought about by these larger aircraft encompasses virtually every aspect of the industry and will be accompanied by some equally far-reaching innovations on the ground – the microwave landing system (MLS) that will speed the flow of aircraft in and out of increasingly congested airports and automated air traffic control that will facilitate the controllers' work.[25]

Futuristic aircraft, hypersonic transports and leviathans carrying a thousand passengers are on the drawing board or in the early stages of study. Some of these aircraft will be operational early in the 21st century; others may not see service before the year 2025, if at all.[26]

For the foreseeable future, aircraft builders are concentrating on extracting the maximum benefits from existing technology and the wide-body fuselage of the Boeing 747. The reasons are largely economic. The cost of new aircraft continues to escalate. Aircraft manufacturers expect that commercial airlines will need to spend more than $500 000 million (in 1989 dollars) for new aircraft until the end of the century, comparable to expenditures on equipment for the 35-year period between 1950 and 1985.[27]

No longer are technological advances engineered by ambitious airline executives like Juan Trippe who encouraged Boeing to produce the 707 which inaugurated transatlantic jet travel in 1958.[28] Gone also are the days when a strong aeronautical industry, subsidised by governments, could spur technological progress and force new designs on the airlines even when it was not always in their best interest. A striking example was the development of the Anglo-French Concorde, a technological triumph for the governments but a commercial fiasco when the time came to take orders.[29] The aircraft of the future will be decided not by national prestige but by economic realities. Nothing illustrates better the new environment in the aeronautical industry than the decision by Air France in 1987 to 'buy American' and order 16 Boeing 747–400s in a $3.5 billion package that was until then the second largest ever for the American firm.

In this context, the announcement by President Reagan in his State of the Union Address in 1986 that the United States would develop a hypersonic aircraft caused few ripples in the international aviation community. Airline executives had more immediate concerns about making the right choices in renewing their fleet while American aircraft manufacturers wanted to make sure they would receive the orders in the face of heavy competition from the Airbus consortium. While the Airbus's share of the world market had been about 17 per cent between 1980 and 1985, it jumped to 44 per cent during the first quarter of 1987.[30] More galling was the European penetration of the American market through the sale of 23 Airbus A–300s to Eastern Airlines on terms which were without precedent.[31]

Boeing and McDonnell Douglas answered the Airbus challenge, complaining that the fight was unfair because of government subsidies their competitor had been reaping from the start. In response, Airbus executives pointed out that the US aerospace firms had benefited from billions of dollars in government defence contracts that enabled the aircraft companies to develop new designs for commercial manufacturing. The US tried to raise the matter in the GATT but apparently without success.[32] The issue simmered down when Boeing and McDonnell Douglas, faced with a backlog of orders, relaxed their pressure for trade action against Airbus.

Beyond this trade war stands the need to finance the sky-rocketing cost of aeronautical technology. Airbus is a prime example of how a multinational cooperative approach can create the resource pool necessary to finance the research, development and production of new aircraft. The governments of the Airbus consortium (British Aerospace, France's Aerospatiale, Germany's Messerschmitt and Spain's CASA) have underwritten the effort with large infusions of cash but the A330/340 models are the last to receive such support. The consortium will have to seek new cooperative arrangements and risk-sharing partnerships.[33]

Looming on the horizon are competitive challenges for the financing of the hypersonic aircraft now that studies by its American sponsors (NASA, Boeing and McDonnell Douglas) show that there is a demand for high-speed civil transport. One study found that such a project will require an international consortium to deal with complex issues of costs, airports and the environment. The report concluded that it is 'economically and technologically impossible for any single country or company to develop [a hypersonic aircraft]'.[34]

With the Americans in the lead, the Europeans do not want to be left behind. The Euromart consortium, led by Aerospatiale and supported by the European Community, initiated a two-year project to study the possibility of a Concorde 2 and a hypersonic Concorde 3. Aerospatiale hopes to put the Concorde 2 in service by 2005, when the life expectancy of the current Concorde expires.[35] The hypersonic model may not be ready before 2015. Many in the airline industry are not ready to bet on such prospects.

ICAO's assessment is one of cautious expectations. It notes that: 'any new SST aircraft will need to have economically acceptable operating costs [and] meet exacting environmental requirements in the noise, sonic boom and emission areas'. In addition while ICAO recognises the significant advantages of cruise speeds between Mach 2 and Mach 3 without the need for new construction materials, 'new fuels or variable cycle engines . . . would involve expensive and risky advances in technology'.[36]

THE ECONOMIC ENVIRONMENT

Airlines have been caught up in a process of change driven by rapidly emerging technology. The changes in the economic environment are an entirely different matter. These developments challenge the basic framework of the regulatory system and are a matter of concern to ICAO to the extent that they impinge on the principle of 'equal opportunity' written into the preamble of the Chicago Convention. Basically, the system has survived without open frictions because governments were not inclined to rock the boat. Bilateral agreements provided sufficient flexibility, and cartel rates set at the IATA tariff conferences were hardly ever challenged by governments. This cosy situation came to an abrupt halt during the fuel crisis of the 1970s when costs began to escalate rapidly as the result of world inflation.[37] The airlines will not soon forget the economic difficulties of the mid-seventies. Knut Hammarskjöld, former IATA Director General, recalled it as a time 'of brutal financial realism when the airlines of the world were being squeezed dry by soaring costs, sky-high interest rates, diminishing yields and nose diving profits'.[38]

The changes in the economic environment are seen in the world-wide traffic patterns. The proportion of the total scheduled traffic carried by the United Kingdom and the United States declined over a thirty-year period (1946–76) from about two-thirds to a little more than a quarter. Over the same period, the number of international scheduled carriers increased from 40 to 180, and the average payload multiplied sevenfold.[39]

The ensuing competitive battle exacted an even greater toll as the rapid growth of low-cost charter flights eventually threw the IATA price-fixing machinery out of gear. The charter (non-scheduled) airlines and tour operators had remained largely outside the regulatory framework. They simply did not exist at the time of the Chicago Conference. Some twenty years later, the first Atlantic 'Skytrain' services of Sir Freddie Laker brought hordes of bag-packing travellers onto the market and helped transform air transport from a luxury to a mass-market product.[40]

This phenomenon resulted in unprecedented overcapacity on key routes, especially over the North Atlantic, a situation which was aggravated when the major airlines countered higher operations costs with larger jets. In 1975 alone, the unused capacity on the North Atlantic was equivalent to 15 000 empty Boeing 747 round trips.[41]

In the face of trends evident as far back as 1970, one would have expected that these airlines would have curtailed their services. However, no major airline was prepared to abandon its share of the market to the competition. As Andreas Lowenfeld has remarked, 'even before the fuel crisis of 1973, the basic Bermuda structure was under severe stress and international aviation was a sick industry'.[42] The first fuel crisis brought about an abrupt change and spurred an American drive for far-reaching changes in the regulatory system. By 1975, as the grumbling of the American carriers became louder, President Carter began a comprehensive overhaul of American aviation policies. What looked straightforward on the domestic front was viewed with apprehension in other countries where airlines were owned by their respective governments and were interlocked with national policy. As Christer Jönsson stated: 'the new policy amounted to a fervent call for international deregulation, emphasising competition, liberalisation of charter operations, no capacity restraints and "marketplace" pricing with minimal government involvement'.[43]

At first, American deregulators had planned to revamp the international system within the existing framework and took pains to reaffirm their belief in multilateralism and the IATA tariff conferences.[44] The policy change was triggered by the British decision to terminate the 1946 Bermuda Agreement and the difficult negotiations in 1977 leading to a new agreement, known as 'Bermuda 2'.

As the cleavage deepened between the United States and most other countries which resisted free-trade policies in aviation, ICAO summoned a Special Air Transport Conference in April 1977 – the most important such gathering since the Chicago Conference.[45] Given the fact that ICAO has long since abandoned attempts to seek a multilateral regime covering economic regulatory matters and had been given no new mandate on that score since the first Interim Assembly of 1946, many were sceptical that the first Transport Conference would do more than bring the issues into the open. The agenda was divided into four headings: the open rate situation and the widespread violations by airlines of IATA-approved fares; policies regarding charter airlines; regulation of capacity in international air transport; and the international mechanisms for setting rates and fares.

The debate at this first conference showed that the 97 governments represented had different perceptions of both the problems and possible solutions. On the question of charter services, which were being offered almost as regular flights, some delegates spoke in favour of an integrated international regime. Others felt that charter operations should be regulated separately. With respect to excess capacity, some delegates suggested that the situation over

North Atlantic routes was a short-term phenomenon due to the introduction of jumbo jets and worldwide recession. The majority, however, thought that excess capacity was a chronic problem due to deficiencies in the regulatory system.[46]

The far-ranging debate showed a wide disparity of views which precluded any kind of a consensus – the United States being very much isolated. The only agreement was that no matter how serious the shortcomings in the system, solutions must be found through bilateral agreements and should not be left to the vagaries of the market.

By the time the Second Air Transport Conference was held in 1980, opposition to deregulation policies was crumbling; the US had already signed bilateral agreements with about 15 countries. All these bilaterals had been negotiated on a one-by-one basis, preventing airlines in a particular region, for example Europe, from grouping together and putting up a common front.[47] This 'carrot-and-stick approach' satisfied American demands for competitive pricing, liberalised capacity and charter provisions and offered greater access to valuable US markets sought by foreign carriers. The stick was represented by threats of traffic diversion as American carriers could easily substitute one European gateway for another to force recalcitrant countries to come to terms.[48]

In these circumstances, the opposition voiced at ICAO Assembly sessions and air transport conferences to the American position had little effect. In Lowenfeld's description:

> These conferences had begun to resemble the United Nations General Assembly: the rule of one country, one vote meant that the developing countries, when united, controlled the conference. Individually, countries such as Mexico, Brazil, Morocco, Venezuela, etc., might make their arrangements in bilateral accords with the United States and other developed countries; as a group in a large conference, however, the developing countries tended to join in the position that free competition means ganging up of the strong against the weak, and threatened the opportunity of each country (or group of small countries) to field an international airline.[49]

Thus at the first two air transport conferences, as Lowenfeld further pointed out, 'the majority favored capacity controls, restrictions on charters, and strict control of fares by IATA. The fact that all these positions put the majority at odds with the United States, was not a discouragement to block voting, nor, in the context of the ICAO Conferences, an invitation to negotiate'.[50]

By the time the Third Air Transport Conference was convened in 1985, regulatory reform as such was no longer an issue as more and more states had joined the deregulatory bandwagon, albeit more out of necessity than out of conviction. The conference took up a host of issues dealing with competition laws, airline marketing and selling, currency transfers and the application of noise restrictions on older jets.[51] The conference urged states to settle their differences through bilateral negotiations and asked the ICAO Council to develop guidelines and recommendations to avoid conflicts over the application of domestic laws. The United States delegate took strong exception to suggestions that ICAO could have a say in the way states apply their basic economic policies. In his view, ICAO's recommendations to states would take the Organisation beyond its appropriate role by questioning national policies with respect to competition laws.[52]

A matter of grave concern raised at this 1985 conference was the abusive use by major airlines of computerised reservation systems (CRS) to control the market.[53] The ICAO Council was mandated to study the problem and to develop recommendations. The ICAO study and analysis contained few surprises. For Chris Lyle, Chief of ICAO's Economics and Statistics Branch, the major question is what to do next to implement the report's conclusions.[54]

Lyle quite rightly states that ICAO has no regulatory authority in the field of air transport and that 'the Organization's conclusions in the field of air transport policy have generally been issued as recommendations to its member states, carrying no binding force but functioning as a more or less effective medium for moral suasion'.[55]

This anomalous situation does not prevent other international bodies from dealing with the issue. It was at this Third Air Transport Conference that a potential conflict was raised between ICAO and the negotiators in GATT who were assessing whether the rules governing trade in goods should extend to air transport and CRS. The 26th session of the ICAO Assembly in 1986 reacted with dismay at such prospects and urgently advised its member states to make sure that their negotiators in GATT are made fully aware of the existing regulatory system.[56]

By the time the ICAO Assembly met again in 1989, a Group of Negotiations on Services (GNS) had held several meetings under the auspices of GATT. The feeling at the Assembly's Economic Commission in the face of the uncertain outcome in GATT was reflected by the Tunisian delegate in two words, 'incomprehension and powerlessness'. The delegates realised that the problem was not one of jurisdiction between GATT and ICAO, but rather, stemmed from the differing approaches to the nature of air transport on the part of trade and aviation policy makers. The ICAO delegates were also pointedly reminded by the GATT observer that any remonstrations by ICAO should not be addressed to GATT but to their own sovereign governments participating in the trade in services talks.[57] Although the ICAO delegates pressed for pertinent studies and an eventual fourth Air Transport Conference to clarify ICAO's role, they realised that given the GATT calendar, any input by ICAO would come too late to influence the outcome; full negotiations on trade in services were scheduled to get under way in 1990.

The upshot of the issues left unresolved at the Chicago Conference is that ICAO cannot deal with economic regulatory matters without an unambiguous mandate. As a high ICAO official stated: 'ICAO's role in air transport is that of a periodic, refined and gentlemanly consideration of civil aviation economic problems, the outcome of which, it is assumed, will be more orderly and globally consistent means of coping with these problems'.[58] Lowenfeld's assessment of ICAO's role is more blunt. In his words, 'ICAO [is] ill-adapted to the task of economic regulation, and unlikely to play a major part in developing new rules of the game'.[59]

CONCLUSION

Looking to the immediate future, air transport will require new forms of international cooperation in technical and economic areas. Whether ICAO's contracting states will respond to the challenge depends on their willingness to sacrifice some of their sovereign rights. The global expansion of air transport and the ever-increasing traffic require new multilateral mechanisms. As a first step, states must decide on the management of a global navigation system that meets the needs of the aviation community without restrictions. In the longer term, states face responsibilities of much greater political significance involving the allocation of sovereign rights in the control and management of the airspace.

3 ICAO in the United Nations Context: A Case History in Functionalism

Peace is no policy . . . The only way to secure peace is to stop bothering about it and begin to work together to carry out together the business of the world.

Salvador de Madariaga

Scholars in the field of international organisation have tried to classify international agencies along criteria which, in theory at least, could provide a better understanding of how the international community administers and organises world affairs. This concern is not surprising. As Inis Claude observed: 'the process of international organisation is a significant feature of the dynamic pattern of international relations in our time'.[1] While scholars have tried in the past to define international organisation in terms of legal arrangements between states there has been a growing recognition that the context is not exclusively political in nature but is also economic, social and technological.[2]

The classification of organisations is not an idle academic exercise for it leads to basic assumptions which over the years become established in the literature. If we accept the proposition that far from being irrelevant, 'theory can play an important role in efforts at improved cooperation by the international community',[3] it becomes then imperative to correct false assumptions as to how these agencies interrelate.

A basic classification divides these intergovernmental organisations between those dealing with peace and security and those concerned with social, humanitarian or technical matters. In the United Nations system, we are dealing with the UN itself and the specialised agencies brought into relationship with the United Nations under Article 57 of the Charter.[4]

In analysing the UN system, one must keep in mind that subsystems are interrelated and that their interaction with political issues cannot be overlooked, even if the political activities of the United

Nations are not examined. This is important, according to Mahdi Elmandjra, because one often encounters the simplified theory which establishes clear-cut divisions between political and other activities.[5]

Leon Gordenker states that the myth of the non-political activities of certain agencies derives in part from a narrow definition of politics. If we confine politics in the international realm to conflicts and the use of military force, then everything else can be seen as non-political. Thus, the United Nations deals by definition with political matters because it is concerned with international security. Everything else can be seen as non-political.[6]

This simplistic dichotomy, as Gordenker explains, fits in very well with a conventional view of the origins of the earliest international organisations born before the United Nations, such as the International Telegraphic Union (later to become the International Telecommunication Union), the Universal Postal Union and the International Civil Aviation Organisation. These agencies were created to meet obvious needs which had nothing to do with peace. Their scope was limited to specialised technical subject matters. They could therefore be considered non-political. But, as Gordenker points out, if a slightly more sophisticated definition of politics is applied to these organisations so as to include the competing claims and demands of states within a system, then even the narrow technical agencies fall under this political rubric.[7]

The artificial division in political theory between the political and non-political concerns of the United Nations can be traced back to the functional approach propounded by David Mitrany and other scholars who rejected the realist view that the United Nations is an instrument by which nations 'protect and promote their respective national interests'.[8] As defined by Claude, the 'functional sector of international organization is that part of the mass of organized activities which relates directly to economic, social, technical and humanitarian matters – that is to problems which may tentatively be described as non-political'.[9] The expectation of the functionalists was a world community based on common needs in which 'interests and activity are congruent and in which politics is replaced by problem solving'.[10]

In the euphoria that led to the creation of the United Nations, peace was to be the highest aim. Elmandjra has noted that peace as a fundamental objective was not merely the absence of war but an indivisible concept to be found in the preamble of the constitutions of most organisations belonging to the UN system.[11] Thus the Convention on International Civil Aviation proclaims in its preamble 'Whereas it is desirable to avoid friction and to promote that cooperation between nations and peoples upon which the peace of the world depends'.

This preamble places the emphasis upon the development of a programme of activity as a means of preventing conflict. This is the functional approach although the drafters of the Chicago Convention did not state this in so many words. At the same time, as Gerald Fitzgerald remarked, they were not unaware of the merits of functional activities as a means of avoiding international friction.[12]

It is one thing to say that all of the actions, activities and programmes of the United Nations system are intended to contribute to peace; it is another to find out how this is done. It is futile to seek empirical evidence for the lofty claims made in the past that 'the more people in the world are able to move around and see each other ways of life, the more quickly shall we arrive at an age of peace and plenty'.[13]

Better communications have undoubtedly improved living conditions in the world, but can one say that air travel has contributed to international security and the maintenance of peace? If we are to believe Quincy Wright, the opposite is more to the point. He points out that 'while aviation has manifested a continuous and consistent trend toward greater efficiency and wider utilization, world politics has been characterized by even greater confusion, inconsistency and violence'.[14]

Claude has posited as a working experiment that functionalism in the United Nations must be assessed on the basis of political questions. He states that 'functional theory invites this kind of examination, since its emphasis upon economic and social matters is explicitly justified in terms of ultimate political impact [and that] functional experience demands it, since the intrusion of political factors is almost invariably one of the earliest facts of life brought to bear upon a fledgeling agency for international cooperation in any field whatever'.[15]

THE SPECIAL CASE OF SPAIN

The pertinence of this statement was demonstrated in the early years of ICAO when thorny questions of membership clashed with the requirements of civil aviation. The first issue concerned Franco's Spain; it complicated from the start negotiations leading to the agreement to bring ICAO into relationship with the UN under Article 57 of the Charter. Spain had participated at the Chicago Conference in 1944 and it subsequently ratified the Chicago Convention. But it was denied UN membership in line with the position adopted at the Potsdam Conference and endorsed by the General Assembly that Spain was unwelcome because of its past support of the Axis powers.

When negotiations with ICAO (still a provisional agency) came before the various bodies of the United Nations, the USSR objected and asked that the talks be suspended until Spain was expelled from ICAO.[16] While other delegations were of the same opinion, the Economic and Social Council, the UN body concerned with the negotiations, felt that relations between the UN and Spain should not hold up the signing of the agreement in accordance with the provisions of the Charter.[17]

The question was finally resolved when the General Assembly on 12 December 1946 recommended that the Franco government be barred from membership in the specialised agencies. A draft resolution to oppose the ICAO–UN agreement was rejected in favour of a draft approving it on condition that ICAO comply with the recommendation. This decision was subsequently adopted in plenary session of the General Assembly without opposition.

ICAO could either refuse to accept the Spanish deposit of the act of ratification of the Chicago Convention or amend that Convention so that Spain could be legally expelled before ICAO formally joined the UN system. The Organisation chose the latter option and decided at its first Assembly on 14 May 1947 that a state 'whose government the General Assembly of the United Nations has recommended be debarred from membership in international agencies established by or brought into relations with the United Nations shall automatically cease to be a member of the International Civil Aviation Organization'.[18]

As Jacob Schenkman wrote: 'Spain's membership confronted the Organization during its first session with the dilemma that it must either amend the Convention so as to expel Franco Spain or run the risk of losing the valuable connection with the United Nations. It was quite obvious that the connection with the United Nations was the more important.' ICAO's action was criticised by certain writers who thought that the Organisation had adopted a political line which did not accord with the real interests of air transportation.[19]

The price paid for the United Nations affiliation was a new Article 93 *bis* to the Chicago Convention approved by the ICAO Assembly at the same time as the UN agreement.[20] As R.Y. Jennings asserts 'the price included the grant to the General Assembly of the United Nations of a general power of expulsion coupled with a veto on readmission in addition to the power of veto already possessed by the United Nations in respect to the admission of certain classes of states'.[21] He further points out that the expulsion of Spain from the Organisation was made automatically on the motion of the United Nations and this 'saved ICAO from the embarrassing task of a formal act of expulsion'.[22]

Spain's response at the first ICAO Assembly was one of bewilderment since it had ratified the Chicago Convention in good faith and complied with all its obligations. As the Spanish delegation phrased it 'the honourable members of the Assembly will deprecate the precedent of blending technical and [political] considerations of a very different nature which, being subject to local turbulent changes, might make delusive any endeavour to reach the goal of cooperation'.[23]

The adoption of Article 93 *bis* by the Assembly did not achieve the expulsion of Spain because under Article 94(a) an amendment does not come into force until it has been ratified by at least two thirds of the total number of contracting states. A draft resolution stipulating that in the meantime Spain should be barred from the Assembly was not put to a vote; that country had already announced its withdrawal rather than become 'an unwelcome guest'.[24]

Considering that Franco remained in power for some 20 more years, not much was achieved as the result of the UN Assembly and ICAO decisions. Furthermore, since Spanish airspace could not be removed from aeronautical maps by the stroke of a pen, some pragmatic way had to be found to accommodate the 'unwelcome guest'. For all practical purposes, Spain was never considered a pariah state within ICAO and when the time came for it to rejoin the Organisation, it was given a seat on the Council. With the change in the general political atmosphere, the attitude towards Spain changed. The General Assembly revoked its previous restrictions in 1950 and decided that since 'the specialized agencies of the United Nations are technical and largely non-political in character and have been established in order to benefit the peoples of all nations . . . they should be free to decide for themselves whether the participation of Spain in their activities is desirable in the interest of their work'.[25]

Following the UN decision, the President of the ICAO Council took immediate steps to resume relations with Spain and on 6 December 1950 the ICAO Council declared formally that all was back to normal. Spain was candid enough to admit that the 'isolation had not resulted in any irreparable damage thanks to the support it received from many countries and the Organization itself'. In fact ICAO had been working behind the scenes to maintain relations with that country.[26]

According to Thomas Buergenthal, the expulsion of Spain offers no useful precedent for determining how the Organisation would resolve similar cases since Spain resumed its membership before Article 93 *bis* came into force.[27] Yet, ICAO's action cast a long shadow over subsequent debates whenever membership became an issue. In particular, the stage was set for ICAO's subsequent dealings with South Africa, another charter member of the Organisation.

SOUTH AFRICA'S STATUS IN ICAO

Few issues have dominated the international agenda for so long and with such persistence as South Africa's policies of apartheid. These policies have come before various United Nations bodies in one form or another since 1946 and have resulted in a wide range of measures aimed at providing political, moral and material support for the black people of South Africa. Sanctions must be viewed in a legal context since punitive measures are taken in response to a breach of legal obligation. Sanctions in the League of Nations and in the United Nations refer to well-defined violations of international obligations, a threat to peace or an act of aggression (Articles 39–51 of Chapter VII of the UN Charter).[28] This legal context is important, as was pointed out by Peter Calvocoressi, because 'where there is a strong legal case against an alleged offender, the burden is on those who want to do nothing to make a convincing case for inaction. Where, however, the legal argument is weak, it is up to those pressing for sanctions to argue their associates into voting for them.'[29]

To the extent that South Africa's racial policies are inconsistent with the United Nations Charter, they are a legitimate reason for action on the part of the world body and specialised agencies whose mandates cover social and humanitarian concerns. When it comes to the technical agencies the question is not as simple. One may ask how apartheid hinders the 'safe and orderly development' of civil aviation, ICAO's primary responsibility? As in the case of Spain, on what grounds should such a technical agency be involved in social domestic policies, however abhorrent these may be?

Demands for sanctions started as soon as the newly independent states of Africa joined the United Nations. Thus, in 1962 the General Assembly in paragraph 4(e) of Resolution 1761 requested all member states to refuse 'landing and passage facilities to aircraft belonging to the government of South Africa'. In 1965, the General Assembly took similar action against Portugal, prompting the ICAO Secretary General to warn that 'in so far as concerns States members both of the United Nations and of the International Civil Aviation Organization, the request is inconsistent with the terms of the Convention on International Civil Aviation'.[30]

When some 20 years later ICAO acted on its own in recommending punitive measures, its advocates justified them as an extension of the comprehensive sanctions called for by the UN General Assembly. The sanctions in fact reflect more the reality of the United Nations than the complexity of international air transport with its welter of bilateral agreements and rights of third states, a global airline system of ticket interlining, contractual arrangements on joint operations and the pooling and leasing of aircraft controlled by the airlines. All these elements provide convenient loopholes in defying sanctions. Under the IATA interlining system, for instance, Air Canada will sell a ticket to London connecting to a South African Airways flight to Johannesburg.

The proposal for a ban on airline links with South Africa was first aired at the Commonwealth's Nassau conference in October 1985 as one of several counter-measures that governments should take if Pretoria failed to dismantle apartheid. The Commonwealth Group of Eminent Persons gave it a further impetus although the co-chairmen recommended banning only direct air links so as to force travellers to fly via Harare or Lusaka.[31] In other words, since South Africa controls trade routes and harbour access of its neighbours the ban on 'direct air links' would deny South Africa access by air to the rest of the world and give its neighbours a useful bargaining card. A complete ban on the other hand would not only affect South African Airways but all the carriers flying into South Africa.

When the 26th session of the ICAO Assembly in 1986 called on all ICAO contracting states 'to ban air links and suspend or terminate bilateral air transport agreements with South Africa' the move brought forth conflicting arguments over the role of ICAO and the use of civil aviation.[32] A number of Western states opposed sanctions on the grounds that the ICAO Assembly was not the proper forum to consider such a resolution and that it should not urge contracting states to act in violation of their bilateral air services agreement or to use these bilateral agreements as a political weapon.

As expected, a majority voted for the resolution (83 in favour, 12 opposed and 19 abstentions). Those who could bring decisive pressure on South Africa condemned apartheid but voted against or abstained. These states included not only the Western states but the 'front-line states' of Botswana, Lesotho and Swaziland which would have the most to lose from a change in the status quo.

The call for a ban of air links with South Africa came after futile attempts to force her expulsion from the United Nations and the specialised agencies. Such moves have been blocked at the Security Council and at ICAO by Article 93 *bis* which makes the decision dependent on the United Nations.

In 1965, the ICAO Assembly rejected a proposed amendment to the Convention designed to permit the suspension or exclusion from ICAO of any state practising 'a policy of apartheid and racial discrimination'. Although supported by a considerable number of states, the amendment failed to receive the requisite two-thirds vote. Many states voted against or abstained because they believed that any move to oust South Africa from ICAO should be initiated by the UN. Instead the ICAO Assembly condemned South Africa's apartheid policies as 'a flagrant violation of the principles embodied in the Chicago Convention'.[33]

In 1971, the 18th Session of the Assembly followed up its condemnation by barring South Africa from attending any meetings convened by ICAO, except for the Assembly itself, and from receiving official documents.[34] South Africa retaliated by reducing its budgetary contribution by 30 per cent. In doing so, it provided the only legal grounds for losing its seat according to Article 62 of the Chicago Convention which provides for the 'suspension of voting power in the Assembly of any contracting state that fails to discharge within a reasonable period its financial obligations to the Organization'. This provision, which had been dormant for some 20 years, was invoked in 1974 to deprive South Africa of its seat.[35]

South Africa has since quietly paid its contributions and regained its vote while accepting the restrictions imposed by the Assembly. Yet, in spite of its status, it is expected to fulfil its obligations to the technical annexes of the Chicago Convention and other ICAO instruments to which it is a party.[36]

APARTHEID AND AIR LINKS

A major consideration in ICAO's dealings with South Africa is that United Nations and ICAO resolutions have had little effect thus far in isolating that country. Moral issues have yet to make a difference in the heavily competitive world of commercial aviation. An editorial in *Airline Business* (October 1986) sums up the point: 'International airlines, unlike banks, are rather good at politics. Bilateral arrangements, and the use of national carriers as instruments of state policy, make such expertise vital. Of course the bottom line justification to playing politics is revenues and profits . . .' Most airlines maintained their services to South Africa and at times jockeyed for a favourable position in the event that their links with South Africa would be cut off. It was a classic example of a zero-sum game in which one airline's loss was another's gain.[37]

It was an altogether different situation when the proponents of sanctions were in a position to influence the outcome. When the African states closed their airspace to South African Airways (SAA) in response to the UN resolution of 1962, they almost grounded its flights to Europe.[38] Cape Verde, providentially, allowed South Africa to build and equip the island airport of Ilha da Sol especially for its airline. In due time, SAA acquired special performance B747s which could fly non-stop around the African mainland to four continents, albeit with additional flight time and considerable loss of intermediate traffic. South Africa later provided technical assistance to Equatorial Guinea whose international airport of Malabo helped lessen SAA's reliance on Cape Verde.[39]

It is evident that South Africa is taking advantage of its vulnerable neighbours with SAA providing maintenance, overhaul and engineering services to their carriers and sometimes even flight crews. The 'front-line states' have built modern international airports, hoping one day to reverse their traditional dependence on South Africa. Harare in Zimbabwe, Maseru in Lesotho, Mbabane in Swaziland and Gaborone in Botswana, all have landing sites in place awaiting more business.

These large modern airports built with massive international assistance underscore a paradoxical situation. If they can be justified on political grounds to help break these countries' dependence on South Africa, these airports are used for traffic to and from South Africa. Lesotho provides the best example. Completely surrounded by South Africa, it embarked in 1979 on a plan to develop air transport including a US$62.7 million international airport which opened in 1985. Whatever the airport's long range objectives, its major user is South Africa. It controls operations since all flights in and out of Maseru must fly over South African airspace. Besides, South Africa controls the entire supply line for aviation fuel. ICAO's Technical Assistance Bureau which planned the airport noted at the time that it was built without assurances that foreign carriers would use the new facility.[40]

THE SPECIAL CASE OF CHINA

The representation of China in the UN system presented another test case for ICAO. In this instance, the Organisation was once more bound to follow the UN position which did not necessarily accord with the requirements of civil aviation. The issue came to a head shortly after the Nationalists fled the mainland and established themselves in Formosa (Taiwan). In November 1949, the People's Republic delegate formally informed the President of the UN General Assembly and the Secretary General that his government repudiated the legal status of the delegation of the 'Chiang Kai-Shek clique', and that this regime had no right to speak for the people of China in the United Nations.

The announcement resulted in an interminable controversy as to which of the two rival regimes – the Nationalists in Formosa or the Communists on the mainland – were authorised to send representatives to act on behalf of the Chinese state. Subsequently, the question of credentials came before each session of the General Assembly and before the other agencies.

As for ICAO, a cable from Peking (now Beijing) informed the Secretary General that 'the Chinese Kuomintang reactionary remnant clique have no longer any qualification . . . and must be driven out from its various organs and meetings'.[41] This telegram to ICAO was dated 28 May 1950. Three days later, the Taiwan regime gave notice of denunciation of the Chicago Convention to take effect one year from that date.[42] In the fourth session of the Assembly which had just started, a controversy arose as to whether the denunciation should be accepted and whether in the first place, it was made by the legal representative of China. The question was left unsettled. China was not represented at all at the Assembly and was not heard from until 2 December 1953 when a second instrument of ratification was deposited with the United States as the depository state, effective 1 January 1954. Four states which had recognised Peking (the United Kingdom, India, Pakistan and Norway) again stated that they did not regard as valid the instrument of denunciation or the second ratification.[43] Since the acceptance of ratification rested with the depository state, it was promptly approved – the United States being at the time the strongest supporter of the Nationalists.

It was evident from informal discussions at the time that China had withdrawn from the Organisation on financial grounds only, and that it made no effort to stay in contact with ICAO under the impression that, to do so, it would be open to criticism for participating in its activities without contributing towards its expenses. It was also evident that the legal fiction of representing the mainland proved to be too costly for Taiwan. When China was reinstated it was allowed to reduce its assessment and to liquidate its arrears in annual instalments.

Even after it had been readmitted in ICAO, China's membership in the UN was the subject of continuing confusion each time the issue was brought up in New York. After unsuccessful attempts to expel it for lack of a two-thirds majority, the UN General Assembly finally resolved the situation when by a vote of 76 against 32 (and 17 abstentions) it decided (on 25 October 1971) to 'restore all its rights to the People's Republic of China, . . . to recognize the representatives of its Government as the only legitimate representatives of China to the United Nations, and to expel forthwith the representatives of Chiang Kai-Shek from . . . the United Nations and . . . all the organizations related to it'.[44]

The resolution deals with the representation of China not only in the United Nations but also in all the UN organisations. ICAO's decision to comply with it is based on solid grounds: (a) Article 58 of the United Nations Charter which states that 'the Organization shall make recommendations for the coordination of the policies and activities of the specialized agencies'. (b) Resolution 396 (V) on the recognition by the United Nations of the representation of a member state which recommends that the General Assembly's attitude concerning any such question should be taken into account . . . in the specialised agencies. (c) Article V, paragraph 1, of the Agreement between the United Nations and ICAO which provides that 'the International Civil Aviation Organization . . . agrees to arrange for the submission, as soon as possible, to its appropriate organ of all formal recommendations which the United Nations may make to it'.

There was, however, a different twist to the case. If the United Nations had expelled a state then that state by virtue of Article 93 *bis* of the Chicago Convention would automatically cease to be a member of the International Civil Aviation Organisation (unless the United Nations recommended to the contrary). China was not expelled from the United Nations. At issue was its representation to the United Nations. As regards ICAO, China had participated in the Chicago Conference and its representatives at the Conference were designated by the Republic of China on whose behalf the Convention was signed and ratified.

The General Assembly decision was therefore of the highest significance for ICAO. The United Nations resolution did not automatically take effect as Article 93 *bis* did not apply. The ICAO Council faced a double choice: it could either decide not to take action and leave the matter unresolved until the next session of the Assembly or it could abide by the General Assembly decision.

The Council at its 74th session decided to take its cue from Resolution 396 (V) of the General Assembly and to recognise the Government of the People's Republic of China as the only representative of China to ICAO. As a result all correspondence and official contact with Taipei ceased immediately. Deprived of his diplomatic status, the resident representative of the Republic of China sent a formal protest on behalf of what had now become in effect a non-state. The note was filed without acknowledgement.[45]

Having disposed of the legal issue, ICAO was now faced with a technical problem because Taiwan was still expected to continue providing services and facilities to international aviation. The government was still recognised by states adjoining its Flight Information Region (South Korea, Japan, United States and the Philippines) which included segments of the major airways in the Far East.

Officially, the ICAO regional office in Bangkok was instructed not to participate in any regional meetings attended by delegates from Taiwan. An alternative was offered to have ICAO convene such meetings and leave a vacant seat for Taiwan.[46] For practical purposes, the Bangkok office has found ways to enter into an unofficial agreement with Taiwan on technical matters through the use of third parties.[47]

As for relations with mainland China, ICAO's policy was one of caution; it wanted Peking to make the first move. In any case, international air links with the mainland at the time were limited to the Soviet Union, Burma and Pakistan. The move came in 1974 when Peking made a bid for a Council seat after signalling that it would henceforth become more involved in ICAO activities.[48] The bid coincided with China's opening to the outside world and was followed by a rapid growth of its air transport and of its airport infrastructure.

FUNCTIONAL FACTORS AND POLITICAL MOTIVATIONS

The United Nations Charter provides that the 'various specialized agencies, established by inter-governmental agreement and having wide international responsibilities, as defined in their basic instruments' shall be brought into relationship with the United Nations (Article 57). The bringing into relationship of the specialized agencies with the UN is not only a legal matter. It imposes also a moral obligation so that the best results can be obtained from such cooperation. Each agency is in fact an 'executive organ' or an 'executive arm' of the UN in the specialised field of its competence.[49]

Agreements between the UN and the specialised agencies follow a standard pattern. They provide for reciprocal representation at meetings; reciprocal inclusion of agenda items when requested; exchange of information and uniformity of personnel procedures; coordination of statistical services as well as budgetary and financial arrangements. Each specialised agency has agreed to consider any recommendation made to it by the United Nations and report on the action taken.

Recommendations from the United Nations to ICAO have dealt with human rights, the status of women, narcotic drugs, population, the peaceful use of outer space, as well as transport and communications. In addition there have been over the years recommendations with political overtones. For instance, in one single year, 1986, ICAO received and sent to the Council for its consideration several reports dealing with apartheid and South Africa, the rights of Palestinians (Assembly Resolution 41/23); cooperation with the Organisation of the Islamic Conference (41/8); implementation of the Declaration on the Granting of Independence to Colonial Countries (41/15); the status of Namibia (41/39) and assistance to liberation movements (41/35). Such recommendations are periodically brought before the Council. They are usually noted without debate since they do not require any specific action. However, the possibility always exists that any Council member can open a debate on any such issues, as has been the case in other agencies.

By signing an agreement with the United Nations, the agencies have affirmed their intention to cooperate to make coordination of the activities of the UN system fully effective. In doing so, each agency accepts the coordinating role of the Economic and Social Council. ECOSOC not only tries to avoid overlapping and duplication of activities among the agencies, but has direct responsibility in initiating and carrying out social and economic programmes sponsored by the United Nations itself.

As Mahdi Elmandjra has stated: 'the question of coordination involves objective functional factors as well as deep political and tactical motivations on the part of the "coordinators" whether they be the governments of the member states, the intergovernmental bodies of their institutions or their secretariats'.[50] Coordination, Elmandjra adds, has been one of the most constant concerns of the UN system and is an ever-present theme in the debates of the General Assembly, ECOSOC and the specialised agencies. It is the subject of thousands of pages of verbatim records as well as hundreds of resolutions.[51]

The problems of coordination at the conceptual and operational level have been dealt with at length in various reports, studies and articles and are briefly covered in Chapter 5 with respect to ICAO's technical assistance programme.[52] At stake is multilateral aid for development which is under criticism for wastefulness and the multiplicity of objectives and national interests. Esman and Cleever remarked that if there were a truly integrated international community in the sense that all nations were prepared to reconcile their particular interests so as to advance a commonly perceived general interest, the United Nations would have become the principal instrument used by the aid-giving countries to harmonise and coordinate their development assistance.[53] The UN is hardly anything of the kind.

Coordination also affects inter-agency relations governed by special agreements on related fields of competence. Fortunately, ICAO's highly technical concerns make it unlikely that other agencies have either the competence or the mandate to challenge its responsibilities.[54] The Organisation has therefore been spared the infighting that has characterised at times the relations between agencies sharing responsibilities in social and humanitarian activities. However, ICAO on occasion has been drawn into conflicts in sister agencies over related aspects of aviation, such as telecommunication.

ICAO's close links with the International Telecommunication Union are essential because radio frequencies allocated for aeronautical purposes are reviewed at the ITU's World Administrative Radio Conferences where aviation must compete for its share of the spectrum with other users. These ITU conferences have been highly contentious, as have been other world meetings in which the North and South have different approaches on the allocation of limited resources.[55] The situation has been made more difficult for ICAO because for a number of reasons, the international aviation community has not been able to use its share of the spectrum. ICAO has been under strong pressure from other users to relinquish some of the spectrum intended specifically for future air navigation needs.

Beyond the specific concerns of ICAO, international telecommunications issues centre on sovereignty, the growing information gap between developed and developing countries and the political nature of the debate. It has been argued that in this debate the ITU has been increasingly unable to carry out its primary functions in the face of political and ideological questions which have been introduced into its deliberations.[56]

THE CONFLICTING INTERESTS OF STATES

Except for the technical cooperation which made possible the remarkable development of air transport, one looks in vain for a common 'functional' interest that shapes the policies of states in civil aviation. 'Functionalism' is motivated by the hypothesis that the cumulative effect of 'functional' commitments will tend to influence governments towards more political cooperation and fewer conflicts.[57] This has not been the case in ICAO and it remains to be seen whether technical cooperation can transcend vested national interests in the other aspects of civil aviation. Anything that is non-technical is likely to be political in nature, even when such issues come up before the Council under the guise of technical problems.

Many problems which have come up before the ICAO Council are part of intractable political conflicts between states. Offshoots of the Middle East conflict such as the Israeli air attacks on Beirut Airport in December 1968 and on the PLO headquarters in Tunis in 1985, various interceptions of civil aircraft and aerial intrusions, and the longstanding dispute between Greece and Turkey over the use of the airspace above the Aegean Sea, are some examples of mixing 'functional' expertise with political issues.[58] The ICAO experience contradicts the assumption that an agency's political and technical activities can be easily separated. Any such expectations, as far as ICAO is concerned, were doomed from the start when it decided to be part of the UN system. As Claude has stated: 'the dilemma of functionalism is that its ultimate impact upon politics may never be tested because of the immediate impact of politics upon functionalism'.[59]

Organisations working in the technical fields are certainly a consoling element in a sombre international landscape. But one would tend to agree with Abba Eban that 'we do them no service when we pretend that they ameliorate the divisions in world society and that they can inspire a loyalty that can be transferred to the political level'.[60] What has happened is that the acrimonies of the political arena have spilled over to the specialised agencies (to a different degree to be sure) and that many of these agencies, including ICAO, have devoted an inordinate amount of time to issues whose outcome they cannot possibly influence.

This lesson has not been lost on successive United Nations secretaries general although they can do little to turn the clock back. As long ago as 1965, U Thant in an address to ICAO said 'it would be a matter of regret for the entire international community if important meetings dealing with essential technical, social and economic questions and depending for their success on the vital element of international cooperation were to fail to yield solid results because of the introduction of political considerations into the work of these agencies'.[61] Some 20 years later, Secretary General Javier Pérez de Cuellar expressed similar views when he stated that 'we must beware of blurring the separate and specific functions of the main organs and specialised agencies by treating them as interchangeable platforms for pursuing the same political aims'.[62]

In conclusion it must be admitted that 'functionalism' as such has not been a complete failure. It has provided a useful instrument for theoretical analysis in the field of international relations, security and peace. Unfortunately, it has not been able to lessen political tension. As Gordenker points out, 'so long as an element of conflict of interests is admitted, an international organization must be seen as a political institution'.[63]

4 Decision-making in ICAO: Who Governs in the Governing Body?

Sufficeth them, the simple plan
That they should take who have the power
And they should keep who can.

William Wordsworth, *Rob Roy's Grave*

The making of policy – those authoritative decisions which carry out the wishes of those with influence – is at the heart of any political system. It is all the more a crucial element in the United Nations system which must articulate the interests of so many states.

The various UN agencies have been set up to carry out a number of responsibilities. Whatever their field of activity, they can be divided into two broad categories according to the way in which they perform their tasks. Some organisations are established to provide a forum for negotiations and decisions, others provide specific services. Actually, many organisations fall into both categories. ICAO, for example, can be considered a service organisation which sets international standards and executes an extensive technical assistance programme but it also serves as a forum to harmonise air transport policies among its contracting states. The distinction between the two types of organisations, according to Cox and Jacobson, relates to the way in which they perform their functions, not to the importance these functions have for member states.

Decision-making as analysed by these authors occurs within a context comprising the functions, the institutional framework and basic procedures, as well as the particular historical development. All these factors make up for the differences which are immediately apparent when one examines the structure and decision-making process of international agencies. Even in the context of the UN, where agencies share a common outlook and conditions of service, each has over the years developed its own mode of operations. Formal powers, voting procedures, allocation of authority and organisation of the bureaucracy may have been prescribed at the time the agency was created. However, once established, these agencies have evolved in ways that could not have been foreseen by their founders.[1]

As pointed out out by Cox and Jacobson, 'the question "who governs" directly implies the question who is likely to benefit most and who least from a particular form of organization?'[2] It matters therefore to know which states are allocated adequate representation in the governing bodies to control decision-making in the political and administrative functions.

A study of ICAO's decision-making process is particularly rewarding. The Chicago Convention not only laid the groundwork for the development of civil aviation, it also established an agency to oversee it. To do so, the Convention prescribed decision-making powers not usually found in other agencies. In the first place, the Council of ICAO is a permanent body unlike the executive board of many other agencies. It functions as a legislative body when it adopts the standards and recommended practices which govern civil aviation worldwide. It also has judicial powers with respect to the settlement of disputes and differences relating to the interpretation of the Convention.

ICAO'S POWER STRUCTURE: THE COUNCIL

The thirty-three-member Council is the executive body of the Organisation, drawn from the contracting states and elected by its Assembly at three-year intervals. Article 50(a) of the Chicago Convention provides that 'the Council shall be a permanent body responsible to the Assembly', thus preserving the illusion that it is subordinated to the plenary body. It is entrusted under the Convention with a number of essential duties, combining executive, judicial, administrative and legislative functions. The Council's executive role as spelled out in article 54(b) is to 'carry out the directions of the Assembly and discharge the duties and obligations which are laid on it by this [the Chicago] Convention'. Among essential duties, which in other organisations are normally assigned to the Assembly, are first and foremost the approval of technical standards to be applied by contracting states, and the appointment of the Secretary General.

Such wide executive and legislative authority provided by the Convention without prior approval of the Assembly, suggests the

Council's status as a primary rather than a secondary source of authority.[3] The Council is also empowered to adjudicate disputes over the interpretation of the Convention although this judicial mechanism has not been used by states for the last seventeen years.

The Council's power is remarkable when compared to that of the governing board of other organisations in the UN system. The Council's ability to adopt technical standards as annexes to the Convention without going through a lengthy process of ratification has made possible the rapid development of civil aviation worldwide. In contrast with ICAO, the International Maritime Organisation (IMO) relies primarily on international conventions which have binding force only on those states which ratify them. Successive amendments to these conventions likewise require voluntary action on the part of member governments. The ICAO Council's role in appointing the Secretary General is also unusual. Only the ILO governing body has such powers, but the resemblance ends here since the ILO, unlike the ICAO Council, is a hybrid body composed of governments, employers and workers.[4]

The Council is therefore a powerful and visible body in international aviation in which membership is a prestigious and coveted plum for most nations. Yet, despite radical changes in the international community due to the influx of new states since the Convention was drafted in 1944, the criteria for membership in the ICAO Council have remained unchanged. These rules still favour aeronautical states of chief importance or those which make the largest contribution to the provision of air navigation facilities. Article 50(b) of the Chicago Convention states that:

> in electing the members of the Council, the Assembly shall give adequate representation to (1) the States of chief importance in air transport; (2) the States not otherwise included which make the largest contribution to the provision of facilities for international civil air navigation; and (3) the States not otherwise included whose designation will insure that all the major geographic areas of the world are represented on the Council.

The inescapable evidence is that large aeronautical states play a preponderant role through their quasi-permanent status in the Council. Seats have been tacitly conceded to these countries although the criteria for selection have never been defined. These states have invariably included Australia, Canada, France, the Federal Republic of Germany, Italy, Japan, the UK, China, the United States and the Soviet Union.[5]

The dominant influence of the large aeronautical states extends beyond Category 1, since states which might aspire to be of chief importance in civil aviation, when they cannot be elected in Category 1, can get into the next category (as in the case of China and Italy, and of Japan in earlier years). Certain states have long held seats on the Council in spite of any considerations other than political. As Christopher Tourtellot has pointed out, Czechoslovakia's long tenure (in Category 2 or 3) has been determined by geopolitical rather than strictly geographical criteria. It is the only Eastern European state aside from the USSR ever to hold a seat on the Council and it has done so uninterruptedly since 1965. The Eastern European group is no more numerous than many other regions of the world, yet it is regarded as deserving more than a single representative on the Council.[6]

Australia has also shifted categories, pointing to a different aspect of the problem. Aside from the second and third sessions of the Council, in which membership was a simple procedure because there were as many seats as candidates, Australia has always held a seat in either Category 1 or Category 2. When unsuccessful in its bid for a seat as an important aeronautical state, it has been virtually guaranteed a seat as a major contributor of facilities or by virtue of its geographical position. Since Australia ranks behind Singapore and the Republic of Korea in international scheduled traffic, wherein lies Australia's aeronautical importance? Aside from its dependence on air transport, not an unique characteristic, Australia has been concerned with the development of air transport from the pioneering days of aviation. As a victorious ally, it was a major participant in the Chicago Conference. As Tourtellot has observed, it is remarkable that Australia has retained its Council status as a major aeronautical power and that China has not yet gained it.[7]

The Third World remains under-represented, cheated by history in the first category and by geography in the second. As a result, regional representation has become the sole possibility for these states to aspire to a Council seat since only by being the official candidate of a regional caucus can a state be assured of election by the full Assembly membership. There being no contest in Category 1 – the number of candidates is generally the same as the number of available seats – a greater number of countries has in recent years vied for seats in the other categories, oftentimes running in both the second and third races.[8] It is interesting to observe that in order to gain a Council seat, states have had to adapt their tactics in ways that were not envisaged by the Chicago conferees.[9]

Political lobbying today is in marked contrast to the club-like election in 1944 when the 20 members of the Interim Council were selected for the first time. When India failed to win a seat, Norway with the backing of the Scandinavian countries formally relinquished its seat. Not to be outdone, Cuba with the backing of the Latin American delegations, took the floor and asked Norway to reconsider its move, offering instead its own seat to India. The Chicago conferees eventually accepted Cuba's offer by acclamation.[10]

Cuba acted less charitably in 1986 when it made its next bid for a Council seat. The Latin American caucus on that occasion failed to present a united front among candidates for two seats held by Jamaica and Colombia which were up for re-election. These two countries failed in their bid and were replaced by Cuba and Peru. Likewise, the 26th session of the Assembly in 1986 saw a spirited contest for the seat held by Lebanon for 33 years. Lebanon lost out to Saudi Arabia in the Category 2 elections and again to Iraq in the final rounds.

While the criteria for elections have not been challenged, the number of seats allocated to each category has been a bone of contention. As Tourtellot points out, 'it was logical that the states of chief importance be represented on the Council. Yet the formal recognition of this elite group raises one of the fundamental dilemmas facing all international organizations: the conflict between the realities of the international scene and the sovereign equality of states'.[11]

Even in 1944, the Chicago conferees perceived that a separate designation of the most important states could eventually breed resentment. Portugal instead proposed states 'which have attained the largest development in civil aviation'. This could be interpreted to refer to progress rather than to an absolute status. Cuba and Mexico, on the other hand, advocated a fifteen-member Council with 'adequate representation' of the most developed states and regional diversity. The United States attempted to sidestep the problem by assigning a specific number of seats to each region while committing the Council to permanent great power representation.

With major aeronautical states firmly entrenched in the Council, there has been pressure over the years to enlarge that body and to find ways to give new states greater opportunities to be elected. When the membership was twenty-one, the Assembly decided that the maximum number of states to be elected in the three parts of the election should be eight, seven and six respectively. In 1950, only twenty states were candidates for the twenty-one Council seats and the Assembly suspended the rule requiring a three-part election. It decided instead that there should be a single secret ballot. The twenty candidates received the necessary majority of votes cast and were accordingly elected. (The vacant place was filled at the next session in 1951 by the election of Spain.) In 1953, there was again a single secret ballot as the number of candidates matched the number of seats. In 1962, 1965, 1968 and 1971, with a Council membership of twenty-seven, there was an even division of nine states being elected in each category. In 1971, Article 50(a) of the Chicago Convention was amended to increase the Council membership to 30 so that in 1974 and 1977 there was again an even division with ten states elected in each category. The rules were once again amended in 1974 to add three more members and to give the three categories respectively ten, eleven and twelve seats. Another move is afoot to dilute further the power of the large states by raising the Council membership to 36.

In enlarging a governing council, increases in absolute size, while logical, are fraught with risks. Beyond a certain limit, such a body begins to lose its character as a small executive and efficient entity and begins to resemble unwieldy universal assemblies. The original ratio of Council seats to ICAO membership was originally 2:5, the high proportion reflecting the low number of contracting states. To achieve the same ratio today with more than 160 states would require a Council of over 50 members. The answer, according to Tourtellot, lies not in attempting to regain the original ratio but in revising the method of election.[12]

A noticeable trend over the years has been for a group of states to share power on a rotational scheme. Thus, the Scandinavian countries have joined forces to be represented by a single candidate for a seat in Category 2. The Benelux countries, Austria and Switzerland, have done the same to be guaranteed a seat in the same category. A similar trend has been evident among the Arab states of the Maghreb with the election of Morocco in 1974 and 1977, Algeria in 1980 and Tunisia in 1986.

THE DOUBLE-HEADED EXECUTIVE

Besides the broad powers invested in the Council, another unique feature of the Organisation compared with other agencies of the United Nations system, is that it has at its helm not one but two top-ranking international civil servants – the President of the Council and the Secretary General. The President is elected by the Council for a term of three years and may stand for re-election. The Council of ICAO has had only three Presidents – Dr Edward Warner (USA) 1947–58; Walter Binaghi (Argentina) 1958–76 and Dr Assad Kotaite (Lebanon) since 1976. Their long tenure is a testimony of the stability in direction of the Council's work as well as a tribute to their outstanding personal and professional qualities.

As Thomas Buergenthal has rightly pointed out, the Council President is the individual most influential in shaping the activities of the Organisation.[13] The personality of the President can have a significant effect on the conduct of the Council's work. His perception of his role, his style, as well as his working methods and techniques, influence the way in which he handles his responsibilities. His duties go far beyond the terse description in Article 51 of the Convention which merely requires him to convene meetings of the Council and its subsidiary bodies, to serve as the representative of the Council and to carry out on behalf of the Council the functions which have been assigned to him. In a most propitious way, each of the three presidents has brought particular skills to bear on the work of that body and been able to mark the evolution of the Organisation at crucial periods of its history.

Dr Warner had been concerned with international aviation long before the advent of ICAO. He was responsible for much of the organisational work that led to the Chicago Conference and took an active part in the work of the technical and economic committees. Afterwards, he was widely credited for putting ICAO on the international map. As an aeronautical engineer, Walter Binaghi was particularly qualified to oversee the drafting of standards in civil aviation at a time of sweeping technological development, including the introduction of jet-powered aircraft. He also oversaw the expansion of technical assistance to the new states. By the time he retired in 1976, legal questions pertaining to hijackings and other conflicts were becoming as pressing as the technical problems. Binaghi's hand-picked successor was eminently equipped to deal with these issues. As the Organisation's secretary general and as a jurist, Dr

Kotaite could draw on his considerable experience to face the kind of political issues which could never have been anticipated in the earlier years.

Shaping his role to fit a need for an international troubleshooter, the current President has rendered good offices in delicate negotiations and helped settle problems before they developed into confrontations on various incidents related to the Arab–Israeli conflict, the Iran–Iraq fighting as well as other issues involving the safety of international air routes in various trouble spots of the world.[14]

Second in status to the Council President is the Secretary General who is charged with the administration of the Organisation. Since ICAO is the only agency within the UN system in which the administrative and political decisions are the responsibility of different executives, the distribution of authority between the two heads is a matter of particular interest. The boundary lines are not set in the Convention, nor have they been defined by the Council. The relationship between the two ICAO executives has been established by evolutionary process according to the personalities of the incumbents.

According to the provisions of the Convention, the President is to 'serve as representative of the Council' but nothing is said concerning his status in the permanent administration or of his relations with the Secretary General. Official documents of the Organisation describe the President as being 'the permanent representative of the Council' and he is placed at the top of the organisational charts designated to illustrate the hierarchical structure of the administration. He is shown as an integral part of it, as he should, since as an international servant, he is remunerated by the Organisation.

For some time in the provisional structure of the Organisation, there was a separate President's Office composed of an assistant and the External Relations Officer who were members of the secretariat but reported directly to the President. As of 1950 this has no longer been the case. The Interim Council in considering the organisational relationship between the President and the Secretary General, had originally described it in the following terms: 'the Secretary General is the chief executive and administrative officer of the Organization that coordinates and directs the activities of the Departments of the Secretariat. He is responsible to the President'. This wording was amended to make the Secretary General responsible to the Council.[15] He reports to the Council through the

President who decides whether the matter can be settled directly or has to be referred to the Council.

The status of the higher direction along with the respective responsibilities of the Council President and Secretary General came up once more in 1956 when the UK proposed that both posts be abolished and replaced with the single post of Director General with functions embracing but substantially enlarged from those exercised by the Secretary General.[16] The proposal noted that the President's duties were deemed to be of a permanent nature when the Council was in constant session in the formative years of the Organisation but that this was no longer the case. The UK proposal was rejected and no further suggestions were ever made regarding the dual leadership.

The boundary lines in the management of the Organisation have become very tenuous as many administrative questions which come before the Council, such as high-level secretariat appointments, have political implications. On some occasions, the Council has even entrusted the Secretary General with tasks that entailed political risks as in the case of the investigation by the ICAO secretariat of the shooting down of KAL 007 in 1983.

Considering the potential for conflict in a double-headed executive, ICAO has been well served in its 45-year history; there has been no evidence of any personal rift between the Council presidents and the secretaries general. In the history of ICAO, the following held the top secretariat post: Dr Albert Roper (France), E.C.R. Ljungberg (Sweden), R.M. MacDonnell (Canada), B.T. Twigt (Netherlands), Dr Assad Kotaite (Lebanon), Yves Lambert (France), and Dr S.S. Siddhu (India) since 1 August 1988.

It would be difficult to generalise on the working relationship between the two heads in ICAO because the office holders have displayed a variety of qualities. The appointment of Dr Roper as ICAO's first secretary general was almost predestined since he had served with ICAN (the International Commission for Air Navigation) – ICAO's precursor. He was succeeded by the head of the Swedish Board of Civil Aviation who in turn was succeeded by a Canadian diplomat without discernible aviation background. He was followed by ICAO's chief of finance who had worked in private business before joining the Organisation. Both Assad Kotaite and Yves Lambert, on the other hand, have had government careers and served on the Council as their country's representative before being appointed secretary general. The present incumbent was also a civil servant who held the top post at Air India. He headed at the same time India's Civil Aviation Administration.

Of these seven executives, two were trained as lawyers (Roper and Kotaite), two were trained engineers (Ljungberg and Lambert), one was a career diplomat (MacDonnell), one had primarily a business background (Twigt). The incumbent holds a doctorate in philosophy. About all that can be deduced from this mixture of backgrounds is that technical training and experience seem less important than political considerations. This is not to minimise their other qualifications.

Political considerations were clearly evident in 1988 with the appointment by the Council of a Third World candidate, thereby ending the unprecedented twelve-year tenure of Yves Lambert. Lambert himself had been elected in 1976 as the result of a split between the Council's Latin American and Asian members. In 1988, these states joined together to replace him in a contentious move widely perceived to have been a show of strength by Third World countries.[17]

THE INTERNATIONAL SECRETARIAT

The political independence and integrity of the secretariat in the United Nations system have been the subject of much debate. In an international public organisation, the bureaucracy is much more vulnerable to political pressures than in national administrations. Nominations, renewals of contract and eventually dismissals depend not only on the decision of the top administrator but can be influenced by the intervention of governments (foreign ministries or national representatives).[18] In the United Nations itself and in some of the larger agencies (UNESCO in particular), such interventions are accepted as a matter of course. This in turn predisposes staff members to turn to their governments for support on matters affecting their personal status. Favouritism, whether sought by governments or the top agency administrator, has long undermined staff morale and reduced the efficiency of these organisations.[19]

In the words of one former UN official: 'probably no secretary general, and certainly no head of a department, is likely to have the Masada instinct necessary invariably to resist these sorts of pressures'.[20] The same official points out that the large majority of member states in the UN system neither understand nor believe in the principle of an independent civil service at home and prefer a 'lusty mixture of politicisation and patronage that produces a bureaucracy serving the interests of the governing political party'.[21]

ICAO, however, has been insulated from these pressures since the staff establishment requires highly-trained specialists and relatively few administrators. Also, the generous granting of permanent contracts has until recently fostered a career system which made personnel practices at ICAO different than in many other agencies where appointments, contract renewals and promotions are the sole prerogative of the director or secretary general.

Cases of nepotism and cronyism are remarkably absent in ICAO. It would be difficult to imagine administrations lobbying for certain posts (except for those of directors) or staff members lobbying delegates or Council members to further their careers. There are, however, political implications in the choice of directors, and the geographical distribution among these five posts is now an accepted policy. In fact, the choice allowed the Secretary General is strictly limited to establishing a short list and basing his decision on the recommendation of the Council. With respect to Soviet officials, the Secretary General has practically no control and accepts the official government candidate. Yet, the Secretary General has been known to resist pressure from the Council and in at least two cases, Yves Lambert has held firm on the appointment of a director to secure his own choice over that of the Council. The problem was even more delicate in that the candidates in both instances were Council members.

The appointment of a director with less than desirable credentials can be disastrous to any organisation. At the very least, it can prove to be an embarrassment for the country which gained the appointment (as was the case when a Soviet bureaucrat who resigned his post of Director of the Legal Bureau before his term was over). Conversely, given the fact that ICAO directors can serve a maximum of eight years, they can wield considerable influence in their area of competence. There are several examples such as the outstanding jurists who headed the Legal Bureau. One such notable person was Dr Eugène Pepin, the first secretary of the Legal Committee who helped draft the Paris Convention of 1919 (the precursor of the Chicago Convention) and as a nonagenarian in the 1980s was still actively interested in ICAO's work.

Besides having a say in the appointment of directors, the Council, acting on a resolution of the Assembly, has initiated personnel policies to bring about a more equitable geographical distribution of the professional staff. In terms of countries represented on the staff, there certainly has been an improvement with 75 nationalities in 1988 compared with 64 in 1978. Nonetheless, the inescapable fact after more than 40 years of personnel recruitment is that the major aeronautical countries still account for the majority of the staff. In 1976, the secretariat breakdown showed 133 nationals from 18 developed countries (or 75 per cent of the professional staff) as against 41 nationals from Third World countries and three from the Soviet bloc. About half of the staff came from four states (Canada, US, France and the UK). Ten years later, the breakdown showed 156 nationals from 19 developed and newly-industrialised countries (65 per cent of the staff). The number of nationals from developing countries had grown to 81, or 33 per cent, while the number of nationals from Canada, US, France and the UK had dropped to 43 per cent.

While in 1976, career contracts were still offered to new staff, this is no longer the case. As a result, appointments on a fixed term makes it possible to replace the original cadre of career professionals with nationals from countries not represented on the staff. While the merit principle still holds, it is nonetheless evident that the nationality of the candidate has become a prime factor in his appointment.

TECHNICAL AND POLITICAL CONSIDERATIONS

No analysis of the decision-making process in ICAO can be complete without examining the Air Navigation Commission (ANC). Of the six subsidiary bodies which assist the Council, two are expressly mentioned in the Convention. They are the ANC and the Air Transport Committee, whereas the Legal Committee, the Committee of Joint Support of Air Navigation Services, the Finance Committee and the Committee on Unlawful Interference with Aircraft were established by the ICAO Assembly. Unlike the standing committees of the Council consisting of Council members or their deputies, the ANC is composed of fifteen individuals (originally twelve) who are appointed by the Council from a list of nominees submitted by the contracting states. They do not sit as representatives of their governments but in their individual capacity with the exception of the chairman who is appointed by the Council. The

Commission can be described as a committee of experts which advises the Council on technical questions, and develops the standards and recommended procedures for adoption by the Council. The Commission is therefore at the heart of ICAO's normative function.

As in the case of the Council, some states have a quasi-permanent status on the ANC (Australia, Canada, China, the Scandinavian and the Benelux-Austria-Switzerland groups, the Federal Republic of Germany, France, Japan, Spain, the UK, the United States and the USSR). The Council is limited in selecting suitable nominees from other countries because of the available pool of individuals having 'suitable qualifications and experience in the science and practice of aeronautics', as spelled out in the Convention (Article 56).

There have been various attempts in the past to increase the membership of the ANC to balance the representation between the large aeronautical states and countries which, in the words of the Council member from Mexico, are less advanced technologically but nonetheless have qualified experts who can contribute to the work of the Organisation. These states mounted a successful drive to have the 1989 Assembly increase the ANC membership to 19 members. The large states tried in vain to stop the move in Council, using the same arguments as in 1971 when they failed to block a first increase from 12 to 15 members.[22] They argued that the Commission's quality was more important than quantity, because as one Council member delicately noted, 'not all ANC members are discharging their functions in an excellent manner'.[23] Most Council members, however, felt that an increase in membership was justified in light of technological requirements.

The Commission is facing a formidable task that is bound to test the qualifications of its members. Planning global navigation systems will require decisions quite unlike what the Commission has been used to. From its earliest days ICAO has been guided by the principle that it must deal with technical issues and problems that are mature and have reached a point at which a global decision can be taken without undue controversy or protracted debate. In the field of air navigation, 'maturity' means that equipment, systems or concepts have been exposed not only to tests and evaluations, but also to sustained operations in one or more countries. This will not be the case with global systems and the elements of the future air navigation infrastructure which will determine the development of aviation beyond the next century.

Since all technical questions come up before the ANC, what is decided in the Commission determines the final outcome in the Council. Given the complexity of issues, the ANC relies on the expert advice of specialists, usually representatives of the aeronautical industry, the airlines and pilots. The Commissioners, who cannot be expected to be all-encompassing experts, are prone to accept such advice or turn to their governments for instructions on important decisions. Moreover, outside actors from the industry have become more active in world affairs, particularly in the fields of communications and transportation. For James Rosenau this means that 'the processes . . . conducted by governments have been supplemented by relations among private individual groups that can and do have important consequences for the course of events'.[24]

Since technical standards can be in conflict with the economic and sometimes the political interests of major aeronautical powers, their interventions are of particular interest. It has been noted that already in its earliest days the Commission was influenced by political considerations in making its recommendations.[25] This is not to say that these decisions cannot be defended on technical grounds. In fact, considering the number of issues and problems before the ANC, one is struck by the few cases when the Commission was influenced by other than purely technical factors. The cases in question dealt with important issues and as such deserve special attention.

To cite the most noteworthy example, in the mid and late 1970s, the ANC considered the adoption of one of several proposed microwave landing systems (MLS) as the standard equipment for airports by the end of the century. In this instance, the competing and incompatible systems were developed by firms in the UK, France and West Germany, and by a joint US-Australian team. Each commercial effort was strongly backed by the government concerned which perceived the economic and technological advantage in having its system chosen worldwide. The French proposal attracted little interest and was withdrawn. Consultations led Germany to back the US-Australian bid in exchange for support of a German technique for other purposes. After this trade-off was completed, there remained only the American-Australian and the British proposals on the table. The British soon charged the US Federal Aviation Administration (FAA) with providing inaccurate data to discredit the British system while American officials accused British commercial interests of engaging in 'vicious lobbying' and impugning the integrity of the FAA.[26]

After years of wrangling at the ANC, the final decision was made in a technical meeting of all states to recommend the US-Australian scanning-beam system over the British Doppler system. The final vote was by secret ballot to assure that delegates would be free to express their preferences without concern for possible political repercussions or prior commitments.[27] The crux of the problem was summed up by a British delegate who noted that 'those participating in the final choice were faced with the impossible task of studying some 2,000 pages of material on complex operational and technical issues and the time did not permit adequate study by those states which had not previously participated in the many years of preparatory work'.[28]

Since many experts concluded that the British Doppler system was at the time more advanced and could have been more rapidly implemented, one must view the decision as being primarily a political choice. The selection process was flawed from the beginning. ICAO named ten specialists to a panel to evaluate the competing systems. Although each specialist was selected on an individual basis and not as an official representative, five came from countries that were in the competition. Each of them consistently took positions favouring his government's proposal.[29] Considering that the prize was worth about $4 billion in equipment sales, such bias might have been expected. Throughout the selection process, the avionics manufacturers concerned were conspicuous at meetings and demonstrations.

It is doubtful that any lesson was learned from the selection process. In fact, the dogfight was a replay of a similar controversy over the choice of the VOR/DME as the standard short-range navigational aid in the late 1950s. At that time, the major contenders were again the UK and the United States, the first proposing the Decca system more suitable to the needs of European traffic, and the US the VOR/DME system. It was evident at the time that the manufacturers were lobbying in favour of their system.

Another illustration of the industry's participation in the ICAO decision-making process concerns airline manufacturers. Since it is a standard practice for these firms to lobby their governments, it is not surprising that they are also active on the international scene. A recent case concerns safety standards for long-range operations by twin-jet aircraft. Manufacturers – Boeing in particular – had been pressing governments to allow the use of newer twin-engined aircraft on longer routes. Since international recommendations were set in 1946 when these aircraft could only be used on short routes, the need for new international guidelines was clearly evident. After initial hesitation ICAO took up the matter with the help of a panel consisting of representatives of national regulatory agencies, the aircraft manufacturers, airlines and pilot associations. The group went over a mass of statistical data on engine reliability furnished by the industry.[30]

Boeing's intense lobbying efforts to relax national and international rules on the use of twin-jets were clearly motivated by commercial considerations. The company had estimated that it could sell an additional 30 models of the Boeing 767 for a potential $1.3 billion if the aircraft could be used on longer routes.[31] As one trade journal wrote at the time: 'Boeing's intentions make its motivation unashamedly clear and Boeing's motivation will be nearly identical to that of Airbus and similar to that of the airlines.' The same publication noted that ICAO as well as the FAA and the British CAA believed that the statistical data was not enough to allow twin-jets to fly on long over-water routes without exception.[32]

In the absence of data based on sustained operations, ICAO took a prudent approach by setting a safety threshold beyond which twin-jets could be used only with special equipment. The decision was justified on the basis of safety risks since the chance of both engines failing independently in the same hour was estimated at 10 billion to one.[33] Yet it would appear that the impossible happened when a British Midland Boeing 737 crashed just south of the East Midland Airport on 8 January 1989, killing 44 of the 126 passengers on board. The crash blamed on faulty wiring caused consternation as the FAA ordered a series of mandatory inspections of all twin-jets built by Boeing since 1980.

In conclusion, decision-making processes in the Council and its subordinate bodies favour the large aeronautical states and by extension their airlines and manufacturers. It would be difficult to imagine the Council or the Air Navigation Commission taking decisions which might be in conflict with the political and economic interests of the large aeronautical states. The power structure in ICAO is stratified to the extent that these major players have the determinant say in major political issues affecting the development of civil aviation.

5 International Aviation and the Third World: The Politics of Equal Opportunity

> *. . . the undersigned governments having agreed on certain principles and arrangements in order that international civil aviation may be developed in a safe and orderly manner and that international air transport services may be established on the basis of equality of opportunity . . .*

Preamble to the Chicago Convention

The international system which evolved from the Chicago Convention and was institutionalised in ICAO was meant to protect the sovereign rights of states and assure the safety, regularity and orderly development of civil aviation on the basis of equality of opportunity.[1] The principle of national sovereignty over the airspace is important in the regulatory context because it is at the heart of the regime governing the bilateral negotiation of traffic rights between states. As Ronald Bickley has pointed out, it ensured wide participation in international air commerce as states seized the opportunity to develop air services which complement their national aspirations and their commercial needs.[2]

Sovereignty in civil aviation has meant little in economic terms for most developing countries. The system, as dictated by the economics of air transport and the interests of major airlines, has failed them in their expectations of equal opportunity for financial assistance. They belong to a system which they cannot use to their advantage notwithstanding Stephen Krasner's assertion that it conforms to their preferences for 'principles, norms, rules and decision-making procedures' which favoured 'authoritative rather than market allocation'.[3]

Civil aviation in developing countries cannot be separated from overall developments in air transport. Indeed, the Third World was the first to feel the impact of changes which have swept the industry in the last decade. Most developing countries under the best of circumstances would have required a long period of protected development for their weak and less efficient flag carriers find themselves more than ever vulnerable in a system which cannot respond to their specific needs. As Ali Ghandour, Royal Jordanian Airline's chief executive put it: 'The Third World, as at present constituted and in so far as these developments in the aeronautical environment are concerned, is essentially a by-stander, willing but unable to influence, let alone participate in, the course of events'.[4]

THIRD WORLD: THE MYTH OF COHERENCE

In a divided world, countries have operated on the international scene in more or less coherent groups. The Third World is the largest such political grouping in the UN system on the basis of shared problems and common expectations. It is the least coherent unit, comprising states which are neither industrialised nor part of what had been the socialist bloc of Eastern Europe, but nevertheless show close political or economic affinities with one or the other grouping.

Because of varying conditions of underdevelopment, Robert Rothstein has stressed the need to distinguish between different groups in the Third World. Differentiation is inevitable, he notes, because of different starting points, resource endowments, growth rates and because differences have been made more salient by the passage of time.[5] These variables are all the more apparent in civil aviation. The obstacles faced by developing countries in air transport are manifold. They are caused by world conditions, problems specific to a particular region and by priorities set by the countries themselves.

The international system affects Third World airlines in different ways depending on how well they have weathered the economic turbulence of the early 1980s. As a group, for the decade 1979–88, they increased their share of the world international scheduled traffic. But however significant this achievement, it has been primarily due to the performance of the newly industrialised countries: Saudi Arabia, the Gulf States, Malaysia, Singapore, Thailand, Korea, and to a lesser extent India, Pakistan, the Philippines and Brazil. (Saudi Arabian Airlines averaged the highest annual growth rate of 10.4 per cent as against the 7.1 per cent world average.) In 1988, these airlines accounted for 15.2 per cent of the world international scheduled traffic and represented a privileged faction in the system. Most other airlines in Asia, Latin America and Africa have barely maintained their share of the world's market or have experienced a decline, plagued as they are by problems of mismanagement, the lack of planning and a shortage of marketing and commercial expertise.[6]

By far the worst problems exist in Africa which contains a large proportion of the world's poorest countries. It is also a continent where international air routes, like its national boundaries, were in many cases inherited from colonial days when the flow of traffic was North–South.[7] A number of airlines were developed under the wing of the national carriers of the colonial powers and some of these links still exist. Complete independence has eluded African carriers for lack of technical resources. As one writer has noted, African airlines fear domination by powerful carriers of the developed countries.[8]

EQUALITY OF OPPORTUNITY: A BRIGHT PROMISE

Theoretically, as proclaimed in the preamble of the Chicago Convention, international carriers operate 'on the basis of equality of opportunity'. In reality, this equality has remained but a bright promise for most developing countries. International air transport services, based on the principle of national sovereignty, reflect national interests extending far beyond the limits of air transport economics. Developing countries cannot bargain from a strong position to exchange trading rights in bilateral air services agreements. Nor can one speak of true competition. A United Airlines flight from New York to Dakar is not the same as an Air Afrique flight from Dakar to New York. The American flight represents a marginal asset while for the African carrier it is a matter of survival.

Christer Jönsson has observed that in bilateral negotiations, small airlines generally face major disadvantages because of high operating costs, small fleets, few routes and poor use of aircraft. Developing countries are for the most part destination points rather than sources of traffic. Moreover, passengers from developed countries tend to travel on their own flag carriers.[9]

Prior to the Chicago Convention of 1944, and even before the Second World War, bilateral exchange of traffic rights was well established. This period was marked by highly restrictive bilateral air service agreements, negotiated in secrecy and diplomatic intrigue. The former colonial possessions were often used as bargaining chips. In addition, some nations astride direct international routings successfully sold transit or overflying rights, or denied such rights to others. The effect, either way, was highly detrimental to air transport development, given the limited operational capability of aircraft at the time.[10] Small countries competed with one another to attract foreign carriers and establish themselves as important air junctions.

For most of the key participants, one of the basic assumptions was that the prewar system of colonies, protectorates, possessions and zones of influence would continue essentially unchanged. Robert Thornton has pointed out that the Chicago Conference and the subsequent bilateral negotiations were concluded on the assumption that bargaining strength based on colonies was permanent. Of course, events have demonstrated that this was not correct. Almost certainly the results would have been quite different had states bargained from their positions in today's post-imperial structure of nations.[11]

One is tempted to speculate, as Bickley has done, on what might have happened had agreement been reached in Chicago on a multilateral exchange of commercial rights. Given the different philosophies advanced in favour of one approach or another, and the fact that no compromise could be reached at Chicago or in the immediate years thereafter, Bickley believes that any agreement reached subsequently in order to pay lip service to the cause of multilateralism would have been doomed to failure. Under present conditions of a liberal multilateral regime, Bickley questions whether developing nations would have had a real opportunity to participate in international air transport, other than by promoting 'flag of convenience' registries with all that this entails.[12]

All speculations aside, it is clear that by not being present or represented in Chicago, Third World states were the major losers in the overall compromise. Because participants in the Chicago Conference could not agree on the nature of an economic role for ICAO, none was formulated and it was left, almost by default, for the airlines themselves to establish the economic rules for international air transport through their trade association. IATA has long been perceived as being dominated by the large carriers. A researcher who has studied IATA's closed-door conference system found that the ambitions that prevailed among the aviation powers in the Chicago Conference were carried over to IATA by the major international airlines. He quoted an experienced chairman of the traffic conferences to the effect that most of the 'constructive work' of IATA was done by about a 'dozen larger carriers whose opinions and examples carry very much weight'.[13]

IATA's decisions affect airlines in different ways, depending on whether they are active members participating in the tariff (passenger or cargo) conferences or in the 'interlining' (inter-carrier transfers) or 'clearing house' services covering currency transactions. Airlines of developing countries have different needs from those of established carriers. They are frequently highly protectionist. The nature of their operations encourages higher tariffs to counter greater costs. Although some carriers in industrialised countries are also inefficient, few would support protectionist measures as extreme as those sought by developing countries. These airlines also face particular difficulties because of weak currencies, and one airline – Nigeria Airways – has been suspended twice in the past from the IATA Clearing House for failing to settle its debts.

IATA has argued that its rate-making machinery reflects the consensus of governments. Since some 60–70 per cent of IATA airlines are government-owned, divergences must be reconciled to avoid 'open-rate' situations.[14] IATA has lately reviewed its conference procedures and allowed the presence of ICAO observers. Its tariff-coordinating conferences have become much more transparent and are now open to government observers in addition to those of regional aviation bodies. Conscious also of criticism from airlines of developing nations, IATA has established a programme to help these carriers become self-reliant.

The post-Chicago bilateral regime has helped important aeronautical states, those strong in a political or economic sense or those located in a sufficiently strategic position or along international air routes. They influence international air transport and play a commanding role in ICAO's governing Council.[15] Developing countries have waged an uphill battle to introduce economic issues in ICAO in order to have a greater voice in formulating regulatory policies. Following up on previous unsuccessful attempts to have the Air Transport Committee deal with such matters,[16] a group of African states led by Kenya proposed at the ICAO Assembly in 1965 a plan for special fares to promote tourism in their countries. Most other states opposed ICAO's intervention in tariff matters and felt that such complex arrangements had best be left with IATA.[17]

The unresolved economic issues which had been submerged for more than three decades resurfaced in the 1970s in the wake of deregulation policies and their application to the international system. The strains on the system led ICAO to call a Special Air Transport Conference in 1977. Third World countries were in a predicament. Whatever their dissatisfaction, they realised that the international system was here to stay, embodied in more than 2000 bilateral agreements, and that whatever its shortcomings, the system was better than none at all. In those circumstances, it would have been counter-productive for the Third World to mount an offensive for a 'new transportation order' as some hardliners might have preferred, along the lines of the New International Economic Order (NIEO) adopted by the United Nations in 1974 and the new information order being advanced at UNESCO. Instead of divisive resolutions that would have challenged the existing world order, the Conference settled for improvements of the prevailing system.

Krasner states that civil aviation was spared the North–South confrontations over the allocation of resources because the existing regime already gave them easy access to air transport. Most of the Third World countries possessed their own airline and had secured a substantial share of their own national markets.[18] Only a few, however, have viable international operations that extend beyond a few routes. The ICAO air transport conferences did not give these countries much encouragement with respect to traffic arrangements. The problems were complicated by the low financial results of airlines, first blamed on oil increases, then on the recession of the early 1980s, and on excess capacity, open rates and widespread tariff violations which were not adequately dealt with in bilateral agreements and IATA tariff conferences.

ISSUE-LINKAGE IN THE CONTEXT OF GLOBAL TRADE

Sensing perhaps that their grievances might obtain a better hearing in the context of global trade issues, a number of Third World countries requested the UNCTAD Secretariat to investigate aspects of civil aviation affecting tourism. The UNCTAD report goes beyond the cautious approach of ICAO in its bold conclusion that 'the aviation interests of developing countries may not be adequately safeguarded'.

This report cites several discriminatory and unfair practices in civil aviation. It finds that in addition to such practices, developing countries have structural disadvantages that restrict the growth of their airlines. Of particular concern are restricted opportunities for development and expansion of traffic rights and exchange of routes without preferential treatment. The UNCTAD report concludes that such denial of traffic rights, which are discriminatory under the Chicago Convention, could be viewed as offering the developing countries less than a fair deal.[19]

The same report finds that the virtual demise of the multilateral airfare structure has allowed the more powerful airlines, with their extended route network, to undercut the fares of less competitive airlines, thus threatening their very existence. This is particularly the case with low fares offered exclusively by the world carriers, which tend to draw off traffic from other routes flown by airlines of developing countries.[20]

The more powerful states can also impose discriminatory taxes and excessive airport and user charges. They exert other pressures through computer information and reservations systems covering bookings, hotels and other services. These computer reservation systems (CRS), owned by the larger carriers, are powerful tools in the competition on lucrative routes. The CRS stakes are high in a distributive system where the great majority of ticket sales for major airlines are made by travel agents. In contrast most Third World airlines still sell their tickets directly to passengers. Combined with other effects of deregulation (such as code-sharing and the control of major hubs [interchange points] by one dominant carrier) the built-in bias of computerised reservation systems can be disastrous for small airlines. A small carrier is doomed unless it can generate traffic of its own in a market dominated by large carriers.

The airlines of developing countries fear that they will be adversely affected by the outcome of almost all deregulation policies. In what seemed a desperate effort to stem the tide, the 20 member states of the African Civil Aviation Commission (AFCAC) asked the ICAO Assembly in 1989 for a multilateral agreement on the regulation of CRS which 'would safeguard the basic principle stipulated by bilateral air transport agreements based on fair and equal opportunity of airlines to compete'.[21]

Third World airlines must also face particular financial burdens which further weaken their competitive position. They have expressed concern over costly security requirements as well as over the cost implications of stricter noise regulations on carriers flying to US and European airports. The ICAO Assembly in 1986 urged states to relax noise restrictions already in effect for older jet aircraft and to defer action on second-generation aircraft until ICAO has had a chance to study the political and economic impact. Preliminary studies at the time showed that restrictions on second generation jets would have drastic consequences. They would affect some 5200 aircraft, many of them with less than twelve years of service or half their average life span. The developing states which can ill afford to modernise their fleet would be most affected.

At the 27th session of the Assembly in 1989, the AFCAC states deplored that the previous Assembly's pleas on noise restrictions had been largely ignored and that their applications for exemptions were generally rejected except for non-commercial flights. This time, the developing countries demanded that no restrictions be imposed that were not mandated under Annex 16 (Environmental Protection). The Assembly, given environmental pressures, could do little more than urge states not to impose blanket or unilateral restrictions and to be more generous with exemptions.[22] The plea is not likely to be heeded in the United States or in Europe where the EC Commission has already made it clear that it wants to enforce noise standards to the full extent.

Considering the overwhelming financial burdens, it may well be asked – aside from national prestige – why a government would want to launch an international airline or compete with other carriers that are more efficient in terms of lower costs and large-scale operations. The usual justification may be found in the school of thought associated with Raúl Prebisch. He has argued that industrialisation is the only possible cure for the low productivity and low per capita income of developing countries.[23] There is also a belief that industrialisation will have a psychological effect on the people of a country and transform a traditional dependence on the production of primary goods, by setting higher goals. Transport policies in the developing countries have been linked with overall aspects of social and economic development.

Although the operation of an airline is not usually thought of as 'industrialisation', it is the kind of thinking which, according to William O'Connor, has led governments to establish an airline with little prospect for it to compete on straight, unsubsidised terms with larger, established competitors.[24]

There is also an overriding reason why developing countries want their own national carrier. They cannot expect that foreign airlines will provide the required domestic services, nor in the case of African countries, is there much reason to believe that unrestricted foreign airline operations will lead to a new pattern of air services, such as new routes linking Africa and the Middle East. It seems more likely that foreign airlines will want to perpetuate the past pattern of north–south routes linking Africa with Europe.

Against such overwhelming odds, it makes economic sense for weaker players to pool their resources. However, such considerations have flown in the face of political realities as shown by the demise of East African Airways in 1976 (replaced by individual airlines in the three states concerned), by the former West African Airways Corporation (split in 1958 into Nigeria Airways and Ghana Airways), and by the problems besetting the multinational Air Afrique which is still flying thanks to massive French assistance in management and technical operations.[25]

Pooling resources is the most promising trend as smaller airlines have started operating joint routes and training and overhaul facilities (such as between Thailand and Malaysia). For Ali Ghandour the choice for developing nations is clear. They can either hold on to the protection of bilateral agreements or face up to new challenges. They must band together to achieve maximum efficiency or remain 'money-losing symbols of national pride'.[26]

One possible solution was advanced by the former chief executive of Air Afrique. He advocated four regional carriers for Africa to cover the Maghreb, the Air Afrique states, East Africa and the southern part of the continent. These carriers would pool their resources and operations and eventually become a pan-African entity.[27] Admittedly, this strategy requires extraordinary leadership at the political level to overcome the handicaps of state-owned enterprises and to provide needed capital and trained personnel. It also requires reassessing the concept of the flag carrier as an instrument of national interest.

AVIATION DEVELOPMENT AND TECHNICAL ASSISTANCE

Air transport plays a vital role in social and economic development. The aeroplane permits fast transport of passengers, freight and mail. Its range is worldwide and its reach is not restricted by oceans and mountains.[28] The air transport infrastructure is relatively inexpensive, but it requires sophisticated equipment, well-trained personnel and rational planning.

It is also recognised that upgrading civil aviation in the Third World is important not only to these countries but to all the airlines which use these facilities and services. This is particularly true for countries strategically located on long-distance routes. They assume regional air transport responsibilities that far exceed their own economic interests.

G. Arthur Brown, the Deputy Administrator of the UN Development Programme (UNDP) and former executive of Air Jamaica, has observed the remarkable shift in the earlier perception that aviation in the Third World serves an affluent minority and is thus a luxury rather than a necessity. He finds, for example, the same attitude displayed towards the tourism industry where it is felt that there is something immoral in providing hotels and beaches for people who will be moving around in shorts, straw hats and dark glasses with cameras strung over their shoulders. Yet, many countries achieve the highest and quickest growth in income by selling their inexhaustible resources: the sea, the sun and the sand.[29] Civil aviation and tourism in this respect suffer from the same misconception on the part of international development agencies.

ICAO has done valuable pioneering work in linking air transport with agricultural and industrial development. An early contribution was a two-year study in 1975 of the potential contribution of civil aviation to African social and economic development. In this multi-disciplinary survey ICAO consultants were assisted by experts from other UN agencies. The study covered 37 countries, from Mauritania in the north to Lesotho in the south. It identified more than 200 potential projects in which aviation could assist African states in their development.[30]

These findings must be credited for a relative increase in allocations from the UNDP, the central agency for voluntary contributions from governments and the major source of funding for ICAO technical assistance projects. It is interesting to note the low priority accorded to civil aviation projects by the UN Expanded Programme for Technical Assistance (EPTA) – the forerunner of the UNDP.[31] The increasingly larger percentage of total UNDP resources earmarked for ICAO (presently at 6.5 per cent) reflects the greater priority and urgency which recipient countries have given to civil aviation projects.

For better or for worse, ICAO's Technical Assistance Programme is tied to the uncertain political fortunes of the UNDP, the world's largest channel for multilateral technical cooperation to some 150 developing countries. Yet, various studies starting with the Jackson Report found that the UNDP's coordination of some 100 different agencies in the social and economic fields is a hopeless task.[32] As a UN inspector wrote:

> This fragmentation of activities is not offset by any real coordination either at the intellectual level or at the methodological and institutional level. Each organization has not only its methods but also its theory on development and on the goals which should be pursued by the recipient countries . . . The system thus relieves UNDP of the need to have its own concept of development.[33]

If fragmentation of resources were not dangerous enough, the executing agencies come to the UNDP as rivals, each one trying to obtain as large a slice of the pie as possible. In this scramble for funds the small technical agencies can never hope to outperform the larger agencies. Donor countries have tended to bypass the UNDP altogether and to allocate funds directly for humanitarian and social programmes.[34] It is no wonder therefore that multilateral aid for development has been under criticism for wastefulness, lack of coordination and poor evaluation. The UNDP has come under fire from its major donor as part of the US belt-tightening offensive against the UN.[35]

The US position further clouds a sombre financial climate at the UNDP where contributions since the early 1980s have fallen short of expectations. As a result, funding for projects executed by ICAO and other UN agencies have been reduced proportionately.[36] All the funds ICAO receives from the UNDP and other sources in one year do not even cover the cost of one jumbo jet. Because of its scant resources, ICAO concentrates its technical assistance on manpower development, leaving it to others – the World Bank, the regional development banks, bilateral funds and the countries themselves – to build the infrastructure and acquire aircraft.

THE LENDERS OF LAST RESORT

The developing countries have turned to the World Bank and its affiliated International Development Association (IDA) as a lender of last resort for building their aviation infrastructure. The limitations of these agencies with respect to aviation are more doctrinal than financial. As William Ascher has pointed out, the World Bank presents the most formally institutionalised features of an international economic regime.[37] It would therefore be out of the question for such an institution to launch new initiatives that run counter to the ingrained concepts of the bureaucracy and to the interests of the major states which hold the purse-strings.[38]

Eliud Mathu, a former chairman of Kenya Airways, has suggested that the World Bank help provide airlines of the Third World with loans for the acquisition of aircraft, the same way airlines in the US and Europe do in the world's market places. He has even suggested that the World Bank set up an International Aviation Finance Association or finance a grant-leasing organisation.[39] Since international aid agencies do not purchase commercial aircraft as a legitimate form of assistance, Third World countries are used as a dumping ground for old aircraft sold at exorbitant prices, or must depend on credit from aircraft manufacturing states or on leasing arrangements through financial intermediaries.[40]

If the international financial institutions have not lived up to the expectations of the Third World when it comes to aviation development, neither have the regional development banks which these countries believed would be better disposed towards them. Krasner points out that these regional banks were created to resist the developed countries' 'hegemony in the world economy', yet they are still largely dependent on the industrialised nations for resources.[41] The only assistance for civil aviation has been a $3 million loan for a project in Lesotho from the African Development Bank, the regional institution which has achieved the most autonomy. The Inter-American Bank and the Asian Development Bank have not shown similar interest in civil aviation.

To make up for chronic deficiencies in funding, ICAO has placed high hopes on funds-in-trust arrangements set up by the recipient state or by another government or donor organisation. Such trust fund arrangements supply equipment and services to the Third World on advantageous terms. However, while several countries, among others Argentina, Colombia, Ecuador, Egypt, Greece, Morocco, the Philippines and Tunisia, have received additional aid, on the whole the scheme has primarily benefited the oil-producing nations. The most outstanding example of charity beginning at home is Saudi Arabia. Its contribution totalling $36.4 million (in 1983 and 1984) represented more than 80 per cent of all trust funds projects executed by ICAO during that time.[42]

Appeals to broaden the base of ICAO's technical assistance programme outside the ordinary budget have met with mixed success. An ICAO Assembly resolution (A24/16) yielded just over $6 million in the three-year period 1983–6 including $1 million from the OPEC Fund for International Development and $1.5 million from Brunei. This represents only 7.3 per cent of the funds obtained from the UNDP in the same period. The situation is not specific to ICAO. A Special Fund for Technical Cooperation established in 1973 by the ITU to meet urgent needs of the developing countries for telecommunications equipment and networks yielded only 426 890 Swiss francs over a ten-year period (1973–83).[43]

Over the years, the developing countries have attempted in vain to create special funds within ICAO's ordinary budget. At the 16th Assembly in 1968, Tunisia with solid Third World support succeeded in having a special fund of $300 000 included in the triennial budget, although the United States, France, the UK and West Germany objected that this would run contrary to their government policy, concentrating all technical assistance resources within the UNDP. This unique experiment was not repeated beyond that one financial exercise. When a group led by Colombia tried once more to create a technical assistance fund for aviation security, the move was quashed in the Council and was not presented to the 26th session of the Assembly in 1986.[44]

ICAO's basic power structure makes the task of processing such demands all the more frustrating. The Third World's power of action is based on a voting strength that has no practical effect on the realities of power within the Organisation.[45] Changes in the power structure would entail amendments to the Chicago Convention, which must be approved by a two-thirds vote of the Assembly and ratified by no less than two-thirds of the total number of contracting states. Raoul Lahogue has rightly observed Article 94 has served to blunt the consequences of the voting power of the Third World since unlike ordinary decisions of the Assembly which are not binding, the developing countries would need to muster two-thirds of the membership to effect essential changes favourable to their interests.[46]

The massive entry of the Third World into the international scene has had a marked effect on the voting patterns of the various agencies but has not affected the basic power structure in the international aviation system where the major aeronautical countries remain the power-brokers. Developing countries are part of a system elaborated without their effective participation. They have little to gain from bilateral bargaining in which they cannot compete on the basis of equal opportunity nor are they benefiting from trade practices serving oligopolistic interests. Their weak airlines can never hope to survive in a deregulated market unless they adopt radically new attitudes on multinational cooperation. Mathu has likened their dilemma to a poker game where all the cards are stacked against them and where the players are asked to play without limits on the stakes.[47] In this kind of game, where much depends on borrowing against future pay-offs, Third World countries are at the mercy of the other players who also control the pool from which they must draw to stay in the game.

The real issue, which has been raised in a controversial UN document by Maurice Bertrand, is whether the world organisation, which spends a great deal of time and effort on international development strategies, is in fact equipped to deal with global issues except in a superficial way. The industrialised countries prefer to discuss these problems among themselves and keep developing countries out of the discussions. Only radical structural reforms leading to the development of an 'economic United Nations' side by side with the political United Nations could solve economic problems with the full participation of developing countries. As Bertrand points out, a favourable political climate is a *sine qua non* even before a start can be made.[48]

6 Civil and Military Aviation: Sharing the Same Sky

And the moral of that is – 'The more there is of mine, the less there is of yours'.

Lewis Carroll, *Alice's Adventures in Wonderland*

Civil and military aviation, which share the same airspace, have learned to live in a symbiotic relationship, each responding to its own rules. The close links between civil and military aviation were well understood when governments were the principal actors in the early days of commercial aviation. These links have been severely strained in what has been called an era of interdependence.[1] At issue are questions about the control of the airspace, security needs, the misuse of civil aircraft and the application of military technology by civil aviation.

HISTORICAL CONSIDERATIONS

At the time of the Chicago Conference, many of the implicit or explicit notions about the importance of civil aviation as an instrument of national defence had been postulated before or during World War II.[2] The fears of aerial invasion and airborne intelligence fed by the example of Lufthansa's activities in South America strongly influenced the delegates at the Chicago Conference. While such threats appeared absurd in the light of sober military evaluations, governments considered it an important military objective to possess a sound commercial air route and control over the use of national airspace.[3]

The Conference never dealt directly with the military implications of the postwar development of air transport. Any fears that the military would lose control of the airspace and air routes to a supranational agency were short-lived. Complete and exclusive national sovereignty over the airspace was enshrined in Article 1 of the Chicago Convention. Proposals for an international entity to operate all international air services and for a supranational allocation of air routes were quickly rejected by the Conference. ICAO was to deal exclusively with the safe and orderly development of civil air transport, technical rules and standards.

Coordination between civil and military authorities was not an issue at the time. The few difficult problems at the end of World War II concerned mainly military aircraft, particularly those of the US Air Force. With the exception of Britain, Switzerland, the Scandinavian states and the Iberian peninsula, the US Air Force operated most flights. It also provided essential ground services and facilities for navigation, communication and air traffic services in Western Europe using equipment and techniques developed during the war to handle the boom in both civil and military air traffic.[4] This wartime development led to the concept of a common system which envisaged that the air navigation systems used by military and civil aviation should be as similar as possible so that during a crisis, civil air transport could quickly be integrated into the military system.[5]

European experience with civil aviation during World War II had been different because commercial operations were restricted to the few neutral states. A spirit of improvisation and flexibility therefore guided developments as civil aviation was slowly building up and ground services were still largely provided by the military.

Despite the numerous military installations which existed in the early 1950s in Western Europe (many of which still exist), the sharing of airspace did not present too many problems. Many airways followed devious routings because their straight alignment impinged on military reserved airspace. Propeller-driven civil aircraft operated in the lower layers of the airspace while an increasing number of military jets flew at 20 000 feet. Coordination problems arose mainly at and around aerodromes used by military jets.

There was one aspect of civil/military coordination which became a major problem. About 20 air forces operated in Western Europe, each one with its own particular way of conducting business. This ranged from differing altimetry during landing approaches to the designation of military flight operations under civil air traffic control. To make things even more complicated, this uncoordinated situation existed in a relatively small area, one quarter the size of the US in the airspace controlled by some 20 sovereign states.[6]

Until the mid-1950s, civil and military aviation co-existed in European airspace on the basis of segregation; the military being the supreme master of the upper airspace. The introduction of civil turbo-prop and jet aircraft changed this situation dramatically. The segregation of civil and military air traffic in the NATO portion of Europe then became impracticable.

The basic problem in the co-existence of two-types traffic is that, on one hand civil operators demand the strict application of separate standards between aircraft and rules to protect the airspace in which they fly, while from a military point of view, predetermined flight paths and stringent separation rules negate the freedom of movement and tactical flexibility required by fighter aircraft. Hence there is a need for states to create civil and military control organisations capable of coordinating these two types of flying in an airspace that cannot grow larger.

The ICAO Assembly in 1956 turned its attention to the problem and adopted a resolution on joint civil military use of airspace and air navigation facilities and services. It called on all contracting states 'to encourage coordination between their various aeronautical activities in order that the common use of airspace and of certain facilities and services be so arranged that safety, regularity and efficiency of international civil air navigation will be safeguarded'.[7] This exhortation, repeated at every session of the Assembly and regional Air Navigation meeting, has had very little impact on military authorities beyond national coordination. To extend coordination at the international level requires political cohesion and a regional mechanism which is lacking except within the NATO context.

THE NATO EUROPEAN AIRSPACE

The need to share the increasingly congested airspace led to new forms of coordination between civil and military services and to the establishment by ICAO and NATO of a Committee on European Airspace Coordination (CEAC) in which each NATO member is represented by one civil and one military representative. The European Office of ICAO and IATA participate in an advisory capacity to represent the interests of non-NATO countries and the airlines.

CEAC, like all other NATO committees and the NATO Council itself, works by consensus or unanimity rule. It cannot impose its decisions upon member administrations. One might believe that this would reduce the Committee to impotence, but this is not so. Over the years, discussions in CEAC have led to a give-and-take mentality among its civil and military members. They have come to understand common interests in a wider context and have achieved a substantial degree of compromise and agreement by quiet persuasion, rather than enforcement of decisions.[8] However, experience has shown that things do not necessarily work out so smoothly in practice.[9] National military authorities are sometimes concerned that ICAO decisions may have military implications on which they have not been consulted.

Since the NATO Supreme Allied Commander Europe is responsible for air defence in NATO Europe, CEAC remains the only civil/military forum where NATO military requirements can be taken fully into account in the management of the airspace. One of the Committee's first and most urgent tasks was to conduct a review of restricted, dangerous and prohibited areas in NATO Europe. This review led to the abolition of a number of such restrictions and the establishment of flexible areas for civil and military use.

Another of CEAC's main tasks concerns large-scale NATO and national air defence exercises. Previously such exercises had imposed severe economic penalties on the airlines, or raised safety concerns. CEAC now establishes a yearly schedule of NATO and national defence manoeuvres and convenes joint civil and military working groups to work out compromises. An important spin-off of this coordination process has been the educational effect on civil and military users and airspace managers.

From the late 1950s the Committee became increasingly responsible for better and more uniform civil/military air traffic control in NATO Europe, including the integration of civil and military systems and the joint use of facilities and equipment. CEAC also seeks through a continuous review of civil and military air traffic systems in member countries to achieve common standards. Progress however has been slower than expected because of differing requirements of civil and military air operations.

Political problems have surfaced at times to mar the generally smooth relationship between NATO members. Greece has repeatedly protested the violation by Turkish military aircraft of international airspace in which it provides air traffic services to civil aviation. Greece claims that these intrusions are dangerous and contrary to a NATO agreement of 1981 on the application of Annex 2 to the Chicago Convention (Rules of the Air) to NATO members.

The standard Turkish reply has been that the Chicago Convention does not apply to state (military) aircraft and that its freedom to fly over the high seas is beyond challenge.[10]

CEAC's interest in joint civil/military communications and navigation aids has been indispensable to ICAO's planning for the entire European area. Since 1961, a working group has updated joint air/ground/air communications, navigation aids and frequency requirements into an overall plan for NATO Europe, taking into account the requirements of non-NATO countries.

Furthermore, the work of CEAC has led to the establishment, outside NATO, of the European Organisation for the Safety of Air Navigation (EUROCONTROL) in the early 1960s. As the first supranational effort of its kind, EUROCONTROL's limited concept seemed somewhat short-sighted at a time when NATO was considering the future in terms of a wider scheme of civil/military air traffic control comprising the entire airspace and using common facilities and equipment. However, it was evident that neither the military nor the civil authorities of the member countries concerned would ever implement such far-reaching goals.

EUROCONTROL, for all its innovation in the field of air navigation and international law, has not lived up to its potential. The agency, however, is headed for a brighter future as an amended convention, a wider membership and new urgent tasks in air traffic control have given it a new lease on life. Some of EUROCONTROL's limitations had been built-in from the start. The agency was to provide services only to traffic flying in the upper airspace although the possibility existed for a state to delegate the control of its airspace below that level. The most significant limitation was that each participating state could take back control over its airspace whenever 'the circumstances' so required. It seemed clear therefore that while civil aviation requirements led to the creation of EURO-CONTROL, its ultimate effectiveness rested with the military.[11]

The scope of EUROCONTROL has long been limited by its membership. Initially, when the first discussions took place at ICAO in 1958, the Benelux countries and West Germany envisaged to integrate traffic control in their upper airspace with France, Italy and Britain joining later. As it turned out, only Belgium, Luxembourg and West Germany decided in 1972 to participate in the first EUROCONTROL centre at Maastricht in the Netherlands. The other states continued to operate their own national control centres under the general supervision of the new agency, although the Netherlands later yielded control of its upper airspace to the agency.

To the extent that civil/military coordination takes place at the Maastricht Centre, there is a good working relationship.[12] Military and civil controllers occupy a parallel suite of identical consoles. Procedures rely on aircraft separation rather than on the traditional airspace boundary divisions or the 'sterilisation' of airspace prevalent elsewhere. Military areas extend across permanent airways in a number of locations as part of an agreement that these airways will not interfere with military operations.

TORTUOUS AIR ROUTES AND RESTRICTED AIRSPACE

Civil and military authorities have long been at odds in many parts of the world where air forces have staked out large portions of the airspace and forced airlines to extend flight routes to avoid prohibited zones. The air route patterns set by governments after World War II for technical, military or political reasons may have been acceptable by the airlines at one time. The situation has changed drastically as the result of cost increases and stiff competition which requires airlines to effect as many savings as possible.

An important source of potential cost saving could be realised by the realignment of the air routes in Europe which are much longer than they need be – 15 per cent on average and as much as 47 per cent in extreme cases – according to IATA.[13] The fragmented airspace due to military training areas forces commercial traffic into limited corridors and restricts altitude options and parallel airways which could reduce congestion. IATA has put forward detailed proposals to ICAO for a realignment of the route structure to give carriers a better share of the airspace. It is relevant to note that in many countries all airspace outside published routes is restricted.

In some countries, through the coordination with the CEAC, military authorities have permitted a flexible use of 'their' airspace either regularly during weekends or by allowing direct flight routings when the restricted area is not in use. Weekend routes through military zones provide considerable advantages at peak hours; unfortunately not many such routes are operating.[14]

When seen in the worldwide context, the civil/military working relationship within NATO is exceptional. In other regions, joint civil/military bodies that coordinate airspace management and air traffic control simply do not exist and where they do, they are mostly consultative and therefore unable to take effective decisions.

According to the ICAO Regional Offices, the present situation leads to the existence of large portions of 'special use airspace' (prohibited, restricted, danger and other areas) which impose additional mileage on international routes. In addition, in certain parts of the world, the lack of liaison and close coordination between civil air traffic services units and relevant military operational control/air defence units poses serious safety risks on certain routes.[15] Two such trouble spots have been the Far East and the Gulf area where in a constantly shifting political climate it has not been easy to devise alternate routings.

After air routes over Vietnam were reopened in 1978, international air traffic in the Far East faced a serious problem as the result of tension between China and Vietnam. In July 1980, China declared four danger areas over the high seas along Route Amber–1 in the vicinity of Hainan Island, forcing international flights to use a costly detour on the Bangkok–Hong Kong segment. The Chinese relented somewhat following consultations with the ICAO Council President, but maintained that they were motivated by safety considerations to prevent aircraft from straying into Chinese airspace.[16] From time to time there have been attempts by China, Japan and the two Koreas to establish shorter air routes between China and Japan over the divided sky of Korea. These consultations were linked to the subtle shifts of relationship that have kept tensions high on the Korean peninsula for more than 30 years.

Flight operations across the Gulf on the important trunk routes from Europe to the Far East were severely affected over recent years by the Iran–Iraq conflict and other incidents. The closure by Qatar of its airspace to overflights in April 1986 as the result of a territorial dispute with Bahrain, caused serious congestions and disruptions affecting all airports in the Gulf area. The situation was made even worse when Bahrain citing unauthorised military activity near its airport, established a restricted area which encroached upon the airspace of Qatar and Saudi Arabia. Qatar, as expected, objected to this violation of its sovereignty. Bahrain dismissed the protest and vowed to continue 'to use the area for its aviation in an unrestricted manner'. It said the restrictions were justified and affected only a small segment of international traffic.[17]

The various route restrictions undoubtedly subjected commercial flights over the Gulf to greater threat of military action than necessary while contingency routings were being worked out by ICAO. Furthermore, the US Navy at various times warned aircraft cleared for landing or departure to maintain a safe distance from the naval forces or identify themselves on an emergency frequency. Pilots in such situations were at risk not knowing where to locate the US Navy or having to communicate in the blind. The airlines through IATA expressed concern to ICAO that the reroutings were decided without the agreement of adjacent states and the carriers.

Following the downing of the Iran Airbus in July 1988, the Council directed the Air Navigation Commission to review standards and recommended practices pertinent to hazardous flights. The ANC found that the Annex 11 provisions of the Chicago Convention relating to such activities were adequate if properly applied. These provisions and more particularly those relating to civil and military coordination could only be of 'a general nature' and could not fit specific conditions in different parts of the world.

The ANC conclusions were not satisfactory to the pilots associations. They felt that ICAO should do more to ensure the safety of flight crews in areas of potential danger. In general, IFALPA wanted the carriers to either stop flights or re-route their aircraft to avoid danger zones. The pilots also wanted ICAO to assume responsibility for designating such areas and defining their dimensions, in the event this was not done by a responsible state authority or where a danger zone is over the high seas. The latter request seems logical as international rules apply over international waters. IFALPA also warned the ICAO Assembly that naval forces in international waters ordered civil aircraft to alter air traffic instructions issued by legitimate civil authorities in accordance with existing ICAO regional air navigation agreements.[18]

DEFENCE INTERESTS AND CIVIL AVIATION

The defence link in civil aviation is the simple proposition that transport systems, both surface and air, are essential to the operation of modern military forces.[19] It has even been argued that 'the national defence function is the origin of the striking but highly plausible theorem that the commercial aircraft is a by-product of the warplane'. According to Geo R. Besse, 'the improved performance of successive generations of civil aircraft cannot be dissociated from research for military purposes or those of strategic defence and, if this is less true now with the advent of missiles, the demands of logistics remain, altering the context but not the substance of the problem'.[20] Military planners have always assumed that in emergencies they will have access to civilian fleets and to a certain extent, as demonstrated in the Falklands episode, this still holds true. Britain chartered Short Brothers Belfast heavy-lift aircraft and pressed its medium-range Lockheed C-130s into long-haul operations as part of its buildup at Ascension Island. The Falklands landing itself was supported by chartered commercial cargo and passenger ships. (British Airways was subsequently awarded a contract to transport the troops.)

The use of airlines for transporting troops and supplies during military conflicts has been normal practice. The Dutch ferried troops and materiel in KLM aircraft to Indonesia to quell anti-colonial disturbances in the late 1940s.[21] Egypt supported its military action in South Yemen with its civil airline during the Nasser period. Both India and Pakistan used passenger aircraft for troop transport in 1971 during their armed conflict. American troops were ferried to and from Vietnam in chartered aircraft.

In some countries it is a common practice for the military to provide partial funding for the acquisition of civil aircraft on the understanding that they will be released for military use in the event of a national emergency. Agreements also exist for the operator to provide flight crews, maintenance and servicing. In this instance it is clear that the flight crews are placed in a rather tenuous legal position.

At issue is the definition of 'state aircraft'. At present there is no internationally accepted interpretation of Article 3 of the Chicago Convention which states that the Convention is applicable only to civil aircraft and not to state aircraft and that 'aircraft used in military, customs and police services shall be deemed to be state aircraft'.

The key to Article 3 is contained in the word 'used'. The status of the flight crew is thus determined by aircraft use rather than by aircraft registration, markings or flight plan identification used. The difficulty arises when a commercial aircraft is contracted out to perform special government transport assignments and the persons on board are no longer covered by the provisions of the Convention and other international legal instruments.

The legal vacuum led the International Federation of Airline Pilots Associations to bring before the ICAO Assembly in 1986 and again in 1989 the following occurrences wherein the status of the aircraft involved was or could have been in question:

- On 10 October 1985 Egyptair flight MS 2843 en route from Cairo to Tunis operating as a VIP Charter to the Egyptian Government was being used to transport the alleged hijackers of the Italian cruise ship *Achille Lauro*. The individuals were travelling under armed guard. Even though the crew had filed the standard ICAO flight plan, the aircraft was intercepted by armed aircraft of the US Navy and forced to land at a US navy base in Sicily where the 'passengers' were detained and the aircraft permitted to depart. There was no subsequent action taken by ICAO or any other international body, apparently because no country made a formal complaint.

- On 4 February 1986 an aircraft registered to Libyan Arab Air Lines departed Tripoli en route to Damascus with Syrian diplomatic personnel returning home from a conference. The flight was subsequently intercepted by aircraft of the Israeli Air Force over international waters and forced to land at a military base. Israel which had suspected these passengers to be wanted terrorists subsequently allowed them to continue their journey. Libya lodged a formal complaint to ICAO and presented copies of the certificate of airworthiness and the flight crew's licences as evidence of the aircraft status. The Council accepted the documents and condemned Israel.

- On 12 December 1985 a DC–8 type aircraft operated by Arrow Airways (a US operator) crashed shortly after take-off from Gander, Canada. The aircraft was under charter to the US Department of Defense for the sole purpose of transporting US Army personnel returning from peace-keeping duties in the Middle East. While the sole use of the aircraft was 'military', the accident was classified as a 'fatal-accident – non-scheduled passenger flight' and investigated accordingly under national provisions.

- On 29 September 1984 a US registered B707 operated by South Pacific Airways was en route to a Middle-Eastern desti-nation with 120 Fijian military personnel on board. During the polar transit from Alaska to Europe the flight crew became lost and inadvertently penetrated the sovereign airspace of Norway. The aircraft is understood to have been under charter to the UN Middle East peace-keeping team but again the incident was investigated and corrective measures were initiated by the US under civil procedures.[22]

In the last two cases, as well as in other instances, a further complication was the fact that the aircraft was used solely for military purposes, albeit in the service of an international organisation. It would seem that Article 3 is open to different interpretations and that states are guided more by political convenience than by uniform application of any international rules, thereby creating difficulties for the flight crew.[23]

'MISUSE' OF CIVILIAN TRANSPORT

A longstanding issue is the use of civil aviation for intelligence and other covert missions. The evidence goes back to the early days when aerial pictures were taken from balloons and from an aeroplane piloted by Wilbur Wright. In later years intelligence specialists have cited Aeroflot as a major culprit. As one of them has noted: 'After all, as the largest airline in the world, it maintains offices in nearly every major city of the Western world and its aircraft (the IL–76 for example) are configured for aerial reconnaissance'.[24]

Jay Tuck provides some evidence of Aeroflot planes 'bristling with antennae' regularly straying from civilian routes to fly over sensitive and restricted Western airspace. In one particular day, on 8 November 1981, two Soviet passenger planes diverted from their planned course. One wandered over a navy base in New London, Connecticut, the other over a General Dynamics shipyard in Groton, Connecticut, where a Trident submarine was under construction. Tuck asserts that Aeroflot has often taken advantage of its landing rights in Luxembourg for low-flying excursions over the NATO military bases of West Germany and almost routinely requested permission for charter flights across the American continent – at times and on routes that coincided with a military manoeuvre or an intercontinental missile launch.[25]

Even before the dust had settled in the KAL incident, there was a news report in April 1984 of an Aeroflot TU–124 en route from Bucharest to Marseille straying off course over the French harbour of Toulon, listed on aviation maps as restricted airspace. At the time, the atomic submarine *Rubis* was in for repairs and the aircraft-carrier *Foch* was being outfitted with a highly sophisticated NATO navigation system.[26]

Although powerful satellites have made intelligence missions by civil airliners redundant,[27] military considerations still keep Cubana Airline from using normal routes over the United States on its flights to Canada. The Federal Aviation Administration has a restriction (FAR 91–103) which forces Cuban aircraft from Havana to Montreal to make a considerable diversion over the Atlantic to avoid overflying the mainland. Cuba has objected to ICAO that this restriction is a flagrant violation of the International Air Transport Agreement and the Chicago Convention. It found a measure of support in a resolution of the Third Air Transport Conference which called on states to abide by their international obligations to allow overflights on a non-discriminatory basis.[28]

If Walter Lacqueur stretches the point when he asserts that virtually all countries use civil aviation 'as a tool or a cover for illicit or questionable operations',[29] there is considerable evidence of the misuse of civilian transport for military purposes. The CIA has actually admitted it used civilian airliners for espionage over East Germany and it is a matter of public record that the agency once owned several airlines – Air America, Air Asia, Southern Air Transport and Intermountain Aviation. It came as a surprise to Richard Helms when he took over as CIA Director to learn that Air America was at one time the largest airline of the world.[30] As late as 1987, the CIA was reported using cargo jets painted 'Santa Lucia Airways' to supply Angola guerrillas from an air base in Zaire.[31]

Some of the covert operations by Southern Air Transport in supplying arms to Iran and goods to the Contras were revealed in the wake of the 'Irangate' testimony. Actually, the role of the Miami-based company would have remained secret but for an occupational hazard: one of its aircraft was shot down over Nicaragua in October 1986 and the sole survivor, Eugene Hasenfus, told interrogators he thought his mission was backed by the CIA.[32]

Nicaragua cited several violations of its airspace as far back as 1983 at the 24th Session of the ICAO Assembly. Nicaragua's chief delegate then charged that in September of that year two civil aircraft attacked a boys' school with bombs of US manufacture. The second aircraft carried a bombing mission on the Sandino Airport. This Cessna 404 was shot down, crashed into the control tower and finally came to a halt in flames in the main passenger lounge. The two crewmen were killed.

The next day, according to Nicaragua, two T–28 aircraft originating from Honduras dropped four high-explosive bombs on Port of Corinto and the adjacent Paso Caballos bridge while three civil aircraft flying in from Costa Rica attacked the Cibalsa military unit in the Department of Rivas. On 10 September, another civil aircraft violated Nicaraguan airspace and was shot down in the Isla La Juana area, near El Castillo, on the Costa Rica border. Nicaragua alleged that in the month of August 1983 alone, there were more than thirty violations of Nicaraguan airspace by US aircraft.[33]

The ICAO Assembly never took and was never formally asked to take a position on these alleged incidents, even though the most charitable interpretation of the Chicago Convention would make them a clear violation of Article 4 of the Chicago Convention. This short Article states that 'each contracting State agrees not to use civil aviation for any purpose inconsistent with the aims of this Convention'. It does not attempt to define such misuse. It has never been the subject of a decision or interpretation either by the Assembly or the Council.[34]

AIRPORTS AND STRATEGIC INTERESTS

Airports classified as civil are open to question in many countries, particularly where these airports have a strategic importance. The general policy from the earliest days was that the evolution of a national airport system plan must begin with the determination of the total national transport demand as a function of economic activity, defence needs and the social objectives of the country concerned.

It would be hazardous to determine to what extent some airports cater to both civil and military needs (albeit separately). To take the case of Bandar Abbas, an Iranian airfield used by civilian and military aircraft, the mixed use of the runways contributed to the USS *Vincennes* mistaking an Iran Air Airbus for an F–14 jet about to attack the ship. The commercial airliner was spotted as an unidentified target. At the time, F–14s regularly used the airfield. Furthermore, the US fleet was not routinely monitoring civilian flights in the area and was not listening to the control tower at Bandar Abbas when the airliner took off.[35]

There may also be powerful economic incentives for some countries to confuse the situation purposely. Anthony Sampson cited the case of Cape Verde which provided landing rights to South African Airways at Ilha da Sal on the long route from Johannesburg to New York and Buenos Aires at a time when South Africa was denied overflight rights in Africa. Cape Verde was oddly indiscriminate in providing such facilities, Sampson added, since the airport was also used by Aeroflot to fly Cuban troops to Angola to defend it from South Africa.[36]

Because the role of military aviation varies considerably from state to state, ICAO does not try to provide advice on civil/military coordination but leaves it to each state to do so in such a way as to permit 'the safe and expeditious conduct of flights of civil aircraft'. (Annex 2/2.13)

The military use of civil airports has led at times to excessive fears as illustrated in Nicaragua and Grenada. In the first instance, American officials were convinced that the Sandinista Government was constructing a large airfield to let the Soviet Union extend reconnaissance flights in the northern hemisphere. They claimed that the airfield with a 10 000 ft runway at Punta Huete, north of Managua, was unnecessary because the Sandinista Government had no aircraft requiring a runway that long and Sandino International Airport, on the outskirts of Managua, would be more convenient than Punta Huete for commercial airlines. Intelligence experts contended that Punta Huete would eventually be used as a landing and refuelling base for Soviet aircraft. That would make it possible for the Russians to fly long-range reconnaissance and electronic eavesdropping flights along the west coast of Alaska and North America from bases in Soviet Asia.[37]

In the case of Grenada, following that country's establishment of diplomatic relations with Cuba in 1979, a technical and economic cooperation agreement was signed for the construction of a new international airport at Point Saline. As the largest Cuban aid project in the Caribbean, the new airport designed for long-haul operations caused considerable concern in Washington. The US Government saw the project as a threat to its strategic interests if it were to become a staging area for Cuban air traffic, including military flights to Angola.[38]

Addressing the ICAO Assembly in September 1983 shortly after it joined the Organisation, Grenada denounced what it called 'an unwarranted geo-political ball-game'. Its chief delegate said the new airport was justified to provide direct access to the island and realise 'our full tourism potential'.[39] Before the year was over, the US military intervention stopped all work on the airport. The construction was completed under new US management.

AIR TRAFFIC CONTROL AND THE KAL INCIDENT

The US offers perhaps the best example of airspace management under one authority as institutionalised by the FAA Act of 1958. Yet, even here, civil/military coordination is not foolproof as illustrated by the KAL incident in which 269 passengers and crew were killed on 1 September 1983. If the report of the investigation by ICAO[40] flatly rejects the Soviet contention that the Korean aircraft was on a spying mission and instead points to a gross navigational error, the circumstances surrounding the flight left much room for speculation and controversy.[41]

The key argument for implicating US authorities in planning a 'spy mission' is why the airline was not warned by air traffic control that it was headed off-course. Soviet officials raised the question first and it has been echoing ever since in a series of politically-slanted articles and books.[42]

The simple fact of the matter is that the kind of coordination between military and civil air traffic control that was assumed to have existed on the North Pacific route system (NOPAC) did not exist at the time of the shoot-down. Shemya Island, the US Air Force base in the Aleutian chain, that should or might have alerted the KAL crew that it was heading off-course, was responsible only for identifying incoming and not outgoing flights on Route R20 which runs close to the restricted Soviet airspace. When the NOPAC system was beginning operations, the US Air Force had agreed also to monitor outbound flights, but this was a temporary measure. At the end of 1982, the FAA let the agreement lapse.

In 1983, no agreements were in force. According to the FAA, the only time the air force ever called the civil traffic control that year was when *incoming* aircraft penetrated the ADIZ (Air Defense Identification Zone). Military radars which might have noticed the course deviation had no reason to suspect that the outgoing plane was in trouble.

A civilian radar unit now operates on tiny St Paul Island off the west coast of Alaska and reports directly by remote control to

Anchorage Air Route Traffic Control Center. Also, since the reopening of Route R20 on 19 October 1983, the military radar on Shemya now screens and checks all flights and relays the data to Anchorage. Murray Sayle, an Australian journalist who investigated all the aspects of the KAL incident, asserts that had the system worked on the night of 31 August–1 September 1983, the tragedy of Flight 007 would not have happened.[43]

The KAL tragedy led to amendments of various annexes of the Chicago Convention. These improved procedures deal with minimum airborne navigation equipment required for flight communications, identification of civil aircraft, surveillance of air traffic and the use of military radar facilities to assist civil air traffic services along sensitive routes.[44]

Any hope that the new interception rules would also apply to military aircraft was dashed when in 1986 the Council adopted Amendment 27 to Annex 2 (Rules of the Air). The Air Navigation Commission – the Council's technical body – which was given the task of drafting the improved procedures was faced at the very outset with the question as to whether ICAO standards could be made to apply to interceptor aircraft.

The rules as first proposed contained specific obligations for interception control units. While a substantial majority of states expressed no disagreement with the binding nature of the proposed standards and saw no problem in applying these regulations to their state aircraft, the US strongly objected on the grounds that their adoption would clearly violate the Chicago Convention, particularly Article 3(a).[45] It would have no objection, however, if such provisions as related to state aircraft were retained as guidance material. The USSR at first did not believe that the procedures were inconsistent with the Chicago Convention but subsequently joined the US in opposing the amendment.

In the end, the Council adopted a watered-down version of the amendment to the effect that 'interception of civil aircraft shall be governed by appropriate regulations and administrative directives issued by contracting States in compliance with the Convention on International Civil Aviation'.[46] It is ironical that the two major protagonists in the KAL incident joined forces to block any move in ICAO that would have infringed the freedom of action of their respective military establishment.

On the positive side, the two superpowers agreed to implement an ICAO recommendation on closer cooperation between US and

Soviet air control units. The Soviet-American-Japanese civil aviation pact announced in Geneva at the 1985 Reagan-Gorbachev summit meeting sets up the first procedures for foreign civil aircraft to make emergency landings in the Soviet Union.[47]

THE CIVIL USE OF MILITARY NAVIGATION SYSTEMS

The KAL incident brought to the fore the use by civil aircraft of a sophisticated satellite navigation system developed for the US Armed Forces. The use by the airlines of military systems is not new since international aviation has long been using the LORAN-C and the OMEGA/VLF system S/I, both originally developed by the US as long-range navigation aids for naval vessels. (The OMEGA radio navigation system is operated by the US Coast Guard in partnership with several countries where transmitting stations are located.)

Sophisticated global navigation systems, like the NAVSTAR-Global Positioning System (GPS) which will deploy 24 satellites and the Global Orbiting Navigation Satellite System (GLONASS) developed by the Soviet Union, are too costly to be duplicated for civil use. Originally conceived for defence purposes, these systems can be expected to have a dramatic impact on civil aviation. NAVSTAR was designed to provide military pilots a position accuracy within 10–20 metres anywhere in the world, in any kind of weather.[48] Given this unique potential, the Pentagon was under pressure to make the system also available to civil aviation without military constraints. Duane Freer, who at the time headed the ICAO Air Navigation Bureau, put the question squarely to an aviation symposium: 'Can the civilian community accept for routine operational use such a military operated system? Could it be a basic element of the international civil infrastructure and, if so, under what conditions? With what understandings? There are a host of additional questions that would need to be answered'.[49]

To be used to its full potential, NAVSTAR would have to provide a position accuracy that cannot be matched by any other system. It is, however, designed to give markedly different levels of accuracy for military and civil use. Originally, the US Government appeared unwilling to offer civil users an accuracy better than 500 metres – later improved to within 100 metres, which might make it suitable also as a non-precision approach aid. Since NAVSTAR was intended primarily for military use by the US and its NATO allies, the Pentagon was not particularly interested in sharing its technology with the Soviet military, although those opposed to the accuracy limitation argued that the Soviet Union would not depend on a potential enemy's navigation system, especially since NAV-STAR can be programmed to cut off its transmissions over the Soviet Union.

Following the Reagan Administration's decision to offer NAV-STAR for civil use in the wake of the Korean Airlines incident a big question was still left up in the air: how would a military system be operated for the benefit of civil users during an armed conflict? The misapprehensions were somewhat eased when the United States and the USSR announced in April 1989 that they would work together, thus avoiding a potential split in the aviation community. It was significant that the surprise announcement was made at the last meeting of the FANS Committee, thereby ensuring a prime role for ICAO in planning the political, financial and institutional aspects of the new system. Its eventual management under ICAO's auspices would guarantee that it would not be cut off by military contingencies.

When the joint NAVSTAR-GLONASS system is fully operational, each with 21 active satellites and three spares, airliners will be able to pinpoint their position with an accuracy of 100 metres. Each system on its own will cover the globe so that together they will provide complete reliability. Aircraft will be able to monitor their position from as many as four satellites anywhere in the world.

While the US and the USSR had worked together in the use of satellites for search and rescue operations even when their relations were at their lowest point, they would not have done so on the more sensitive aspects of air navigation before glasnost. The agreement was a technical as well as a political breakthrough and the first concrete result of the Reagan-Gorbachev summit meeting in Moscow. To be sure, the US would keep the exclusive use of NAVSTAR's high-level accuracy for its specially-equipped military aircraft but the second-level service would be offered without restriction to civil aircraft. This agreement between the US and the USSR could not have proceeded without the assent of the military establishment in both countries. It remains to be seen whether this exemplary cooperation between civil and military authorities can be extended in other fields of civil aviation such as managing the airspace and preventing the use of force against civil aircraft.

THE BASIC RULES OF THE GAME

Civil and military cooperation reflects a state of affairs in which, to use R.O. Keohane's description, 'the rules of the game include some national rules, some international rules, some private rules and large areas of no rules at all'.[50] The players, however, have at least agreed on three basic rules.

First, Article 1 of the Chicago Convention is based on the complete and exclusive sovereignty of states over their airspace. This airspace is managed according to national legislation which gives military authorities control over areas essential for defence. Second, Article 12 of the Convention states that the rules of the air as laid down by ICAO are applicable over the high seas.[51] The rare instances of civil aircraft intercepted over international waters do not invalidate the rule since these actions have been condemned by the international community.[52]

A third rule concerns the obligation of states to refrain from the use of weapons against civil aircraft in flight and to ensure that in case of interception, the lives of persons on board and the safety of the aircraft must not be endangered. If this rule has always been implicit in customary international law, it has been codified as a principle of general international law in Article 3 *bis* in the wake of the KAL incident.[53]

It can be argued that this last rule is not fully accepted by all players and that some of them will act according to their own rules as shown in the next two chapters in various cases of civil aircraft being shot down.

The coupling of the general rule on the use of force against civil aviation in Article 3 *bis* with the obligation by states 'to take appropriate measures to prohibit the deliberate use of any civil aircraft . . . for any purpose inconsistent with the aims of this Convention . . .' (paragraph d) leaves wide open the legal vacuum with respect to civil aircraft used as 'state aircraft', let alone the deliberate misuse of such aircraft. Legal arguments regarding aerial intrusion have never been put to a test. The real issue therefore is not whether a state has complete sovereignty over its airspace, but how that state will respond. The response will depend on whether the aircraft is civil or military, on its apparent hostile or peaceful intentions and on the existing political climate.[54]

THE WAR AGAINST DRUG SMUGGLING

The role of military forces may expand to policing the sky. In an all-out effort to cut drug supply routes from Latin America, the United States wants to send military radar units into the mountains of Colombia, Peru and Bolivia to supplement local police strikes against producers.

As proposed, these US military units would help local authorities pinpoint the hundreds of small airstrips which drug smugglers use to pick up and deliver their cargo. These authorities lack the drive and resources to locate the clandestine facilities which multiply faster than they can be destroyed and to confiscate or shoot down the planes used in drug smuggling. But the remote Andean region is also home to cattle ranchers who use primitive landing strips for routine transportation. Officials concede that distinguishing between the small planes used by these ranchers and those used by drug smugglers will be a nightmare. Peru at one point considered declaring certain airspace off limits to have better military control over air traffic.

Given the great sensitivity over the presence of American military personnel, especially after the Panama invasion, the United States is holding in abeyance its plan for an extensive electronic surveillance of air traffic in the Andean region. The Pentagon is understandably reluctant to undertake this task without the full support of local authorities.

There is also apprehension in the United States about policing the sky. The Senate, with the support of aviation lobby groups and the Justice and Transportation Departments, rejected an amendment to a drug bill that would have allowed Customs and Coast Guard pilots to open fire on private aircraft suspected of drug smuggling. 'It looked good on paper, but missiles do go astray', Samuel Skinner, the Secretary of Transport, was quoted as saying at the time.

Considering that according to ICAO's estimates general aviation accounts for 80 per cent of all drug shipments by air, smuggling has been a major concern in international aviation to the extent that technical solutions can be found.[58] The Chicago Convention encompasses various aspects of the problem, including control of the landing and departure of aircraft (Article 10), lawful clearance of cargo (Article 13), the right to search aircraft (Article 16), the right to prohibit the transport of certain items (Article 35), and provisions dealing with rules of the air and air traffic services. The problem is that the drug smuggler does not fly by the rules. He rarely files a flight plan and when he does, diverts to another airport at the last moment. Most often, the smuggler evades surveillance by flying in total darkness and radio silence and landing in the most unsuspected places. There have also been reports of smugglers with lights out mixing with commercial aircraft and getting away because air traffic controllers are reluctant to clear airspace for surveillance aircraft.

The Air Navigation Commission has reviewed procedures particularly as they relate to flight information and coordination between air traffic services and law enforcement agencies. New requirements have been added to facilitate the detection of illicit flights. For instance, while pilots entering the United States must file a flight plan beforehand, some Caribbean and Latin American countries are slow to transmit them with the result that legitimate flights can be inadvertently flagged as suspicious. The ANC has called for better communications links and the use of civil and military radar to maintain closer surveillance in the airspace most frequently used by drug smugglers. The help of military forces, while welcomed, is bound to add another burden on civil/military coordination.

CONCLUSION

Satisfactory answers to a rational use of airspace are still elusive because of large restricted areas around the world, the steady increase in commercial traffic and the ever-present danger of navigational errors and 'misuse' of civil aviation. In the words of one expert: 'Close coordination at the highest level will be more than ever necessary in terms of airspace and air traffic control and close day-to-day liaison will be required at all operational levels.'[55]

ICAO's ultimate goal in respect of civil and military air traffic control is full integration, a single system capable of meeting civil and military requirements. It is not a vision of the airspace at present shared by the military rulemakers and until such time as it is, the use of the airspace by both civil and military aviation will continue to be a source of conflicts and possible mishaps.

7 International Conflicts and the Safety of Air Travel

Prudence may dictate platitudes. Votes may counsel vagueness.

Lester Pearson, *Diplomacy in the Nuclear Age*

With nation-states fiercely protective of their sovereign rights and national interests, it is no wonder that so much of the politics of international aviation has revolved around the use of the airspace. For all its expanse, the sky has definite limits for civil aviation since airlines require the safest and shortest routes to their destinations.

The basic rule of law which gives a state full and absolute sovereignty over its airspace also gives it the right to exclude foreign carriers from its territory. In the absence of a multilateral system governing air services, most states have agreed to allow overflights and technical stop-overs on a non-discriminatory basis and to reserve commercial rights for bilateral agreements. Conflicts of interest are inevitable when political claims take precedence over the principle of freedom of navigation and a state closes its airspace for reasons other than hostilities or national emergency, thereby denying rights previously enjoyed by other states.[1]

Conflicts also arise when states defy international agreements and claim control over airspace which is not within their jurisdiction. The airspace around the world is divided into a series of contiguous Flight Information Regions (FIRs) within which air traffic control and flight information services are provided. Unless states decide to delegate responsibilities, they are expected to provide these services not only within their national airspace, but over oceanic areas as determined by the ICAO Council in accordance with regional air navigation plans and the capability of each country.

Conflicts are aggravated when the state which provides air traffic control fails in the event of disruptions to institute contingency measures to ensure the safety of international flights. ICAO will step in and work out alternate routings with adjoining countries only when the national authorities cannot adequately discharge their responsibilities or when specifically requested to do so by the state concerned. It cannot do so without their consent or cooperation.

Flight Information Regions over the high seas may give the illusion of sovereign power beyond national territory causing states at times to act as if they own the airspace in which they provide services. While a state has complete freedom to organise its national airspace as it sees fit, so long as it conforms with established procedures, it is not a free agent over the high seas and in airspace of undetermined sovereignty. The Council is specifically empowered under Article 12 of the Chicago Convention to apportion these areas on the basis of regional agreements and technical and operational requirements. FIR boundaries are not demarcation lines which shift according to the changing political winds. A pilot must be able to rely on clearly-defined charts so that before he takes off he knows exactly what to expect in the way of navigation and communications facilities. Since undefined or contested boundaries can create safety hazards, the aviation community cannot tolerate confusing situations brought about by states extending their rivalries over the airspace outside their jurisdiction.

Since a state is the only judge of its actions when it contests ICAO-approved boundaries or when it closes its airspace to press a political claim, it is up to other states to protect their interests and ensure the safety of air travel. Those who doubt the ability of states to settle their disputes through bilateral negotiations or mediation, look to the conflict management mechanism in the system to bring about solutions.

THE COUNCIL AS A TRIBUNAL

Under the provisions of Chapter XVIII of the Chicago Convention, the ICAO Council is specifically charged with adjudicating disputes between states over the interpretation or applicability of the terms of the Convention and its annexes. This first postwar mechanism for the pacific settlement of disputes incorporated in an international instrument was hailed as a significant innovation in international law.[2]

Specifically under Articles 84–88, the Council is empowered to adjudicate disputes between contracting states which cannot be settled by negotiation. The Council must hear a complaint 'on the application of any State concerned in the disagreement'. The Council's decision may be appealed either to the International Court of Justice or to an *ad hoc* international tribunal whose judgment shall be final and binding. The Council under Article 66 also assumed judicial functions (including the settlement of differences and the hearing of complaints) with respect to the International Air Services Transit and Air Transport Agreements. Several other multilateral conventions signed under the auspices of ICAO refer to the Council's jurisdiction for the settlement of disputes.

The judicial cases before the Council had in common the arbitrary suspension of overflights. Under Article 9 of the Chicago Convention each State is free to restrict or prohibit the aircraft of other states from flying over certain areas of its territory provided that the same applies for its own aircraft. The qualifying criterion is that such prohibited areas should be of reasonable extent and location so as not to interfere unnecessarily with air navigation.

In the first case, presented in 1952, India alleged discrimination under Articles 5 and 9 of the Chicago Convention. It claimed that it was not allowed overflights over a prohibited zone along the Pakistani border with Afghanistan when aircraft of other countries were permitted to do so. The second case, in 1967, involved the United Kingdom against Spain over a prohibited zone in the Bay of Algeciras opposite the airport of Gibraltar. In 1971, it was Pakistan's turn to file charges against India after that country suspended all overflights by Pakistani aircraft over its territory.

The Council did not take any decision in the first case, although it helped the parties reach an amicable settlement. The second case was adjourned indefinitely when the parties decided to negotiate their differences. Michael Milde has noted that technically the Gibraltar case is still pending before the Council and could be revived at any time.[3] The underlying political problem has long since shifted to the UN Fourth Committee and to the EC where the status of Gibraltar Airport almost brought to a standstill plans for the liberalisation of Europe's air transport system.[4]

The third case was the most contentious. It arose against the background of armed hostilities and the alleged complicity of Pakistan in the hijacking and destruction of an Indian aircraft in Lahore in full view of cameras. The confrontation over Kashmir led India to suspend overflights by Pakistani aircraft, thereby cutting off air communications between West and East Pakistan. India questioned the jurisdiction of the ICAO Council arguing that the suspension was the result of hostilities. Eventually the case went to the International Court of Justice which ruled that the Council did have jurisdiction to entertain Pakistan's application. After the creation of an independent Bangladesh in East Pakistan, both countries dropped the proceedings.[5]

Early misgivings as to whether the Council could fulfil its judicial mandate in a political confrontation proved to be well-founded in the last case.[6] At one point in the proceedings, several Council members requested a postponement on a vote to seek instructions from their respective governments. When Chapter XVIII was drafted in 1944, the participants in the Chicago Conference had visualised that the Council would become a tribunal composed of impartial judges to settle disputes between states. It was an unrealistic expectation because Council members do not act in their individual capacity but only as spokesmen of their respective governments. As Milde has pointed out, 'the Council cannot be considered to be a true judicial body composed of judges who would be deciding strictly and exclusively on the basis of respect for law'.[7]

It is significant that in none of the three cases in which the judicial machinery of Chapter XVIII has been invoked, did the Council take any decision on the merits of the case. Equally significant is the fact these were aviation disputes arising against the background of a larger political conflict. Hans Morgenthau in discussing problems of reconciling legal claims with conflicts of power, concluded that those political disputes which affect the overall distribution of power between two nations cannot be settled by judicial methods.[8]

The disuse of the Council's judicial process is shown in the way India has handled further grievances against Pakistan. In a complaint to the Council President, India in 1985 accused Pakistan of arming the hijackers of an Indian Boeing 737 during a stop-over in Lahore. The Boeing with a full complement of passengers was taken over by Sikh extremists after it took off from Lahore and subsequently flown to Karachi for refuelling and on to Dubai where the incident ended with the release of the passengers and the arrest of the offenders. Citing Pakistan's 'encouragement and cooperation with the hijackers', India requested ICAO to take appropriate measures but did not call for a Council meeting, so there was no follow-up on its complaint.[9]

THE NON-JUDICIAL MEANS FOR SETTLING DISPUTES

Short of invoking the judicial machinery of Chapter XVIII, states can rely on other provisions in the Chicago Convention to air their grievances before the Council. Under Article 54, it is incumbent on the Council to report to contracting states any infraction of the Convention and to report to the Assembly any infraction where a State has failed to take appropriate action within a reasonable time after notice of the infraction. Under the same Article (n), the Council must consider 'any matter relating to the Convention which any contracting State refers to it'. The latter provision is so broadly worded as to invite any type of grievances ranging from the strictly technical or legal to those with obvious political implications.

Milde has rightly observed that the proceedings under Article 54(n) have been used when adjudication would have been fully justifiable. A typical example is the protest of Nigeria in 1967 against Portugal concerning flights from the then Portuguese territory of Sao Tome to Port Harcourt to supply rebels in Biafra with arms and other supplies. According to Milde if the allegations were proved true, Portugal would have violated provisions of the Chicago Convention with respect to the sovereignty of Nigeria (Articles 1 and 2), misuse of civil aviation (Article 4) and violation of a prohibited zone (Article 9). While the Council procrastinated for some 18 months, fact-finding questions were addressed to both parties. Finally in June 1969, Nigeria requested that the matter be postponed *sine die* by which time the situation in Biafra was settled. Nigeria's action, however, did have a positive outcome in that the controversial flights stopped shortly after the filing of the complaint.[10]

It is clear that when the alleged infractions are part of a political dispute, states are more inclined to seek redress through the political process under Article 54 than through the judicial process, the more so if they can be assured a majority vote on the Council.

The Organisation has been understandably careful not to take sides even when states have designated restricted zones in apparent violation of international procedures. In one such case, Chile in 1978 abruptly deleted a segment of an international route which provided the most direct routing for the ten weekly flights between La Paz and Santiago. Chile's action caused heavy penalties to landlocked Bolivia. Allegedly taken to relocate radio navigational aids, the move was clearly political. Bolivia had just broken off diplomatic relations after protracted negotiations for access to the sea. In the meantime Bolivia had imposed restrictions of its own but was quietly dissuaded from bringing a complaint before the Council. The issue was therefore never raised officially and does not appear in official records.

At times states may be too far on a collision course to settle their differences informally. Thus, Panama went ahead with a complaint under Article 54(n) alleging a series of violations by US military aircraft from a base in the Panama Canal Zone.[11] Since the dispute involved two members of the Council, that body could do little else than urge further bilateral talks. Panama's new civilian government withdrew its complaint in the aftermath of the American intervention in December 1989.

THE CHANGING ROLE OF THE COUNCIL PRESIDENT

As ICAO became involved in a growing number of conflicts, the Council President gradually assumed a more prominent role as an arbiter and conciliator. This is unusual because he is not specifically assigned such a role under Article 51 of the Chicago Convention which spells out his responsibilities. Not only is the Chicago Convention silent on the President's good offices, but the Council, in defining the circumstances for making good offices available in cases of unlawful interference with civil aviation, specifically limited the scope of ICAO's action. It decided that 'good offices shall be made available to Contracting States only if the Council satisfies itself that in the specific case ICAO is not likely to be involved in questions of a political nature or in disputes between two or more States . . .'[12]

Notwithstanding the limitations imposed on his authority as an agent of the Council, the current President (Assad Kotaite) has increasingly used his influence to restrain the parties in a dispute from interfering with international air operations. Most of the President's missions have been concerned with the safety of air routes in various trouble spots of the world. He has on numerous occasions been able to moderate conflicts before they developed into confrontations.

As soon as he took office, Assad Kotaite was asked by the Council to use his good offices in a dispute between Senegal and Cape Verde over flight information services for the heavy northwest/south-east traffic flow between Dakar and North America. The case was sensitive because it affected major air routes and brought into conflict a small outsider which wanted to reap the economic benefits of this traffic and francophone states operating a joint air traffic control system created with French help. The President's mediation efforts resulted in a compromise that split the disputed flight area between Cape Verde and Senegal.

Such good offices have also resulted in opening an air corridor in the South China Sea after China closed its airspace in the vicinity of Hainan Island, affecting traffic on the main air route to Hong Kong. Efforts are still under way for opening a shorter route between China and Japan over the divided sky of Korea – the President acting in this case as the middleman between states which do not have diplomatic relations. His success depends on the willingness of the parties concerned to extricate the purely technical problems from their political context.

DIPLOMATIC MOVES IN THE FAR EAST

These diplomatic efforts have resulted in the improvement of the route structure over the Indo-China peninsula and the South China Sea particularly on the Amber–1 route. This airway which carries heavy traffic between Europe and the Far East had been discontinued following closure of the airspace over Indo-China in 1975. As a result, ICAO found it necessary to establish a network of contingency routings over the South China Sea to avoid the peninsula. The unification of Vietnam allowed Hanoi to reopen the direct route Bangkok–Danang–Hong Kong on Amber–1 following talks in Vientiane in February 1978 between the Council President and Thailand, Laos, Vietnam and the United Kingdom representing Hong Kong. The successful outcome of the meeting also opened the way for Vietnam to join ICAO in 1980.[13]

The reactivation of the Far-Eastern segment of Amber–1 was followed by the opening later that year of the more direct routing Manila–Lubang–Danang–Bangkok which resulted in a considerable saving in time and fuel for the airlines. Military skirmishes between Thailand and Kampuchea on the one hand and between Kampuchea and Vietnam on the other prevented further improvements.

International air traffic in the Far East faced more serious disruptions in 1980 when as the result of renewed tension between China and Vietnam, China designated four danger areas over the high seas around Hainan Island.[14] International flights were forced to use a costly detour on the Bangkok–Hong Kong route. The Chinese relented following consultations with the Council President and agreed to allow flights at certain hours as well as to other temporary measures to improve operating conditions.[15]

More complicated are the negotiations with China, Japan and the two Koreas for the purpose of establishing shorter air routes between China and Japan. These talks concern a northern route Beijing–Tokyo through Pyongyang, a middle route Beijing–Tokyo through Taegu (Republic of Korea) and a southern route Shanghai –Tokyo over the high seas. After prolonged consultations, the President was able to report that all the parties had accepted the southern route, thereby reducing the flying time between China and Japan.[16] The corridor allows nearly 100 flights per week, one-third of them operating non-stop to Beijing pending the opening of the shorter northern route.

North Korea agreed to opening its airspace for a northern route to all civil aircraft (including US carriers) without discrimination but required bilateral negotiations with the states concerned.[17] The route has not yet been inaugurated. The settlement hinges on agreement by North Korea to the middle route via Seoul which would mean its tacit recognition of the existence of two separate states. South Korea's acceptance of the northern route is conditional on Korean Air Lines being given the right to fly over North Korea in order to compete with airlines using the trans-Siberian route between the Far East and Europe.

The real issue is that the northern route favoured by North Korea has the support of China while the middle route over South Korea is supported by Japan. North Korea seems motivated by ambivalent feelings towards Japan. While seeking closer ties, it has criticised Japan for its friendly relations with the US and South Korea. The biggest stumbling block, however, is the continued animosity between the two Koreas.[18]

The airlines operating to and from Hong Kong which use a circuitous route over Pakistan have also complained about route restrictions on the Central Asia segment of Amber–1. After initial talks with representatives of Afghanistan, India and Pakistan in 1983, the President reported that Afghanistan had agreed to a more direct routing between Delhi and Kabul via Islamabad.[19] These efforts, however, have not yielded the expected results due to sporadic tension on Pakistan's northern border with Afghanistan.

MILITARY AND POLITICAL MANOEUVRES OVER THE AEGEAN SEA

For years, ICAO has been trying to resolve an intractable issue between Greece and Turkey concerning the realignment of an air route linking northern Europe to Greece to ease congestion on an important holiday destination. While on the surface this realignment is operational and technical in nature, it involves traffic over the Aegean Sea (between Limnos and Mesta) which Turkey claims affects its freedom to conduct naval and air exercises. Turkey further contends that the geographical configuration of the Aegean Sea does not provide other sites for such exercises.

Even though Greece and Turkey are members of NATO, the dispute has led to countless complaints by Turkey of harassment and interceptions by Greek fighters during military manoeuvres in Greek-controlled airspace in spite of prior clearance having been obtained and flight plans filed according to ICAO procedures. The fact that the realignment had first originated in the European Air Navigation Plan in line with a Council resolution did not deter Turkey. It considered the move 'predominantly political' with the 'objective of excluding Turkey from freely using the international airspace of the Aegean'.[20]

The problem is part of a broader conflict over Turkish exploration rights on the Aegean continental shelf claimed by Greece, the limit of Greek territorial waters, the militarisation of the Greek islands off the coast of Turkey and finally the unresolved problem of Cyprus which brought the two countries to the verge of war a number of times.

The issue of airspace control arose as a result of the 1974 crisis on Cyprus. Turkey challenged arrangements existing since 1952 and contested a presidential decree extending Greek airspace to ten miles beyond the coast so as to cover the Limnos terminal area and the NATO operational control areas. On 4 August 1974 Turkey advised all carriers operating in the region to contact Izmir instead of the Athens control centre when approaching the Turkish coast. Since this unilateral action by Turkey affected international flights over several Greek islands, Greece closed the Aegean air corridors as unsafe. These air corridors were reopened in 1980 as part of the reintegration of Greece in NATO.[21]

The issue of airspace control in the Aegean placed ICAO in a predicament since the Organisation is committed to speeding the flow of traffic on the congested air routes of Europe. It has been a recurrent headache for the ICAO Regional Office in Paris, which coordinates such efforts, and for the Air Navigation Commission which has tried to find a solution acceptable to both parties. The ICAO Council itself has been loath to take a firm position on the matter and to exert sufficient pressure on the two NATO partners to settle their differences.

It is a case which would require arbitration to reconcile conflicting interpretations of the Chicago Convention. Neither party in the conflict has so far shown an inclination to do so. Unlike the sea-bed issue which almost resulted in a military confrontation in April 1987 there are with respect to the airspace no hard-core economic issues involved. Technical questions could be resolved by arbitration taking into account the obligations of states under the Chicago Convention and Annex 11 (Air Traffic Services). There have been intermittent attempts to seek a negotiated settlement on some of the issues at the level of technical experts and in the context of the seasonal NATO meetings. However, Greece's preference is for the adjudication of outstanding issues and Turkey for a political settlement.[22]

RIVALRIES IN THE CYPRIOT SKY

Cyprus has been a burden to the UN ever since a peace-keeping force was installed on the island in 1964 to separate the embattled Greek and Turkish communities. It became a perennial issue as well for ICAO from 1974 when Turkey launched a large-scale military operation and established a *de facto* Turkish Cypriot government in a northern enclave of the island.

Turkey meanwhile tried to assert control over the airspace and requested pilots to contact the Ankara Area Control Centre (ACC) while operating within the Nicosia flight region. This was followed in March 1977 by the establishment of 'ERCAN' as the only author-ised flight information centre in the area.[23]

The existence of two flight information centres inevitably created confusion for airlines using the air corridors over the region. Turkey's insistence that all aircraft take guidance from 'ERCAN' although this service was not recognised by ICAO brought repeated complaints from Greek and Cypriot authorities as well as airlines and pilots' associations.

ICAO's position outlined in a circular by the Council President (18 March 1977) was that the creation of 'ERCAN' was illegal and that the responsibility for providing air traffic services lay with the Nicosia Area Control Centre in accordance with established ICAO provisions.[24] The International Air Transport Association entered into the picture when Turkish Cypriot authorities refused to discuss the matter. IATA advised its member airlines to comply with the ICAO position and refuse instructions from 'ERCAN' without informing the Nicosia Centre.

The International Federation of Airline Pilots' Associations has been particularly concerned in the past about the deadlock and its effect on safety. An IFALPA memorandum notes that 'pilots overflying the northern Nicosia FIR maintain two-way radio contact with at least two and often three air traffic control centres simultaneously. The combination of heavy traffic congestion in a small area, the absence of coordination between adjacent control centres and the assignment of conflicting flight levels to aircraft in the vicinity can only jeopardize the safety of flight operations throughout the whole area'. In 1982 and again in 1984 IFALPA classified the northern position of Nicosia FIR and adjacent air spaces as 'critically deficient'.[25] Since then radar facilities have been installed or ordered to alleviate these deficiencies.

Cyprus has raised the illegal operation of the 'ERCAN' station at various ICAO Assemblies calling it 'the most flagrant violation of international procedures and practices'.[26] So far, the aviation community has learned to live with the political status quo. The periods of crisis and lulls seem to follow an established pattern according to the prevailing political climate and the ups and downs of Greek–Turkish relations.[27]

THE GULF WAR AND THE INTERNATIONAL ROUTES

Civil aviation's worst trouble spot has been the Persian Gulf area where hostilities have at times caused severe disruptions along air routes. ICAO has also been enmeshed in a web of conflicting defence interests and boundary disputes over flight information sectors.

The conflict between Iran and Iraq became a concern for ICAO when the two countries threatened to interfere with international traffic over their airspace. This threat was particularly ominous for airlines flying dangerously close to the Iranian airspace in the Gulf area along the Amber–1 route to the Far East.

Air safety had already become a concern in the turmoil that preceded the takeover by Ayatollah Khomeini in February 1979. With erratic air traffic control and communications provided by the military or being improvised by the airlines, air operations were so risky that IFALPA urged that all flights be stopped except for evacuation purposes. Flights over Iran had already been suspended. IATA sent a mission to Teheran which found the situation worse than expected. As a result, the Council President sent an urgent cable to the Iranian Foreign Affairs Minister on 12 January 1979, offering 'all possible assistance by ICAO in the interest of safety of operation of international civil aviation'.[28] No acknowledgement was ever received.

With a number of airlines suspending operations into Iran and avoiding Iranian airspace, the Council President secured the cooperation of Bahrain to provide air traffic services to international flights over the water portion of the Teheran FIR, thus assuring direct routings between Europe and South East Asia.

Fast-moving developments required the Council President to take immediate action on his own. This was the case when Iran on 26 November 1979, at the height of the US Embassy hostage crisis, warned international air carriers overflying Iranian territory to maintain altitudes of more than 15 000 feet and not to stray from established airways or face the risk of being shot down by air force fighters. Iran's decision requiring airlines to establish contact with Iranian Air Defence or submit a flight plan caused consternation given the history of poor communications control in the area. The day after the order was issued, the Council President told Iran that international carriers would find it difficult to comply with the requirements. He called attention to Annex 2 (Rules of the Air) forbidding intercepting aircraft to use weapons against civil aircraft. The admonition was effective; Iran rescinded its threat.[29]

There were, however, still grounds for concern. Iran was using old interception procedures no longer familiar to most airline pilots. The situation was somewhat eased when Iran advised airlines operating into its airspace that their fears were groundless and that interception would be used only as a last resort and according to ICAO-approved procedures. To overcome communications deficiencies, the Council President formally requested Bahrain to provide air traffic control services along Route R–21 within the Teheran flight region. He received the accord of Bahrain in spite of that country's continuing suspicions of Iran's intentions.[30]

The semblance of normalcy in air operations was shattered when the border dispute between Iran and Iraq erupted into open warfare on 27 September 1980. Immediately after hostilities started, Iraq and Iran closed their airspace to commercial flights causing delays on the trunk route (Amber–1) at a time of heavy traffic during the Haj pilgrimage season. Problems were also encountered on other routes over the Gulf.

Following urgent consultations with Iran, Iraq and the Gulf States, Bahrain was once again called upon to assume temporary responsibility for services on the high seas portion of international routes (B–56 and R–21) originally assigned to Teheran.[31] There was concern when Iranian military authorities threatened to fire upon any aircraft overflying Iranian offshore installations. The area presumably included the important routings outside Iranian airspace but within the Bahrain Flight Information Region. As a result, the airlines felt the threat covered all civil operations over international waters in the Gulf. Because of safety concerns, Bahrain closed its sector of Amber–1. The situation was finally resolved when the Iranian civil aviation authorities assured airlines that the warning had not been authorised by the highest military authorities.[32]

Notwithstanding the fact that there had never been a formal declaration of war, Iraq officially notified ICAO in October 1980 that a state of emergency existed under Article 89 of the Chicago Convention and that it would therefore not be able to comply with the Convention. At the height of a battle for control of a strategic road to Basra, Iraq warned all airlines to stay out of Iranian airspace or face the consequences. The Iraqi Notice to Airmen (NOTAM No. 9016) issued on 17 March 1985 was immediately circulated to the ICAO Council along with a strong protest by Iran while the Council President asked assurances from Iraq that there would be 'neither interruption nor cessation of civil flight operations on international routes'.[33]

The gravity of the situation was underscored when an Iraqi military spokesman announced that Iranian airspace would be 'a prohibited war zone' and that Iraq intended to continue air attacks on Iranian cities and would not be responsible for the safety of commercial aircraft. The Iraqi NOTAM had a chilling effect on airlines still operating in Iran, leading them to cancel their operations. The warning also caused renewed concern for international flights using the important Amber–1 trunk route to and from the Orient.

While developments in the Iran–Iraq conflict were left to the discretion of the President, Iran felt that the Iraqi threat because of its 'extra-territorial extension of authority and unlawful interference with civil aviation' required Council action. It therefore requested an urgent meeting of that body under Article 54(n) of the Chicago Convention.

The ICAO Council took an even-handed attitude when it debated the Iran–Iraq issue. After a two-day extraordinary session (22–23 April 1985), it unanimously urged both countries to take immediate steps to assure the safety of civil aviation along international routes. It was left for the Council President to seek the withdrawal or cancellation of the controversial Iraqi NOTAM.[34] There followed numerous cables and repeated complaints from Iran about Iraq's non-compliance with the Council's decision. Without formally withdrawing its NOTAM, however, Iraq gave formal assurances that international traffic would not be affected.[35]

Unrelated to the Iran-Iraq conflict, but very much central to the safety of the air routes over the Gulf, was the mini-dispute involving Qatar and Bahrain over the ownership of the tiny Fasht al Dibal island which led Qatar to launch a military attack and dismantle the sandbar in April 1986. The otherwise minor incident had immediate effect on civil aviation given the strategic importance of the Gulf States in assuring the flow of air traffic in the area. Qatar's closure of its airspace to overflights in April 1986 because of defence considerations caused serious congestion and disruption affecting all airports in the Gulf.[36]

The Council President expressed the concern of the airlines in personal visits to the four Gulf States in March 1987. He asked them to return to the status quo existing before the restrictions or seek adjustments in the approved Air Navigation Plan through the normal process of securing agreement of all the parties concerned. Even after his goodwill mission, the United Arab Emirates banned overflights of its oil installations, thereby forcing all traffic into a single airway. Qatar and the UAE eventually accepted the proposals of the Council President and agreed after a meeting in

Abu Dhabi to help transfer traffic to other routes. Bahrain also temporarily lifted some restrictions.[37]

THE MISSING LINKS WITH THE MILITARY

The US military build-up in the Gulf to protect reflagged oil tankers threatened new perils to the congested air routes over the Gulf. In a special NOTAM issued on January 1984 and relayed to aeronautical stations in the Middle East, the US Navy instructed civil aircraft cleared for approach or departure to stay clear of its naval forces and maintain contact on a special frequency, or be held at risk by US defence measures. Iran immediately protested in a telex to the Council President that the NOTAM was 'invalid and unacceptable' and that it constituted a 'clear violation of international law and common practices regarding the freedom of flying over the high seas'.[38]

The US warning, combined with route restrictions already in effect and realignment of other routes at variance with the ICAO Regional Plan, led the Council President to issue a stiff reminder that lack of coordination between air traffic centres in the region and the military and naval activities in the Gulf created a hazard to civil air traffic. His warning addressed to all the Gulf States outlined specific steps to ensure coordination at every level in the management of the airspace and air traffic control in line with relevant ICAO provisions.[39]

Even before the attacking of Iran Air Flight 655 by the warship USS *Vincennes* on 3 July 1988, ICAO had been informed of several cases of potential disasters when pilots were ordered by the US Navy to proceed on a course not approved by the traffic control centres. In the most serious case on record, a British Airways flight on an approach to landing in Dubai was told to reverse course, a manoeuvre that would have caused a midair collision with an aircraft taking off from Sharjah Airport. Fortunately, the BA pilot refused to comply.[40] The Emirates immediately lodged a complaint with the United States.

Earlier, on 26 May 1987, Iran Air Flight 635 en route from Shiraz to Doha on the same route taken by the ill-fated Flight 655, was instructed by a US warship to divert from the standard corridor. With the help of the Bahrain air traffic control centre, the captain managed to land in Doha. Iran reported the incident to the Council

President with a request for appropriate action. In response, the President assured Iran that the matter had received his personal attention. Again, on 1 August 1987, Iran protested that these 'violations and breaches of international rules created chaotic and dangerous situations for civil air transport'. The President repeated his earlier assurance without a further indication of any specific action.[41]

ICAO's immediate concern, however, was not with the US Navy whose personnel seemed oblivious of civil flights and air traffic requirements in the region. By the term of its mandate, ICAO could work only with civil aviation authorities. A small but welcome step involved the detailed coordination measures between the Emirates and Bahrain, Muscat and Iran following a meeting of the parties concerned in the Paris Regional Office of ICAO in January 1986.[42] This was followed by another meeting in December 1987 aimed at opening alternate routes to relieve the congestion caused by the closure of airspace. While that meeting focused on the necessity to move air traffic away from potential danger zones, it could hardly address the major issue of civil/military coordination since the parties with military forces in the Gulf, in particular the United States, were not present. Likewise, the major protagonists in the conflict – Iran and Iraq – were absent.

The downing of the Iranian Airbus in an approved air corridor underscored the difficult task of assuring the safety of international routes in a zone of military activities. An extraordinary session of the Council which met at the request of Iran in July 1988 could do no more than ask the states concerned to improve civil/military coordination in the Gulf and implement decisions of the Paris meeting.[43]

Since the major issue facing air traffic in the Gulf was the presence of a military task force which did not abide by civil aviation rules, one might question the extent of ICAO's role in a military-political confrontation. The agency is directly responsible for the airspace over the high seas, yet it cannot overrule military practices that violate its provisions on the safety of air routes. Military and civil air traffic coordination is a formidable task in the best of circumstances.[44] In the Gulf, permanent solutions require nothing less than the ending of tensions and the withdrawal of naval forces from the Gulf.

However persuasive his admonitions, the Council President's authority is strictly limited. He can only request states to fulfil their obligations and to implement approved rules to ensure the safety of air travel. In dealing with the states around the Gulf, ICAO must contend with specific security problems which are in the way of an overall solution. There have also been other disputes in the region involving flight information region boundaries. Saudi Arabia and the People's Democratic Republic of Yemen are at odds over boundary lines between the Aden and Jeddah FIRs, the result of undetermined borders in the area. In another such dispute, Iraq has long claimed jurisdiction of disputed airspace over the high seas assigned to Tehran. In this case, dissemination by Iraq of confusing aeronautical information to pilots forced the Council President to send a stern reminder to Iraq that it was acting against the provisions of Annex 11 covering Air Traffic Services and relevant Council decisions.[45]

CONCLUSION

Conflict-management mechanisms exist and are not used as shown in ICAO's case. If so, an organisation must find pragmatic solutions which are not challenged by its members. Thomas Buergenthal has noted how ICAO has demonstrated an unusual capacity for reshaping its constitutional charter without going through a cumbersome amendment process.[46] The reluctance of states to resort to the judicial process in ICAO, as envisaged in the Chicago Convention, and the inability of the Council to resolve conflicts which are essentially political in nature, have brought about a gradual evolution of the office of the Council President. The President, whose authority flows from the Council, has had to shape a new role as an arbiter in a growing number of conflicts on the Council's agenda. While he has tried to exert a restraining influence in critical situations, he cannot be expected to resolve political differences unless the parties concerned are favourably predisposed or can agree on their technical aspects.

Regardless of his personal qualities and the perception he has of his role, the Council President is too much an agent of that body to perform as an autonomous actor in the international system. Nevertheless, when the need arose, he has acted with skill and he has effectively used his good offices to uphold the principles and norms which guarantee the safe and unrestricted movement of people and goods across international routes. These attributes, however, cannot make up for the failure of the Council to act decisively against states which do not comply with their international obligations. At best, as has been said of the UN Secretary General, 'he can only speak with the voice of a universal conscience, even if his voice is muted, his admonitions faintly heard and his advice often unheeded'.[47]

8 Flying Targets: Armed Attacks Against Civil Aviation

Controller: Do you see the target.
Pilot: Roger, it is a civilian airliner.
Controller: Destroy the target.

Transcript of conversation of Soviet pilots involved in the downing
of Korean Airlines Flight 007, 1 September 1983

Since armed attacks against civil aviation have been a major pre-
occupation of the Organisation for more than 25 years, ICAO's
responses to such incidents can provide a better understanding of
how the international community reacts when confronted with difficult political issues. Debates in the ICAO Council seem to demonstrate that over the years a majority of states have come to view
certain issues of civil aviation as an integral part of international
politics and to believe that technical questions cannot be separated
from the political context.

THE ARAB–ISRAELI CONFLICT: TECHNICAL PROBLEMS AND POLITICAL ISSUES

Few issues in postwar international affairs have been more explosive
than the continuing Arab–Israeli conflict. Even before the first
hijacking in the Middle East in the summer of 1968, the unsettled
political situation in the area began to affect the running of regional
air services. As soon as Israel joined the Organisation in April
1949, for example, Egypt let it be known that 'technical considerations' would in no way change the state of war that existed.[1]

Difficulties soon arose because of the presence of Israeli delegates
at Middle East regional meetings and the refusal of Arab states to
accept reports and recommendations to which Israel was a party.[2]
Israel subsequently charged before the Sixth Session of the ICAO
Assembly that Arab states were withholding flight information and
jamming air communications as well as denying Israeli aircraft per-

125

mission to fly over their territories. Faced with a conflict arising, on the one hand from a ruling of the Security Council (1 September 1951) that the Arab–Israeli armistice was permanent and that neither party could claim a state of belligerency and, on the other hand, from notifications from Arab states that a state of national emergency existed under Article 89 of the Chicago Convention, the Assembly decided against acting on these charges because of their political aspects.[3]

An even more serious challenge was the arbitrary arrest and detention of Israeli passengers in transit in Arab airports. In the first such case in 1954 involving the detention during a stop-over in Baghdad of three Israeli passengers on a British aircraft flying from Nicosia to Teheran, the Council President (Edward Warner) merely transmitted an Israeli protest to Iraq with a request for 'any observations on this matter'.[4] It was only through the intercession of United Nations Secretary General Dag Hammarskjöld that the Israeli passengers were finally released in exchange for seven Iraqi soldiers captured by Israel in the war of 1948.

These early incidents created a dilemma for ICAO because they were instigated by member states rather than individuals and were targeted solely against a country with which they were still in a state of war. Israel itself chose not to bring up the incidents before the Council either under the judicial machinery of Chapter XVIII or under Article 54. Within ICAO, the incidents were perceived as an unfortunate by-product of the Arab–Israeli conflict rather than as violations of the Chicago Convention which might have elicited a more forthright response.

The hijacking of an El Al airliner on 23 July 1968, in the aftermath of the Six Day War, plunged the international community into a 'complex and ominous international crisis' in the words of United Nations Secretary General U Thant. It was also, as U Thant recalled in his memoirs, a bizarre episode in which he refused to negotiate for the release of captured Arab guerrillas in exchange for the 21 passengers detained by the Algerians.[5]

All through this crisis, U Thant kept in touch with ICAO, the International Air Transport Association (IATA) and the International Federation of Airline Pilots Associations (IFALPA). The latter group became actively involved when it threatened a boycott unless Algeria released the Israeli crew and passengers. (Those of other nationalities had been flown to Paris). IFALPA relented after receiving assurances from Algeria that this would be done as soon as it completed its investigation of the circumstances of the hijacking.

The same day that the El Al aircraft was forced to land in Algiers, the Israeli Minister of Transport cabled the ICAO Council President (Walter Binaghi) asking his help in obtaining the release of the passengers and crew. This was followed by another request that a special envoy be sent to Algiers to safeguard their security and effect their immediate release. In response, the Secretary General of ICAO expressed regret that the Organisation was unable to comply because the Tokyo Convention of 1963, which spells out the obligations of a state in the case of a hijacked aircraft, had not yet come into force.[6] Israel found this legalistic approach 'deeply disturbing' since the Chicago Convention provided ample justification for ICAO's intervention.[7]

By the time the Council President did intervene with the Algerian authorities two weeks after the Israeli request, the stage had already been set for the release of the Israeli passengers and crew. After 39 days of captivity – the longest hijacking in history – Algiers released the Israeli crew and passengers as well as the aircraft, while Israel subsequently freed 16 Arab prisoners. But the incident had been resolved behind the scenes through the good offices of the Italian Government and not through the actions of ICAO or the UN. U Thant had, however, expressed his displeasure at the events by refusing to attend a meeting of the Organisation of African Unity meeting in Algiers at the time.[8] He later reflected on this episode somewhat dejectedly, stating that his role was not publicly mentioned by the parties concerned and that he had been left completely in the dark about the final outcome.[9] The lack of firm responses at the United Nations and ICAO could only reinforce the view, first tested in Baghdad, that holding passengers for barter would not provoke much action from either organisation.

No sooner had the Algiers hijacking been resolved, than events thrust ICAO even deeper into the heart of the Arab–Israeli conflict. On 26 December 1968, two terrorists at Athens Airport threw several bombs at an El Al airliner which was preparing for take-off and killed one passenger. A complaint by Israel elicited a message of sympathy from the ICAO Council President but no action. In contrast, the Director General of IATA (Knut Hammarskjöld) issued an appeal to all governments, and particularly those of the United States and the USSR, to prevent the escalation of attacks against air transport.[10]

In retaliation for the Athens attack, Israeli helicopters landed at Beirut Airport and destroyed thirteen aircraft belonging to Lebanon, including at least one Boeing 707 and two Caravelles. The 45-minute commando raid led to an urgent United Nations Security Council session at which Lebanon described the raid as a flagrant aggression and called for sanctions and compensation for the damage estimated at more than $50 million. Israel countered that the Athens raid had been carried out by 'a paramilitary organisation which operated quite openly in Beirut with the full knowledge and blessing of the Lebanese Government'.

The unanimous view of the Security Council was that Israel had overreacted. It condemned Israel and issued a solemn warning that if such acts were to be repeated, the Council would have to consider further steps. It was the strongest resolution yet adopted by the Security Council on a breach of the peace in the Middle East, though it avoided any suggestion of forcible sanctions under Chapter VII of the United Nations Charter.[11]

In contrast to its previous stance, the ICAO Council took swift action. Upon receiving a formal complaint by Lebanon on 1 January 1969, the president of the Council decided to convene an extraordinary session to examine this 'serious violation of the Chicago Convention'. A counter move by Israel to have its own grievances aired at the same session failed to obtain a sufficient majority in the Council, prompting Israel to protest that the ICAO Council showed a lack of objectivity when in fact the Security Council had acted favourably on a similar motion.[12]

The Lebanese case was forcefully presented by its delegate Assad Kotaite (later to become Secretary General and subsequently President of the ICAO Council). He called on the Council to 'vigorously and unhesitatingly condemn Israel and apply the appropriate sanctions'.[13] Israel argued that the Council was not empowered to apply sanctions and that the raid was an incident in the state of war openly proclaimed by Lebanon. In the ensuing debate, most members condemned or deplored the Israeli raid but felt the Council should deal with the overall problem caused by acts of violence against civil aviation from whatever quarter and not just this single incident. Only four countries (India, Czechoslovakia, Tanzania and Tunisia) supported the Lebanese proposal for a strong condemnation of Israel. Some Council members, particularly the United States, the United Kingdom, Canada, the Netherlands, Italy and West Germany, rejected the motion for sanctions and wanted the debate restricted to technical matters, arguing that the political issues should be left to the Security Council.[14] After three successive adjournments, the Council decided not to take any action on Lebanon's complaint. Lebanon found this regrettable, but did not press for Israel's condemnation when it became clear that the United States would not support such a move in ICAO despite its vote in the Security Council. Israel took comfort from the fact that the ICAO Council had resisted condemning the attack.[15]

The Council's failure to move in step with the United Nations Security Council was surprisingly out of character. However, as Edward McWhinney has noted, the ICAO Council had no competence or jurisdiction to decide if there had been an aggression, this being the role of the United Nations Security Council. The Lebanese case rested more on the eloquence of its delegate than on the law.[16]

Considering that so many hijackings and other attacks against civil aviation were carried out in the name of the Palestine Liberation Organisation until its chairman, Yasser Arafat, formally renounced 'all forms of terrorism', it is ironic that the PLO was granted official status by the ICAO Assembly in 1977 in line with similar moves in other specialised agencies. If this could be justified in the United Nations on political grounds, there were no technical reasons for the PLO to sit as an observer in ICAO Assembly sessions. It controlled no territory and operated no aviation facilities. It reflects the political climate of the time that Israel alone condemned the PLO's preposterous bid for a status in ICAO. In the end, only three States (Israel, United States and South Africa) voted against its admission to observer status; most Western countries, including those which had been recent targets of terrorist attacks, chose to abstain.[17]

The PLO's more recent drive to become a full member in the UN agencies has been temporarily blocked by the US threat to withdraw from these agencies. Whatever the outcome elsewhere, the US holds an effective veto over the admission of the PLO in ICAO since as the depository power of the Chicago Convention, it can simply refuse to accept the PLO's instrument of ratification. In the meantime, in ICAO as in other UN agencies, the PLO observer sits behind a plate marked 'Palestine'.

The frustrations of dealing with terrorists in the absence of an international police force or a consensus on collective sanctions has been all too apparent during the attacks and hijackings of the past two decades. The dilemma is all the more cruel for countries concerned with protecting their nationals. It is not perhaps surprising, then, that some states have been prepared to take action to rescue their nationals in defiance of international law.

The first such case was the Entebbe incident of June–July 1976 in which the Israeli passengers of a hijacked Air France Airbus were being held captive in an old terminal at the airport surrounded by 'protective' Ugandan soldiers under the command of Idi Amin Dada who had supposedly taken charge of the situation. In a daring raid on 4 July the passengers and crew were finally rescued by Israeli commandos after a skirmish with the Ugandan security forces. This incident did not come before the ICAO Council, but in the United Nations Security Council (9–13 July), in reply to Uganda's charge of the violation of its sovereignty, the Israeli delegate claimed 'the right of a State to take military action to protect its nationals in mortal danger' and quoted from several authorities in international law to justify its action. Israel further charged Uganda with collusion and with failing to carry out its obligations under The Hague Convention on the unlawful seizure of aircraft. Israel's argument must have carried some weight because a motion of censure failed for lack of support.[18]

The following year (in October 1977), following a cycle of murder and kidnappings in West Germany, four Arabs hijacked a Lufthansa Boeing 737 bound from Mallorca to Frankfurt and ordered it to fly to Rome and on to Cyprus, Bahrain, Dubai, and Aden, where the hijackers demanded the release of 11 people held in West German prisons. Following rejection of these demands, the hijackers shot the pilot, then ordered the co-pilot to fly to Mogadishu, Somalia. There a West German commando team stormed the aircraft, killing three of the hijackers and rescuing the 86 passengers. No legal questions were raised because the German commandos operated in cooperation with Somalia.

Conflicts between fundamental principles of law were again apparent in two more recent interceptions. The first involved the four hijackers of the Italian cruise liner, *Achille Lauro*, who were captured over the Mediterranean in October 1985 when United States Navy jets intercepted an Egyptian Boeing 737 carrying the terrorists and forced it to land at a United States naval base in Sicily. Two PLO leaders, including Abu Abbas who had accompanied the hijackers, were let go while the others were turned over to the Italian authorities to face trial. This case never came before the United Nations or ICAO, although if it had, the United States probably would not have been censured. As one legal scholar has said: 'the scourge of international terrorism required extraordinary action, and, at least where successful, countries that take action to capture those who have unambiguously committed acts of terrorism will not be condemned.'[19]

It is not clear to what extent the successful capture by the United States of the *Achille Lauro* hijackers set a precedent in the court of international opinion. Would the response have been different had the seizure turned out to have been a mistake, as was the case in a second incident in February 1986 in which the Israelis diverted a Libyan executive jet over the Mediterranean which was thought to have George Habash as a passenger? As in 1973, however, the PLO leader was not on board.[20] The passengers were Syrian politicians who were set free after being briefly detained at an Israeli military base. (Their seizure was generally admitted to have been the result of faulty intelligence.)

In contrast to the American action over the *Achille Lauro*, this incident was brought before both the United Nations and ICAO. While the Security Council had unanimously condemned Israel's 1973 interception, the United States vetoed a similar resolution in February 1986, explaining its position as follows: 'As a general principle the United States opposes the interception of civil aircraft . . . At the same time, we believe that there may arise exceptional circumstances in which an interception may be justified.'[21] Nor did any of the United States' allies in the Security Council vote to condemn Israel on this occasion. When the matter was brought before the ICAO Council at the request of Syria and Libya, Israel asked that the Council debate at the same time the reported threats by Colonel Khadafy to intercept Israeli airliners over the Mediterranean. The debate drew the predictable denunciations by the Arab states, the Soviet Union, India, Pakistan, Senegal, and China. As it had before the Security Council, the United States asserted that as a general principle it opposed the interception of a civilian aircraft, but that this should not mean that giving terrorists sanctuary in an aircraft was acceptable. The ICAO Council condemned the Israeli action – the United States casting the only opposing vote – and took no action on the related Israeli complaint.[22]

This vote showed how far the Council had moved in the years since the Beirut airport raid of 1968. Then it did not take any action on a much more serious incident. Now it condemned an action on which the Security Council had been sharply divided. This shift to activism on the part of the Council had led to growing concern on the part of Western states that ICAO was becoming too involved with political issues. They felt that the Council should restrict itself to technical matters or else it would risk losing its credibility. Four months earlier the Council had debated a complaint by Tunis over an Israeli air strike on the PLO headquarters and had condemned this violation of Tunisian airspace.[23] On that occasion, the United States, in dissociating itself from the consensus, said the issue had already been debated in the United Nations and argued that its resurrection was 'an abuse of ICAO's jurisdiction'. Indeed ICAO Council meetings were coming to sound much like repeat performances of Security Council sessions on Arab–Israeli issues with Council members seconded by professional diplomats and members of their respective United Nations missions.

AERIAL INTRUSION: ATTACKING STRAYING AIRCRAFT

Every state has complete and exclusive sovereignty over the airspace above its territory as spelled out in Article 1 of the Chicago Convention. Consequently, no aircraft is normally entitled to enter the airspace above the territory of a foreign state without the latter's permission. In an early study of aerial intrusion, Oliver Lissitzyn set out the basic argument: does the principle of sovereignty over airspace mean that any aircraft entering a country's airspace without such permission is completely at the mercy of the territorial sovereign?[24] The Chicago Convention recognised that on occasion, civilian aircraft stray over restricted areas, and Annex 2 set out rules for them to be directed back to their assigned flight path or instructed to land. These rules provide that interception of civilian aircraft should be avoided and undertaken only as a last resort and that 'intercepting aircraft should refrain from the use of weapons'. Yet there have been instances in which aircraft were fired upon or downed by missiles. A report compiled by the International Federation of Air Line Pilots' Associations in 1986 lists 33 incidents of hostile action against civil aircraft in which 746 people lost their lives since 1947.[25]

Among such attacks were those on an Air Rhodesia Boeing 737 shot down by rebels in 1979, resulting in the death of 49 passengers, and on two TAAG (Angola Airline) aircraft, including a Boeing

737 which crashed with 130 people on board (8 November 1983). An Argentinian-registered aircraft bound for Iran disappeared in 1981 near the Iran-Turkish border.[26] A year later, an Algerian plane bound from Cyprus to Teheran also disappeared under mysterious circumstances. More recently, a Sudan Airways airline with 60 passengers on board was shot down by Sudanese rebels in August 1986. Guerrillas in Afghanistan have used rockets on several occasions against transport aircraft.

In November 1988, an Afghan civil aircraft carrying 30 passengers was downed by the Pakistani Air Force during a flight from Kabul to Jalalabad. The Pakistani Defence Ministry confirmed that the aircraft had inadvertently intruded into Pakistani airspace and was shot down and that everyone on board had been killed. More startling was the revelation by Pakistani authorities, as reported in the press (*The New York Times*, 22 November 1988), that this had been the fifth such incident in less than one year along the 1400-mile-border with Afghanistan. No report of any of these incidents was ever received by ICAO as would normally be the case with an ordinary accident.

Most of these attacks occurred in areas torn by civil strife, while others took place in areas otherwise considered safe for travel. In one such incident, an Air France airliner on a flight from Frankfurt to Berlin along the Berlin corridor was attacked by two Soviet fighters in 1952. It managed to land safely at Tempelhof, although the attack caused injuries to several passengers. In 1954, a British Cathay Pacific airliner flying from Bangkok to Hong Kong was shot down by Chinese fighter pilots who reportedly did not know they had attacked a commercial airliner. The aircraft ditched in the sea and several passengers drowned.

Four particularly serious incidents came before both ICAO and the United Nations Security Council. In each case the response of the international community appears to have been dictated more by the identity of the culprit than by the particular circumstances of the violation.

On 27 July 1955, an El Al Constellation en route from London to Tel Aviv strayed into Bulgarian airspace and was fired upon by two intercepting fighters. The aircraft crashed, killing all 51 passengers and seven crew members. Israel immediately notified the ICAO Council president but did not request formal action on the part of the Council in order not to detract from the judicial pursuit of the case. It asked, however, that the matter be brought before the United Nations General Assembly under an agenda item dealing with the safety of commercial aviation inadvertently crossing international frontiers. The General Assembly subsequently adopted a resolution which called upon all states 'to take the necessary measures to avoid such incidents'.

While claiming that the Israeli aircraft had ignored orders to land, Bulgaria admitted that its air defences acted somewhat hastily 'and did not take all necessary measures to compel the aircraft to surrender and land'. There were in fact no mitigating circumstances because the attack did not take place in a danger zone but in a regular air corridor open to foreign travel with no security restrictions. Although Bulgaria at first expressed regret and promised to punish those responsible as well as pay compensation, it then changed its position, disclaiming all responsibility and proposing instead to make payments in Bulgarian currency. The case ultimately went before the International Court of Justice with the United States, Israel, and Great Britain submitting memorials. Bulgaria refused to yield to the jurisdiction of the Court, however, and the case had to be dismissed.[27]

The outcome was quite different when a Libyan Boeing 727 was downed by Israeli fighters over Israeli-occupied territory in the Sinai desert on 26 February 1973. The mishap cost the lives of the 106 passengers and three French crew members. The aircraft apparently had blundered into the forbidden airspace in the midst of a sandstorm which had grounded all commercial flights in the area, leading the Israeli air defence system to assume that the aircraft was on a hostile mission. The incident happened at the time of a war of nerves when Arab terrorists had vowed to use commercial aircraft in suicide attacks on Israeli cities. Even though Israel expressed regret immediately after the incident and offered to make payments to the families of the victims, Libya, Egypt, Lebanon, and Saudi Arabia asked for immediate action on the part of the ICAO Council.[28]

The Council considered the matter of sufficient gravity to call an extraordinary session of the Assembly at United Nations Headquarters on 27 February 1973. ICAO's supreme body, by a vote of 105 to one (Israel) and two abstentions (Colombia and Malawi), condemned Israel and requested a fact-finding investigation. The debate was brief and, as the vote indicated, Israel received little sympathy for its explanation that the incident was the result of a series of errors and omissions on the part of the Libyan aircraft and the Egyptian control centre. Some Western delegates, while voting for the condemnation, did note however that there was a certain inconsistency in doing so before an official investigation.[29]

This inconsistency became even more obvious in the way the Council dealt with two subsequent attacks by the Soviet Union and the United States: the KAL incident of 1983 and the downing of an Iran Air flight in 1988.

THE SUPERPOWERS IN THE DOCK: THE KAL AND IRAN AIR INCIDENTS

Whether or not Korean Air Lines Flight 007 en route from Anchorage to Seoul was an innocent passenger jet that had strayed off its course or, as the Soviets still claim, a civilian airliner spying over highly sensitive military installations, three facts are uncontested. First, regardless of whether the crew was guilty of gross negligence or 'willful misconduct' as a US Federal Court jury ruled six years later, the airliner with 269 people on board was shot down by Soviet fighters instead of being forced to land as in a similar incident in 1978.[30] Second, Soviet air traffic stations did not know the plane's flight plan; nor were they supposed to because the flight's intended course was outside Soviet airspace. Under the system in effect at the time, there was simply no procedure for contacting Soviet military or civilian authorities to rectify the situation, even if the crew and American or Japanese traffic controllers were aware of what was happening – clearly, a loophole that needed immediate correction. Third, the USSR has so far steadfastly refused to assume legal responsibility for its action and to pay compensation. Glasnost notwithstanding, why has the USSR so far refused to apologise and assume legal responsibility for the KAL disaster? The reason may be that whatever the weight of legal authority, there is a distinct Soviet position regarding aerial intrusion based on the strict application of Article 1 of the Chicago Convention and its own air code. That position seems to be that an intruding aircraft shall be made to land *under any circumstances*. As John Phelps has written: 'hostile action would be taken against any civil or military intruder that refused to obey instructions to land'.[31]

Following the initial expressions of revulsion and calls for sanctions and boycotts, after the high-level rhetoric and political exploitation of the incident in the United States, and after the United

Nations Security Council debate and Soviet veto, the Council of ICAO met in extraordinary session on 16 September 1983 at the request of the Republic of Korea and Canada. For the Soviet Union, the technical facts in the incident were clear. There had been a blatant violation of its sovereignty. The KAL crew had refused to follow the instructions of the interceptor fighters to land and ignored the rules established in Annex 2 of the Chicago Convention for such a case. The official Soviet version of the incident had already been outlined in an unusual press conference in Moscow by no less a figure than the chief of the Soviet general staff, Marshal Nikolai Ogarkov.[32] The initial United States contention was that the act had been deliberate and that the Soviet Union had known the aircraft was a civilian airliner and not a military target.[33]

Over Soviet objections, the Council approved a resolution deploring the destruction of the aircraft and the loss of lives and called for an immediate investigation with the cooperation of all parties.[34] Immediately afterwards the Secretary-General of ICAO announced that he would appoint a team of experts from within the Organisation to report directly to him. In spite of United States pressure, the Council in this instance refused to condemn the Soviet Union or to prejudge the case before all the facts were in. The report of the investigation which was given to the Council members later that year explicitly rejected the contention of a spy mission advanced by the USSR and found no evidence that the Korean crew was ever aware that its aircraft was off course or intercepted. Further, the report found no evidence that the deviation was deliberate and instead concluded that the crew had incorrectly set its automated navigation system and allowed the aircraft to stray off course for almost five and a half hours. The report concluded that the aircraft was hit by at least one or two air-to-air missiles fired from one of the USSR interceptor aircraft whose pilot had been directed by his ground command and control unit to terminate the flight. The aircraft was subsequently destroyed on its impact with the sea.[35]

The report's credibility has been challenged by various proponents of the 'spy plane' theories, yet its conclusions have withstood the test of time and scrutiny for lack of any factual evidence as to what could have caused the aircraft to veer off its course. As Seymour Hersh points out, the ICAO report remains the most comprehensive document on the incident. That it was undertaken at all by an international team of ICAO experts, that it was pieced together in record time, and that it was made public in the face of opposition from one of the superpowers directly implicated is a rare occurrence in the annals of the United Nations.[36]

With all available data at its disposal and still without the promised report of a Soviet commission of inquiry, the ICAO Council took final action on 6 March 1984. The resolution formally condemning the USSR for its use of armed force against the Korean airliner constituted an unprecedented vote against a superpower.[37] More important than apportioning blame, however, was the question of avoiding future incidents. This was to be accomplished through an amendment to the Chicago Convention specifically banning the use of force against civilian aircraft. In addition to calling an extraordinary session of the ICAO Assembly to approve such an amendment, the Council also decided to improve interception procedures and the coordination between military and civilian communications systems and air traffic control agencies.

With respect to air law, the amendment (Article 3 *bis*) to the Chicago Convention banning the use of armed force against a civilian aircraft did not break new ground since it only formally recognised a generally accepted principle in international law. Even so, in view of the conflicting principle of sovereign rights embodied in Article 1 of the Chicago Convention, a successful outcome of this extraordinary session of the Assembly could not be assured. Nor was it certain that the Assembly would draw the required quorum of 77 states or the two-thirds majority of the contracting states required to approve an amendment to the convention.

Even before the meeting took place (in April 1984) different draft amendments were circulated, one by Western countries favouring a specific prohibition on the use of force against a civilian aircraft and another by the USSR reaffirming 'the principle of complete and exclusive sovereignty of a State over its airspace' and proposing to incorporate a new provision in the Chicago Convention against the 'misuse of civil aviation'. The Council president can be credited with achieving unanimity on a compromise that gave satisfaction to both camps. The amendment recognises the existence in international law of a specific prohibition on the use of weapons against civilian aircraft in flight and gives satisfaction to the USSR on measures to prohibit the deliberate misuse of civilian aircraft.[38]

Technical amendments to the various annexes of the convention only needed Council action to become effective. They posed no problem since they dealt mainly with improved procedures for communications, coordination, and identification of civilian aircraft, for surveillance of air traffic, and for the use of military radar facilities to assist civilian air traffic services along sensitive routes. A proposal to extend ICAO provisions to 'state aircraft' (that is, interceptor aircraft) was opposed by both the United States and the Soviet Union, ostensibly because these aircraft are beyond the scope of the Chicago Convention, but more likely because their respective military establishments would not feel bound anyway.[39]

An immediate and practical outcome of ICAO actions was the aviation agreement announced at the 1985 Reagan–Gorbachev summit meeting in Geneva. This bilateral agreement sets up, for the first time, procedures to allow a foreign airliner to make an emergency landing in the restricted areas of the Soviet Union. Commercial aircraft straying over the north Pacific in areas closer to Soviet territory than to American or Japanese airfields are now able to contact Soviet authorities for instructions. A crucial element in the accord is the direct telephone link-up between air traffic control stations at Khabarovsk and Tokyo. Ironically, the KAL incident which led to some of the harshest rhetoric between the superpowers produced one of the few tangible accomplishments of that first summit meeting between the two leaders.

With the downing of an Iranian Airbus on a routine flight from Bandar Abbas to Dubai on 3 July 1988, it was the turn of the United States to be cast as the villain. The facts were undisputed. A cruiser of the US Navy, the USS *Vincennes*, while battling several Iranian speedboats in the Strait of Hormuz, shot down the airliner which exploded in the air, killing all 298 people on board. At first, the incident seemed like another confrontation in the Gulf between the naval forces of the United States and Iran. But the incident, the deadliest attack yet against a commercial aircraft, quickly developed into something far worse as the details of the blunder became known.

The tragedy invited immediate comparisons with the KAL incident because Iran accused the United States of a deliberate attack. There was also something familiar about the sight of a top-ranking military officer describing in military jargon how an airliner had turned into a threatening target. Admiral William Crowe, then Chairman of the Joint Chiefs of Staff, was quick to dismiss parallels between the two incidents, however. The Iranian airliner, he pointed out, had flown into a combat zone at its own risk and peril unlike Flight 007 which had merely strayed into Soviet airspace. The admiral also emphasised that the tragedy had to be viewed against the growing hostilities in the Gulf and the Iraqi missile attack against the USS *Stark* in May 1987 in which 37 seamen had been killed.[40] The rules of engagement, allowing a captain to fire first in defence of his ship, made United States commanders determined not to be caught off guard.

Whether the shooting down of the aircraft was an 'understandable accident' (President Reagan's description) or a tragic act of negligence, the United States, unlike the Soviet Union, quickly expressed regret and offered to pay compensation to the families of victims. By then it had become clear that the United States did not have much of a case. First, while the United States originally claimed that Flight 655 was outside the commercial air corridor over the Strait of Hormuz, it had to admit that the airliner was flying well within its assigned corridor. Second, while the navy originally claimed that the aircraft was descending towards the *Vincennes*, other data confirmed that the aircraft was cruising at a normal altitude. Third, while the Iranian air force had been known to use commercial airlines for transport,[41] this was clearly not the case in this instance since the Airbus was on an international flight and was sending its signals on open radio channels. Nor could the aircraft's failure to respond to challenges from the ship justify the action taken. A civilian plane does not necessarily receive warnings sent over military frequencies and, as was the case in the Gulf, such challenges had been frequently ignored by pilots who would not be monitoring the right channel.

Iran, for its part, had a strong case. Its aircraft had not strayed into someone else's airspace. It was flying where it was supposed to and was shot down while obeying all the prescribed rules. To be sure, because the Strait of Hormuz was a danger zone and Iranian forces were engaging United States ships at the time, the Airbus might have taken a long roundabout route as it had done on previous occasions, or Iran's civil aviation authorities could have cancelled the flight or closed the route. Iran would have considered such actions only as a last resort because it would have meant legitimising the presence of the United States task force in the Gulf.

These were the underlying issues when the ICAO Council met in an extraordinary session on 13 July at the request of Iran. The Council found itself cast in an unprecedented political role in that it was meeting *before* the Security Council. In the past Security Council debates on such major issues had provided Council members with a guide to their state's position on the incident under discussion. In this instance, however, the Security Council meeting, scheduled for the day before, had been postponed because the, private consultations had not been completed. The ICAO meeting was therefore the first direct confrontation between the United States and Iran in this affair.

With each side represented by seasoned diplomats, the tone of the debate was what might have been expected in the Security Council. The debate focused on the responsibility of each party, with Iran insisting that the United States should withdraw its forces from the Gulf and the United States laying the blame on Iran's failure to comply with a United Nations resolution on a ceasefire in the Iran–Iraq war. Iran's specific demands were straightforward. It wanted an explicit condemnation of the attack, a recognition of the fact that the United States must bear responsibility, and a fact-finding investigation by ICAO.

Except for the opening exchanges, there was no hostile rhetoric. Even the Soviet intervention was subdued. The mood clearly was not in favour of reviving the superpower confrontation which had marked the Council session over the KAL incident. In the end, only four of the 33 Council members (the USSR, Czechoslovakia, China and Cuba) spoke in favour of Iran. By consensus, the Council agreed to take all necessary measures to arrange for effective coordination of civilian flight operations and military activities as well as better routing arrangements. It also agreed to institute a fact-finding investigation, a step already welcomed by the United States. Instead of a condemnation, the Council approved a statement drafted by the President expressing regret and deploring the use of weapons against a civilian aircraft.[42]

The statement differed in subtle ways from the one issued in the immediate aftermath of the Korean incident. Then, the Council issued a resolution. This time, it decided to issue its statement as a 'decision' which was seen as possessing less authority than a formal resolution. This curious formula was in fact a concession to the United States which let it be known that it would not go along with any text that would invite comparisons with the KAL affair. One week later, the Security Council adopted a similarly mild text that avoided direct criticism of the United States. The resolution merely expressed 'deep distress and profound regret' over the loss of innocent lives.[43]

While the United States welcomed the ICAO decision, the

Iranian delegate blamed the outcome on pressure tactics. 'The United States does have its influence and power', the official told a press conference. 'It is not easy for member countries to speak openly, frankly, decisively against the United States even when it commits a very serious crime'.[44]

Considering the magnitude of the blunder, the ICAO response was surprisingly mild. The United States was not even taken to task for what was clearly a violation of ICAO rules on air traffic coordination. Annex 11 of the Chicago Convention provides that 'the arrangements for activities potentially hazardous to civil aircraft, whether over the territory of a State or over the high seas, shall be coordinated with the appropriate air traffic services authorities'. There are no indications that United States naval vessels in the Gulf ever complied with this rule. On the contrary, the warships did not routinely monitor civilian air traffic and were not ordered to do so even after the flight 655 incident.[45]

By the time ICAO's investigation got under way, international attention had shifted to the Security Council where Iran announced its acceptance of United Nations resolution 598 which it had rejected until then. While war-weariness or military reverses were the probable reasons for Iran's acceptance of a ceasefire, the destruction of its airliner provided a face-saving excuse for seeking a political solution to the war. As United Nations peace-keeping forces moved into position to monitor the ceasefire, the Pentagon released the findings of a military inquiry which confirmed that, in the stress of battle, the radar operators on the *Vincennes* had convinced themselves that the aircraft they had spotted on their screens was hostile and intended to attack the ship.[46]

The ICAO report of the incident confirmed the findings of the US inquiry board that faulty communications and the lack of monitoring facilities had made it difficult for the US warships to differentiate between 'friendly and hostile unknown aircraft'. ICAO investigators found that eleven warnings had been sent but that only the last challenge from another ship had been coded specifically to be received by Iran Air Flight 655. The other challenges were not received because the flight crew was not monitoring the proper frequency or did not identify their flight as the one being challenged.[47]

ICAO's own investigation went beyond the Pentagon's conclusions in pressing for practical steps to prevent such mishaps. ICAO had already recommended that military authorities in the

Gulf be given radar codes to identify civil air traffic operating in the same airspace as military aircraft and that the code used by the military to identify 'friendly forces' be made available for use by civil air traffic controllers.

The ICAO report placed more emphasis on corrective action than on apportioning blame. In a closed session on 7 December, the Council disposed of it by sending it to the Air Navigation Commission for further study and recommendations.[48] Iran, backed by the Soviet Union, China, Czechoslovakia and Cuba, tried once more to have the Council condemn the United States, but was unsuccessful. When the Council received the Commission's recommendations, the debate resumed in a decidedly more militant mood on the part of Iran, possibly in the aftermath of internal political conditions. The Soviet Union moved again to condemn the United States and this time obtained the support of two more countries. However, its resolution was defeated by a lopsided vote of 16 to six with six abstentions.

Instead, the Council adopted an innocuous resolution which deplored the incident and reaffirmed ICAO's policy condemning the use of weapons against civil aircraft without, however, referring specifically to the United States.[49] Following the vote, the US delegate praised the 'balanced judgment' of the Council. For his part, the Iranian delegate wanted his pound of flesh and threatened unspecified moves against the US in the face of the continued presence of US naval forces in the Gulf.[50] Less than three weeks later, an Iranian-backed group claimed responsibility for the bomb explosion that destroyed Pan American Flight 103 over Lockerbie in Scotland.[51]

The Council's cautious attitude in the Iranian affair inevitably invites comparison with its forthright condemnation in the two previous cases involving armed attack against civil airliners. In the view of Edward McWhinney, a member of the Permanent Court of Arbitration, the Council should have done no less in the Iranian affair than in the earlier KAL incident regardless of the United States' apology and its admission of a blunder. For him, no claims of self-defence or mistake can legally countervail the absolute legal obligations under the Chicago Convention to respect the safety and security of international aviation. He points out that the claim of self-defence under Article 51 of the UN Charter is weak because the US was not legally at war with Iran at the time and the US was operating in the Persian Gulf without any legal licence from the UN Security Council or from any other competent international authority to carry out hostile military operations.[52]

Iran's case against the United States did not rest with the Council's resolution. It sought legal redress in the International Court of Justice, contending that the resolution of the ICAO Council was erroneous and that the United States had violated international laws. Iran's application to the court was based on the Statute of the court as well as on Article 84 of the Chicago Convention, whereupon the President of the Council informed that body of ICAO's eventual participation in the court's proceedings. Whereas this unprecented case recalls the Israeli–Bulgarian affair of 1955, the question put before the court at that time did not involve a decision of the Council. Furthermore, Bulgaria did not accept the court's jurisdiction in the matter. The United States, which could have done the same, decided not to contest the case. In its suit, Iran asked the International Court to overturn the Council's resolution which exonerated the United States and to order that country to pay damages for the loss of the aircraft, its passengers and crew.[53]

While the ceasefire has eased the immediate concerns over air traffic in the Gulf, the major problem is the continued presence of a military force which must be made to abide by the rules applying to civil aviation. ICAO can work only through the civil aviation administrations of individual states. They in turn must seek the agreement of their respective defence establishments. As demonstrated in the KAL incident, military authorities are not easily persuaded to apply regulations which limit their freedom of action.

9 Terrorism in the Sky: Setting Security Standards

Aviation security is only as strong as its weakest link.

Assad Kotaite, President of the ICAO Council

While technological advances have produced a remarkable degree of safety in air travel, unparalleled by any other means of transport, criminal attacks against airlines have posed a man-made threat for which there are no simple technical solutions. The aviation community has looked to ICAO for vigorous leadership in dealing with all aspects of the problem. Yet from the start the Organisation has had a hard time living up to this model role beyond setting minimal security standards and providing advice and training.

THE HISTORICAL CONTEXT

Before dealing with the provisions of Annex 17, it is important to review the historical context which led to its adoption. The first international convention mentioning hijackings was signed in Tokyo in 1963. It spelled out minimal obligations to ensure the security of passengers and crew and the return of the hijacked aircraft to the lawful commander. No security measures were imposed on states. At this early date, the expectation was that hijacking could be stopped by legal deterrence. There was a general feeling that passengers should not be alarmed or inconvenienced by highly visible security measures.[1] Most states were inclined to believe that they were not immediately affected and that hijacking was too remote a possibility to give security a high enough priority.

By the time the 16th Session of the ICAO Assembly met in Buenos Aires in 1968, it had become clear that the Tokyo Convention was inadequate. In that year alone there were 33 hijackings. The number jumped to 91 in 1969. Even so, the ICAO Council spent many hours debating the creation of a special Committee on Unlawful Interference under Article 52 of the Chicago Convention.

144

It finally did so in April 1969 and it made sure the new body would have a subordinate role.[2]

Previously, at its sixty-fifth session held late in 1968, the Council held a lengthy debate on security which revealed a greater concern for legal subtleties than substance. At one stage in the proceedings, the Council had before it a draft resolution in which it noted 'with concern the adverse effect on safety in international air transportation of the increasing number of acts of forcible and unlawful seizure of aircraft'. This first draft in its final paragraph urged 'Contracting States to take all possible measures under their national laws to discourage acts of unlawful seizure of aircraft and ensure prosecution of those who commit such acts and, if necessary for such purposes, to enact adequate legislation'.[3]

The resolution as finally adopted showed some important changes. The Council replaced the words 'adverse effect on' with 'serious threat to'. The last paragraph was substantially changed so as to urge contracting states to 'take all possible measures to prevent acts of unlawful seizure of aircraft and, where appropriate, co-operate with any State whose aircraft has been the subject of such a seizure'. In a significant move, the Council dropped the reference to the prosecution of hijackers. One argument advanced (by the Lebanese representative) was that the Council should not play the role of an attorney general. The watered-down resolution achieved a broad consensus with 23 Council members in favour and one abstention. Three members were absent.[4]

By 1973, it was recognised that a separate Annex in the Chicago Convention was needed to deal specifically with security matters. Annex 17 was adopted by the Council on 22 March 1974 after a prolonged process involving the Air Navigation Commission, the Air Transport Committee, the Committee on Unlawful Interference, member states and international organisations.[5] Considering that there were 319 hijackings during the four-year period between 1969 and 1972, it may come as a surprise that it took until the early 1970s for the first countries to apply effective security measures.[6] This state of affairs has been blamed on complacency, bureaucratic inertia, lack of imagination and foresight as well as costs and stalling tactics.[7]

As a regulatory text, Annex 17 is unique; it is designed to preserve the safety of international civil aviation from a threat which is non-operational in character or origin. This slim document of 18 pages is primarily concerned with the administrative and coordination aspects of security. It requires each member state to establish its own civil aviation security programme with such additional security measures as may be proposed by other appropriate bodies.[8] In order to maintain confidentiality Annex 17 contains only broad statements of policy on what is required, leaving each state to decide how these measures are to be applied.

Annex 17 provides that each state shall require airlines flying from its airports to adopt a security programme and to ensure that it is compatible with the prescribed airport security measures. The obligation lies with the state to make sure that carriers comply with Annex 17. Accordingly, states will not escape liability if they fail to comply with its provisions.[9]

As a minimum, each carrier's security programme must provide measures to protect checked baggage, cargo, mail and stores, prevention of unauthorised access to aircraft, procedures for the crew and other staff. The operator's programme must also include procedures for the inspection and screening of passengers and cabin baggage if it is specifically assigned this responsibility by the state.

More detailed security recommendations are spelled out in the Security Manual for Safeguarding Civil Aviation against Acts of Unlawful Interference. This elaborate document was drafted by security experts from Brazil, France, Switzerland, the United Kingdom and the United States, together with representatives of the Airport Associations Coordinating Council (AACC), the International Air Transport Association (IATA) and the International Federation of Air Line Pilots Associations (IFALPA). They recommended that aviation security be the responsibility of a national civil aviation security committee comprising representatives of government agencies concerned with aviation, law enforcement, immigration, customs, postal inspection and foreign affairs as well as representatives of airlines and airport administrators.

Because there are so many international aviation operations the Security Manual does not attempt to seek uniform measures among ICAO's contracting states. Each state and airport administration must make an assessment and decide upon the plan or combination of plans best suited to its needs. The emphasis is on exchanging information among states and international bodies concerned with aviation security such as IATA, the International Criminal Police Organisation (ICPO/INTERPOL), IFALPA, the Universal Postal Union (UPU), and the two airport organisations – the Airport Operators Council International (AOCI) and the International Civil

Airport Association (ICAA). As a restricted document, it is available only to national agencies and persons directly responsible for implementing security provisions. It is distributed only through the national authorities.

Annex 17, as first published in 1974, provided at best a basic security programme consisting of minimal obligations in the form of ten standards and eighteen recommendations. Over the years and in response to various events, the text became more specific as several amendments were introduced. It also became more demanding as the result of seven amendments to tighten various provisions.

The first amendment, adopted in 1976, upgraded certain recommended practices to standards that are binding on states. Moreover, it requires that all states provide detailed reports relating to acts of unlawful interference to which they may have been subjected. The second amendment, adopted in 1977, set out new standards for the control, transfer and transit of passengers and their cabin baggage. The third amendment, adopted in 1978, added various rules to be applied during stop-overs. The fourth amendment, adopted in 1981, completes the Annex with regard to the transportation of persons in custody, and to leased aircraft. The fifth amendment, adopted in 1984, deals with the transportation of weapons, whether authorised or not.

The sixth amendment, adopted in 1985, replaced many of the specifications in the text. It modified all the chapters, introduced new provisions and made certain existing practices more stringent particularly those dealing with transfer and transit passengers and access to the aircraft. An important new standard (Article 5.1.4) was added requiring that the baggage of passengers who have registered but not reported for embarkation be removed from the aircraft. Other improved provisions require each state to implement security checks of mail and supplies taken on board. The last amendment, adopted in June 1989, restructured the Annex once again to avoid choosing whether airlines or airport authorities are responsible for implementing provisions. The Annex now simply refers to the measures that must be taken and leaves it to each state to apportion responsibility.

The last two amendments were rushed through with a greater sense of urgency than all the others, as the result of a spate of incidents in the months preceding their adoption. The Council's agenda in June 1985 was particularly grim. That month alone, a

TWA aircraft (Flight 847) was hijacked, one of its passengers brutally murdered and 39 others held hostage for 17 days, under harrowing conditions; a Jordanian airliner was hijacked and blown up in Beirut; a bomb killed three passengers and damaged a terminal at Frankfurt Airport while another explosion killed two baggage handlers at Narita Airport in Tokyo. Finally, in the worst incident of all, a bomb in an unaccompanied piece of luggage placed on board an Air India jumbo jet exploded off the coast of Ireland killing all 329 people on board.

On 14 June, the day of the TWA hijacking, the ICAO Council had on its agenda a report on the implementation of various Assembly resolutions dealing with hijackings and sabotage. The Council deplored the latest incidents and called on states to comply with their obligations 'to combat effectively acts of unlawful interference . . . and to make more effective preventive measures'. The situation clearly demanded more than the usual pleas by the Council.[10] The continued detainment of the TWA passengers in Beirut after the piecemeal release of others and the suspicion that the Air India jet went down as the result of sabotage propelled the Council into action at an extraordinary session attended by top government officials of the states concerned.

Speaking for the Reagan Administration, the US Secretary of Transportation, Elizabeth Dole, said ICAO should not only review existing security procedures but also monitor their implementation at airports around the world. The strongest speech was made by the British Minister of Aviation, Michael Spicer, who sounded an ominous warning: 'It seems probable that we are now facing extremists with high technical understanding or knowledge of precisely where to place an explosive device so that it has the most efficient and horrific and disastrous effect'.[11]

In addition to ordering a review of existing practices in aviation security, the Council instructed the Secretary General to present a plan of action to reinforce other aspects of the programme. As part of this plan, ICAO would analyse implementation problems, provide more training, and devise new techniques for screening and inspection of passengers. The Committee on Unlawful Interference would undertake this task assisted by a panel of experts.[12]

Yet, for all its speedy deliberations, the Council followed the path of least resistance. No action was taken on establishing within ICAO a special team to evaluate compliance by states of ICAO's standards, as requested by Secretary Dole at the Council meetings and repeated in an urgent cable to the Council President.[13] Also, while the plan of action provided for additional resources, it did not address a French recommendation for the creation of a security cell manned by highly specialised personnel and with appropriate technical resources to be made available in hijacking incidents.[14]

The most ambitious plan was put forward by Israel which, with good reason, wanted to contribute to the debate. It recommended that the rigorous procedures in effect at El Al Israel Airlines be applied world-wide. These measures include the screening of suspicious passengers at the check-in counter and a thorough search of all baggage and of the aircraft itself before departure and at every intermediate stop.[15]

There is no evidence that these suggestions were ever acted upon. Israel's Transport Minister remarked somewhat bitterly that 'these initiatives were not successful because of political motives . . . Had they been accepted by the international community, these proposals would have assisted in the elimination of terrorism'.[16]

Apparently discontented with the pace of efforts to improve security, the United States enacted legislation to empower the Secretary of Transportation to 'withhold, revoke or limit' the operations into the United States of any airline which fails to meet minimum ICAO standards. This power has been exercised only once against Lebanon in the aftermath of the TWA hijacking. It effectively grounded Middle East Airlines which until then had bravely maintained some services in spite of chaotic conditions at Beirut Airport. In addition, the Foreign Airport Security Act gives the FAA unprecedented power to assess security standards at foreign airports served by US carriers. The FAA can issue warnings and ban flights by US airlines until deficiencies are corrected. The United States has issued a warning once, in 1986 in the case of Manila International Airport. The move apparently had the desired effect because after subsequent inspection, the airport was found to have brought its security up to ICAO standards.

Security measures must be assessed according to agreed criteria. Yet, there is no established international standard against which the competence of passenger screening can be tested, this in spite of the large sums of money spent and efforts made by states, airlines and airports on this most visible security operation. Few countries, according to IATA, have made any attempts to lay down national criteria.[17]

ICAO's cautious approach in dealings with criminal attacks

against civil aviation has left it vulnerable to criticisms that it failed to appreciate the nature and scope of international terrorism.[18] While security standards have been made more stringent, these have come about largely as the result of incidents which revealed obvious loopholes in the security network. It must be stressed, however, that ICAO's standards are minimal requirements leaving states free to apply stiffer measures if they feel specifically threatened. Such measures can go as far as the physical search of all passengers and cabin and hold-baggage (in addition to normal X-ray), the security control of all personnel and equipment servicing of an aircraft, the posting of security guards in and around aircraft, a complete search of aircraft before boarding and the use of in-flight security guards.

ICAO's security provisions clearly reflect a compromise and a consensus governing all aspects of the Organisation's activities. Furthermore, unlike a national regulatory agency, ICAO cannot enforce its rules. It cannot set more stringent standards than its individual members are willing to implement. The Air Navigation Commission and Council sessions have at times been the scene of sharp divisions on how to secure a common approach. A case in point was the difficulty in implementing the new provision (Article 5.1.4) to match baggage with passengers. There were different views in Council as to whether this should become a standard in the Annex or a recommended practice, as favoured by the Committee on Unlawful Interference. However, Canada strongly urged that the provision be upgraded to a standard but that it would not be applicable until the development of better technology.[19] In the end, the compromise called for the adoption of a standard applicable in two years, although states were encouraged to implement it earlier.

When the Council reviewed the matter in 1987 it was again divided as to how to approach the problem. Canada, while recognising that a full application of the standard might not be possible, felt that another delay would encourage further acts of violence.[20] The Council again compromised by requiring that the standard be made applicable to passengers changing aircraft on the same airline and delaying the implementation date for interline flights until 1 April 1989 to coincide with the introduction by IATA of an industry-wide system of computerised baggage tags.

The fact that technology has lagged behind security requirements is clearly a drawback in setting worldwide standards. Conventional security systems were designed to prevent the hijackings of the

1970s but were not meant to deal with the airline bombings of the 1980s. The Lockerbie tragedy proves the point. The bomb planted aboard Pan Am Flight 103 may have consisted of no more than 300 grams of explosives concealed in a way that made its detection by conventional means practically impossible at most airports. X-ray and metal detectors can spot guns and grenades but plastic explosives cannot be detected either by X-ray machines or trained dogs. Instead of the old-style metal bomb timers and wiring which show up on most X-rays, terrorists have used miniaturised components disguised as parts of radios and cassette players. In addition, passengers are no longer the only suspects. Weapons and explosives have been placed on board aircraft by airport employees who have access to the ramp.

Devices that can identify both low (plastic) and high (metal) density materials, and other techniques to 'sniff' the nitrogen in plastic explosives are in various stages of development. They are not as yet in practical use and are too costly for large-scale application. The latest technique – thermal neutron activation (TNA) – can detect the presence of explosives by bombarding luggage with neutrons but each unit would cost from $750 000 to $1 million. US Government officials have told Congressional hearings that several such units would be needed at each airport before comprehensive searches of all baggage could be carried out. It has been suggested that as many as 200 units would be needed around the world for use by US carriers.[21]

Aside from its high cost, the major problem with TNA is that the technique is not foolproof. If, as reported to the Congressional hearings, TNA has a better than 95 per cent success rate, it would still cause too many false alarms. As the former chief scientist of the US Department of Transportation pointed out, with 10 billion pieces of baggage passing through major airports every year, even a one per cent margin of error would cause 100 million false responses.[22] During a one-year test period with real explosives, the TNA repeatedly failed to detect small bombs.

A promising development as a result of Lockerbie is an international instrument on the marking of explosives to facilitate their detection. It is particularly significant that one of the countries that gave this instrument a high priority in ICAO is Czechoslovakia, a major producer of plastic explosives. However, here again, the group of ICAO specialists who came up with this possible solution sounded a note of caution and recommended that it be part of an overall strategy.[23] For one thing, the specialists have yet to select a tracer. Furthermore, it takes several years to put an international instrument into effect. The bottom line will have to be a combination of techniques and devices. Just as surely, those bent on sabotaging an aircraft will find ways to circumvent security devices. In any case, technology cannot provide all the answers. Even the best equipment is meaningless without highly trained personnel. As an ICAO report makes all too clear: 'since potential terrorists can be expected to be well informed on the latest commercial technology, the human factor which takes in training, motivation and alertness is the most important component of security'.[24]

THE LOCKERBIE TRAGEDY

The bombing of Pan Am Flight 103 on 21 December 1988 showed that in the absence of adequate implementation, global security procedures cannot prevent well-trained terrorists from going through such tight-security airports as Heathrow or Frankfurt. As investigators combed through the debris at Lockerbie, they already suspected that the explosion that killed a total of 270 people on the jumbo jet and on the ground was an act of sabotage. Sixteen months later a US commission on aviation security issued a report which blamed both the FAA and Pan Am for negligence.

This tragedy called attention once more to the difficulty of enforcing existing security measures and revealed that the weak link can exist close to home. Immediately after the bombing, the UK Transport Department said that primary responsibility for providing security at airports lays with the airport operator and secondarily with the airline. British Airports Authority plc (BAA), the privatised operator of Heathrow and other major British airports, referred all security questions to the Transport Department, the agency responsible for security operations. Department officials pointed out that while their department was responsible for setting standards, 'how these are implemented is up to the airport operator in conjunction with the police and the airlines that use the airport'.[25]

The Pan Am bombing was followed by frantic displays of tightened security at many airports around the world. The FAA issued new rules requiring, among other measures, a physical inspection of all checked baggage while the UK Department of Transport imposed such procedures at all British airports handling US airlines.

The measures imposed by the FAA on US airlines operating in Europe and the Middle East could not easily be imposed on foreign carriers used by half of the American travelling public. This anomaly led Richard Lally, a top official of the Air Transport Association, to remark that 'beefing up security only for US carriers would be like having policemen patrol only odd-numbered streets'. The frustration of US carriers was evident as they pressed the US Government to demand yet another review of Annex 17. 'The ultimate would be to strengthen ICAO so that it would serve as the world police force', explained Lally. In addition to seeking US support for stronger security standards, he made it clear that the airlines wanted ICAO to have sufficient authority to ensure that the standards are properly applied and that 'if they don't work, then ICAO should have the authority to do something about it'.[26]

IATA had previously recommended a similar role for ICAO with little success. Not to be undone, the Geneva-based International Foundation of Airline Passengers Associations (IFAPA) proposed the creation of a world aviation security fund with a $1 per flight passenger ticket surcharge to be administered by ICAO. According to IFAPA the fund, which would raise $1 billion in 18 months, could be used to develop high technology detection systems, provide better security training and pay for international security inspection teams.[27]

As officials were being pressed by their parliamentarians to arouse international efforts, both the US and the UK lobbied frantically to bring other transport ministers to a high level ICAO Council meeting. A preliminary discussion showed that some Council members did not take kindly to being upstaged by ministers who, as one Council member put it, 'would give the impression that the present level of representation is incapable of adopting measures which may be necessary'.[28]

More to the point was the statement of the Council member from Argentina. He questioned the purpose of a high-level session devoted 'to seeking solutions to a problem without a clear definition of the problem'.[29] Behind the rhetoric, there was a concern that further improvements in aviation security, particularly in the detection of explosives, would be too costly for the developing countries to undertake without the assurance of financial help.

When the Council met on 15–16 February 1989 with 12 ministers in attendance, there were two draft resolutions, one presented jointly by the US and the UK and a more modest proposal from a group of developing countries led by Argentina and Mexico.[30] The US and the UK acting as gadflies wanted stronger measures on matching baggage and passengers, stricter rules for cargo, mail bags and courier services and new measures to detect explosives and sabotage devices. The other resolution called for stronger security provisions 'as resources permit' and also called for financial assistance.

The US objective outlined by FAA officials at a Congressional hearing before the Council session, was 'to reach agreement on strengthened international security standards and to consider how they can be expanded and applied uniformly'. US Secretary of Transport Samuel Skinner told the Council meeting that the American plan was a two-tiered security system based on stronger Annex 17 provisions applicable to all international operations and additional measures in 'high risk' situations. This would mean that foreign airlines operating within the US would have to apply the same high standards already imposed on American carriers. This US proposal drew immediate fire from the French who saw in it an infringement of national sovereignty.[31]

The UK position paralleled the American demand for stronger provisions in Annex 17 and a more forceful role by ICAO. Paul Channon, then UK Secretary of State for Transport, stressed the need for new rules to inspect electronic equipment carried on board aircraft. The highlight of his intervention was a carefully-timed announcement on 16 February, coinciding with a press briefing by the senior investigating officer in Lockerbie, stating that the bomb which blew up Pan Am Flight 103 had been concealed in a radio cassette player and loaded aboard the plane with other luggage in Frankfurt.[32]

In the end, the two initial resolutions were amalgamated into a single draft presented by the Council President. It instructed the Council's subordinate bodies to prepare detailed recommendations based on the US–UK plan of action.[33] For the time being, states in need of financial assistance would have to content themselves with vague promises of help. The US and UK could be satisfied with the Council instructions to improve the screening of checked and carry-on baggage, to control access to the ramp by airport employees and to search mail bags and commercial courier bags. These tasks had already been approved as part of an ongoing review of Annex 17.[34] The Council also decided to take a closer look at the various devices for the detection of explosives with the help of a group of specialists.

As for the search of electronic equipment, the US and UK did not wait for new Annex 17 provisions to issue guidelines to their carriers. They were confident that other carriers would follow suit. It was probably all that the US could expect in the way of a worldwide concerted action. This left the FAA to ponder once more the limitations of a global strategy and to consider the need to impose its own standards on foreign carriers in 'high risk' situations. Even before Lockerbie, the FAA had wanted foreign airlines flying into the US to submit security plans to the agency for approval. It made the rule official in April 1989. At the end of the year, only 52 of the 134 carriers operating in the United States had received official approval from the FAA.

The FAA rule with respect to foreign carriers did not go over well in Europe where it prompted ECAC to send a diplomatic note to Washington. ECAC did not dispute the right of the United States to impose security measures on its own carriers but considered the extra-territorial application of these measures to foreign carriers constituted an infringement of Article 1 of the Chicago Convention. The arguments presented by ECAC were simple enough. Unlike the United States, security measures in Europe were the responsibility of state authorities and not of the airlines. If the United States had a problem, it should discuss it bilaterally or multilaterally through ECAC or ICAO. What made the United States directive even more galling was the feeling that security measures at many European airports were stricter than those at most United States airports.

However strong the sense of common purpose, this first Council session at the ministerial level was more of a successful media event to reassure the public and parliaments than it was a breakthrough in the fight against terrorism in the sky. Whatever the success, it proved to be a short respite for the British and United States participants who soon found themselves at the centre of a public controversy over their handling of warnings of sabotage attempts against United States carriers.

Efforts to obtain better security were not made easier by the open debate over publicising such threats so that travellers could make their own choices. Crank calls would merely compound security problems and public bulletins would quickly become routine. Disclosure of all threats would bring chaos to air transport and leave it open to blackmail. Most importantly, unwarranted disclosure of intelligence information would put at risk the work of INTERPOL, whose responsibility it is to assess security threats and issue alerts so that preventive measures can be taken.[35]

A major question left unresolved after Lockerbie is ICAO's larger role in assessing how states implement standards. The question has been raised before and undoubtedly will be raised again. At issue is whether ICAO can act beyond its mandate without amending the Chicago Convention. The French put back on the table a proposal for creating a security cell which they had previously made in 1985. A much more ambitious proposal by the UK Transport Secretary, which found little support, called for an international team to undertake systematic inspections of airport security, possibly in cooperation with IATA. Such suggestions that ICAO take over the watchdog role now performed to a certain extent by IATA, the pilots' associations and by the FAA, however justified, do not address the regulatory constraints imposed on the Organisation, in respect of Article 1 of the Chicago Convention and of the legal status of the Annexes.

REGULATORY CONSTRAINTS

The most important regulatory constraints contained in the Chicago Convention concern the legal status of ICAO Annexes. Annexes adopted under Article 37 contain standards and recommended practices, the former being necessary for the safety of aviation, the latter merely desirable. The notification of differences in the case of standards is, as stated in the official foreword of ICAO Annexes 'compulsory under Article 38', whereas, in the case of recommended practices, member states are merely 'invited' to make such notifications. Recommended practices are what they say they are, namely recommendations. They have no legally binding force in international law.

The status of standards is, however, more complex. In contrast to the technical standards adopted under the 1919 Paris Convention on Aerial Navigation, the standards adopted by ICAO are not regarded as an integral part of the Chicago Convention. They are designated as Annexes merely 'for convenience' and therefore do not share the same legal status as the Convention.[36] The obligation that states have assumed under Article 37 is merely 'to collaborate in securing the highest practicable degree of uniformity in regulations, standards and procedures'. Article 38, however, stipulates an unconditional obligation for each contracting state to notify ICAO immediately of any differences between its own practices and those specified by standards in the Annexes. Notification of differences can be made either before or after an Annex has come into force. Furthermore, states may decide at any time not to comply with a given provision, the sole exception being the rules of the air over the high seas in Article 12 of the Convention. These must apply without exception.

Some scholars believe that ICAO standards are not independently binding save for such specific cases as Article 12. Therefore ICAO members cannot be irrevocably bound by ICAO rules nor can they be made to apply standards against their will. This, according to Professor Bin Cheng, was done deliberately in the drafting of the Chicago Convention.[37]

Are ICAO standards in fact being applied as presumed? The question boils down to knowing what happens when a member state has not made the required notification. In strictly legal terms if, by the date on which the Annex or an amendment becomes applicable, a state has not notified ICAO of differences, it must be presumed that it has complied in all respects. It is therefore bound to comply with the provisions for as long as it does not notify differences. ICAO experience has shown that this does not happen as was shown in a sampling of states with respect to the status of implementation of selected provisions of Annex 17.[38] The sampling followed the adoption of Amendment 6 to Annex 17 and the dispatch of a state letter on the filing of differences. While replies were received from 87 states, only seven contained differences. Although the number of replies was encouraging, it was generally felt that many states had refrained from filing differences on security provisions unless assured of confidentiality.

Assessments carried out in twenty states showed that only seven appeared to fully implement Annex 17 provisions, the remainder to a lesser extent. Further analysis shows that such factors as cost, higher priorities, geographical location, low traffic volume and the perceived absence of a threat may be the reasons for the lagging efforts. The data also showed that states scored better in implementing provisions in Annex 17 which were the subject of particular efforts such as the screening of passengers and training of personnel at airports.[39]

Beyond the particular problems revealed in the samplings, ICAO faces a dilemma on the filing of differences to the security provisions of Annex 17. Article 38 of the Chicago Convention clearly spells out the requirement to notify ICAO of differences. These are then published and sent to all states. However, in respect of aviation security, the need to publicise differences has found the Council divided. Those members in favour of confidentiality have argued that such information could endanger civil aviation by identifying the areas of weakness within the international security system. Those opposed argue that potential terrorists do not rely on such information to 'case' an airport for security lapses.

CONCLUSION

Lacking the means to enforce its own decisions, an international regulatory agency can only exercise moral influence, and risks losing much of its effectiveness. As Evan Luard pointed out, without such enforcement authority, an international agency must resort to a variety of techniques to secure the cooperation of its member states. These states are pledged to cooperate in a general way with international agencies and may find it to their advantage to do so, but they cannot normally be compelled to comply with international rules.[40] To reach its objectives, ICAO has relied mostly on staff missions and on its own reports on how states comply with security standards. It has never been the practice to report cases of non-compliance before the Council. Without regular inspections which ICAO cannot undertake, it is impossible for the Organisation to assess deficiencies.

By far the most effective means of securing compliance with ICAO's standards has been pressure from outside the Organisation. In the absence of an international control mechanism, it has been up to IATA and the pilots' associations, and to the US acting on its own, to ascertain that ICAO's security provisions are being applied at international airports. IATA has established teams of experts who regularly visit airport facilities and make recommendations which are sent to national authorities. In 1986 alone, IATA teams visited twenty-four airports in various parts of the world.[41] The shortcomings were traced to lack of equipment and trained personnel but also to inexcusable instances of laxity and lack of proper coordination. The best example of effective pressure was

Athens Airport which came under heavy criticism from the US and from the airlines after the TWA hijacking in 1985. After a boycott by American travel agents, security was quickly brought to ICAO standards.

As Edward McWhinney has stated, global solutions require a strict application of security measures and a plurality of controls, national and international, including diplomatic pressures and economic boycotts.[42] Total security may never be achieved except at an inordinate cost to airlines and travellers and by turning airports into armed camps. However, the technical means exist to improve the standards of aviation security to the level achieved by the best national systems. The problem is that while each country knows what is best for itself, there is no political consensus on what is best for all.

10 Terrorism in the Sky: Loopholes in the Law

International law is a permanent incitement to hypocrisy.

Raymond Aron, *Paix et Guerre* (1984)

Global strategies to counter terrorist attacks against civil aviation include security measures and a legal framework to ensure that offenders are arrested and severely punished. The four legal instruments drafted specifically to cover all aspects of unlawful interference with civil aviation were predicated on the assumption that most states would ratify these accords and that they would faithfully abide by their provisions. The first assumption proved correct, the second not quite.

The tepid attitude of too many states in their dealings with hijackers has long amounted to a sorry record of equivocations, coddling, and at times secret dealings to win immunity from terrorist groups. Brian Jenkins, a political scientist with the Rand Corporation, who has studied the record concludes that 'governments are making all sorts of deals on the basis of one simple criterion: is it productive?'[1] The problem is compounded by the open or covert support some countries have given to terrorist activities. A North Atlantic Assembly report finds that:

> addressing the problem of state sponsorship of terrorism is very difficult because the sponsoring governments often operate secretly, wishing to conceal any direct connection with terrorist groups. Furthermore, it is often hard to present a solid case of evidence that will provide concrete unassailable evidence of a particular state's involvement in terrorist activities . . . Despite these difficulties, however, most commentators have identified three states in the Mideast as active supporters of international terrorism: Libya, Syria and Iran.[2]

CLEAR SIGNALS AND CONFUSING RESPONSES

Acting on solid grounds, some states have taken swift action without receiving much support from the international community. The Reagan Administration found little encouragement when it attempted to halt all flights to Beirut in the wake of the TWA hijacking in June 1985 which showed collusion between the hijackers and various political factions in Lebanon. The US raid on Libya in April 1987 was also widely criticised by friends and foes alike in spite of the 'irrefutable evidence' (President Reagan's own words) of Libya's involvement in several terrorist attacks in Europe. Robert Oakley, the top US State Department official dealing with counter-terrorism, recalled that the widespread view in Washington was that despite repeated approaches, the Europeans – aside the United Kingdom – had waited too long and done too little to have any hope of deterring terrorism.[3]

A direct Syrian connection with aviation terrorism in Europe can be found in two separate attempts to blow up El Al airliners. At Madrid Airport in June 1986, the airline security people detected the bomb before it could be placed on the aircraft. The suspect was arrested and later sentenced. There were indications that he belonged to a Palestinian splinter group created with Syrian help and headquartered in Damascus. The most direct Syrian connection was shown at the trial of a saboteur arrested in another attempt two months earlier at London's Heathrow Airport.

Britain's bold stand against Syria at the time received only mixed support when it might have been expected, after all the rhetoric against terrorism, that here at last was 'the smoking gun' justifying a firm response from the international community.

A British jury had found a Syrian agent, Nezar Hindawi, guilty of plotting to kill 375 passengers on an El Al airliner and of tricking his pregnant girl-friend into carrying the time-bomb in her luggage. Trial evidence showed that Hindawi (1) travelled on an official Syrian passport under a false name; (2) received two visas endorsed by the Syrian Foreign Ministry; (3) met with the Syrian Ambassador in London after the bomb was discovered; (4) spent the next night in a Syrian safe house where his hair was clipped and dyed, and only then surrendered to British police when it occurred to him that his would-be protectors were might-be killers.[4]

Citing the 'conclusive evidence', Britain broke off diplomatic relations and air links with Syria and asked its friends to do likewise as a clear, collective signal that Syria's involvement in terrorism would not be tolerated. Yet, at their initial meeting in Luxembourg, the foreign ministers of the EEC could not agree on anything more than sympathy. Half of them did not even attend the session. The senior French and West German diplomats were at a 'cultural summit' in Frankfurt and had to be contacted at the opera to approve a final statement. The European Community retrieved some credibility when two weeks later it approved a ban on arms sales, a close watch on Syrian diplomatic missions, and surveillance of Syrian airline operations and personnel. The significant fact was not that these steps fell short of what Britain sought, but that the EEC agreed on any sanctions at all.

The British action was a calculated risk in the sense that it might simply have called for the withdrawal of the Syrian envoy. Instead it imposed sanctions which were more harmful to its own interests than to Syria's. The suspension of commercial flights between the two countries did not isolate Syria which was still served by more than 20 international airlines, including such British competitors as Air France and Lufthansa. On the other hand, the closure of Syrian air space forced British Airways and British Caledonian to divert their flights to the Far East, adding to operating costs and travel time.

Britain had no choice but to act alone if necessary to uphold the law, for as *The Economist* (1 November 1986) put it: 'To go it alone is better than consensus at all costs'. In Hans Morgenthau's words: 'an alleged rule of international law against the violation of which no state reacts or is likely to react, is proved, by this very absence of probable reaction, not to be a valid rule of international law'.[5]

The United States and Canada had already complied with Britain's desires by withdrawing their ambassadors from Syria. Thus, the United States could do no less than it did with respect to Libya earlier that year. It subsequently announced supplementary sanctions against Syria, including a ban on the sale of aircraft and spare parts and the cancellation of an air agreement with Syria which formalised an earlier suspension of flights between the two countries.[6]

The Western response to Syria, for all its wavering and dubious effectiveness, was still remarkable in the absence of wider support except for a threat of a 48-hour boycott of Syria by the International Federation of Air Line Pilots' Associations. The response of the airlines group was muted. Just before the EEC ministers' meeting, IATA at its annual gathering urged governments to take 'further steps' to combat terrorism directed at civil aviation, but it did not see fit to bring up the attempted sabotage against one of its member airlines. Some IATA delegates, however, noted that several signatories of the international conventions, including Libya and Syria, had been accused of being havens for terrorists.

At the United Nations, there was official silence in sharp contrast to the self-satisfaction following the unanimous adoption of a General Assembly resolution condemning all acts of terrorism as criminal. The resolution, hailed by Secretary General Pérez de Cuellar as 'a major move having universal implications', called on states 'to refrain from organizing, instigating, assisting or participating in terrorist acts in other states or acquiescing in activities within their territory directed towards the commission of such acts'.[7]

There was no official comment from ICAO. Israel was reported to have sought a condemnation of Syria, but apparently could not muster enough support to press its case before the ICAO Council. This is hardly surprising; ICAO's governing body earlier in the year had condemned Israel for its unlawful diversion of a Libyan executive jet bound for Damascus with what Israel suspected were top terrorist leaders.[8] Syria's retaliatory threats were largely ignored at the time.

Terrorist attacks against civil aviation have led to a number of lofty statements and proposals calling for international sanctions against states which harbour known terrorists. *The New York Times* (14 May 1986) voiced the prevalent opinion that such sanctions would command wide support. The editorial concluded with a blunt question: 'are the democracies finally willing to impose collective aviation sanctions instead of just talking about them?' The clamour for action reached a new pitch in the wake of the Pan American explosion in December 1988. Among others, the foremost American aviation magazine *Aviation Week* (9 January 1989) in a lead editorial stated: 'if the US is unable to secure the support of its allies for prompt action, then it must be prepared to go it alone'. Among the steps recommended was a five-point plan advanced by IATA calling for a United Nations police force, an international court and international detention centre to take the onus off individual nations.

The editorialists and commentators,[9] for all their justified indignation, misread the problem. Every attempt to effect collective sanctions over the years has come to naught because of opposition by various groups of countries. International conventions reflect the most that can be achieved on the part of the international community and this consensus does not include punitive action outside the framework of the Chicago Convention.[10]

When delegates met in Chicago in 1944 to draft the blueprint for postwar aviation development, the need for cooperation between states was so obvious that it overrode any consideration that some states might have to be coerced to do so. Hence, the notion of imposing sanctions to enforce collective decisions was never under discussion at the time. In any case, historic precedents of the League of Nations were not in favour of those who might eventually have been contemplating sanctions. Ever since, the question of sanctions at ICAO has been a divisive issue, the only exception being South Africa, for reasons that have nothing to do with civil aviation.

International law does not provide the means for international organisations to enforce their decisions apart from using the agencies of national governments for that purpose. In other words, enforcement of international rules is left to individual member states. J.L. Brierly has pointed out that the creation of any general scheme of sanctions being at present a very distant prospect, 'this absence of an executive power means that each state remains free . . . to take such action as it thinks fit to enforce its own rights'.[11]

THE TOKYO CONVENTION: A MODEST BEGINNING

As a first attempt to deal specifically with hijackings, the Convention on Offences and Certain Other Acts Committed on Board Aircraft (signed in Tokyo on 14 September 1963) spells out the obligation of a state to take all appropriate measures to restore control of the aircraft to the lawful commander, to permit the passengers and crew of hijacked aircraft which land on its territory to continue their journey, and to return the aircraft and the cargo to the persons concerned. There was no obligation to extradite or prosecute an alleged offender. These measures fell far short of the expectations of those who wished to see the acceptance of an earlier draft requiring the punishment of hijackers.

As Edward McWhinney stated: 'Faced with the practical dilemma of political choice between a comprehensively drafted multilateral convention that would really have teeth in it, but which presumably would attract fewer ratifications, and a vaguer or more modest draft that might reasonably be expected to obtain more ratifications, ICAO clearly opted for the second choice'.[12] McWhinney has even argued that, so far as its substantive obligations go, the Tokyo Convention created a legal pleonasm since these already existed in customary international law. The Tokyo Conference may have weakened the rule of law by implying that the security of passengers and crew and the return of the aircraft were new obligations which would be binding only on those states which ratify the Convention.

During the 1960s the international community showed little enthusiasm for combating hijacking. The Tokyo Convention was to come into effect 90 days after the date of deposit of the twelfth instrument of ratification. However, it was to be six years before the twelfth country, the United States, ratified the convention, and by October 1970 only thirty states had done so.

By the time the ICAO Assembly met in Buenos Aires in 1968, it had become evident that the Tokyo Convention by itself would not curb the problem. In that year alone there were 33 hijackings, and in 1969 the number jumped to 91. Even so, the debate in the ICAO Council to establish a special committee on unlawful interference was long and arduous. Its terms of reference, as approved by the Council, were so limited that when Leila Khaled and an accomplice hijacked a TWA jet to Damascus in August 1969, all that the committee did was to cable Syria for a report of the incident. In reporting back to ICAO, Syria did not state that two passengers were held as hostages in exchange for Syrian pilots in Israeli prisons. Nor did the report mention that the aircraft had been partly destroyed and that the hijackers were released.[13]

ICAO was finally jolted into action by the mid-air explosions on the same day (21 February 1970) of two aircraft, one belonging to Swissair and the other to an Austrian airline. These incidents, in which 47 passengers were killed, led to the extraordinary session of the ICAO Assembly in Montreal in June 1970 which laid the groundwork for Annex 17 (Aviation Security) and also paved the way for the two conventions which now constitute the major legal weapons in dealing with hijackers.

Going far beyond the cautious approach hitherto displayed, the Convention for the Suppression of Unlawful Seizure of Aircraft (signed at The Hague on 16 December 1970) and the Convention for the Suppression of Unlawful Acts Against the Safety of Civil

Aviation (signed at Montreal on 23 September 1971) establish universal jurisdiction over offences against civil aviation both in the air and on the ground. The basic concept underlying both conventions is that an offender, regardless of his motives, should not be allowed a safe haven and must either be extradited or punished. The Hague Convention obliges states to make such offences punishable by severe penalties (Article 2). Article 7 obliges the state-party in whose territory the alleged offender is found either to extradite the individual or to submit the case 'without exception whatsoever' to its competent authorities for the purpose of prosecution.

The system of extradition established by the convention makes it clear that the unlawful seizure of aircraft is 'deemed to be included' in any extradition treaty existing between states and also obligates state-parties to include the offence as an extraditable offence in every new extradition treaty to be concluded between them. Last, the convention contains provisions obliging state-parties to give one another judicial assistance in any criminal proceedings brought in respect of an offence (Article 10) and to report to the Council of ICAO any relevant information in their possession (Article 11). The Montreal Convention establishes similar provisions for a series of acts, mostly committed on the ground, which are likely to cause the destruction of an aircraft or otherwise endanger the safety of aircraft in flight.

No doubt the 88 hijackings and 13 incidents of sabotage which took place in 1970 helped to galvanise states to act. In early September of that year, four aircraft (belonging to TWA, Pan Am, Swissair, and BOAC respectively) were hijacked. The result was the destruction of four aircraft and the capitulation of four governments to the demands of the hijackers. The detention of scores of passengers in the torrid Jordanian desert stirred worldwide indignation. At the United Nations, even the Arab delegates were angered.[14] In one of the shortest sessions ever held (seven minutes), the Security Council on 9 September 1970 unanimously called for the release of all passengers and crew.[15] This was accomplished ten days later.

PRESSING FOR STRONGER ACTION

Even as The Hague Convention was being prepared, both the United States and Canada were pressing for stronger action. One of seven aims President Nixon announced on 11 September 1970 to deal with aircraft hijacking was to seek multilateral agreement – specifically on the suspension of air services – against states refusing to extradite or punish perpetrators involved in international blackmail. US Secretary of Transportation John A. Volpe formally proposed such sanctions at an emergency session of the ICAO Council (in September 1970) in cases where offenders are not extradited or prosecuted. He also asked that the ICAO Legal Committee prepare a convention to formalise procedures for consultation and joint action by states.[16] Canada formally proposed that states include a special clause in all bilateral air agreements spelling out international obligations regarding offences committed on board an aircraft and allowing for the suspension of the agreement if the other party fails to implement these obligations.

On 1 October 1970, the Council directed the ICAO Legal Committee, then in session in London, to consider the possibility of developing an international convention aimed at imposing sanctions on a state that detained a hijacked aircraft or its passengers or crew for the purpose of international blackmail, or that gave haven to hijackers. As the new proposals went through the bureaucratic mill and jurists grappled with fundamental questions of international law, the complex issues to a large extent became a smoke-screen for fundamental disagreements. Some argued that sanctions would be ineffective, unless most or all states participated in them, so that it would be better to have no agreement at all than to have an ineffective one.

A more fundamental attack was made by those who questioned ICAO's competence to prepare a convention involving sanctions. This was felt to be a matter within the exclusive competence of the United Nations Security Council which, under Article 41 of the United Nations Charter, 'may decide what measures not involving the use of armed force are to be employed to give effect to its decisions'. These measures 'may include complete or partial interruption of air and other means of communication'. The sharp division of opinion in the ICAO Legal Subcommittee in early 1971 led to an inconclusive report and as a result, the Assembly in

Vienna later that year decided to play down the whole question of sanctions.

Even if ideal conditions had prevailed at ICAO, the legal complexities in reaching a common agreement would have required long and arduous negotiations. As L.C. Clark pointed out, there are indeed serious questions to be resolved, such as whether an enforcement system should be based on a multilateral convention, bilateral air agreements, or upon a combination of both. The particular interests of states would need to be ascertained and their participation secured in any scheme of international cooperation on sanctions. Furthermore should the decision to suspend services be made by majority vote, by weighted voting, or unanimously? Other issues involve national authorities and international airlines and air transport facilities affected by the suspension of services. Since commercial flights may involve a stopover in the defaulting state, suspension of services would also affect the rights of other states under the Chicago Convention and the Air Services Transit Agreement. Finally, who is to judge when a state is no longer in default? As Clark concluded, no coordinated approach would in fact resist the commercial and economic pressures for a resumption of services.[17]

The unrelenting attacks against the safety of civil aviation led ICAO to revive the question of sanctions within the framework of the Chicago Convention so as not to run afoul of Article 41 of the UN Charter. After preliminary work by the ICAO Legal Committee, the international community was confronted once more with the same issues at the extraordinary session of the Assembly and International Conference on Air Law held simultaneously in Rome in 1973 to consider various amendments to the Chicago Convention, as well as various other instruments and draft protocols to The Hague and Montreal Conventions. The Jamaican delegate to the Assembly perhaps best summarised the hopeless situation in what he termed the singular paradox 'that the success of The Hague and Montreal Conventions as legal instruments directed against the misconduct of the individual has been matched by an alarming reluctance on the part of states to submit their own conduct to scrutiny and assessment'.[18]

High on the agenda of the Assembly was a proposal by France to amend the Chicago Convention so as to allow the Council to investigate and make recommendations in cases of violations. The French draft also proposed that Article 94(b) be applied so that a state which did not ratify this amendment within one year of its coming into force would cease to be a member of ICAO and a party to the Convention.

The United Kingdom and Switzerland, on the other hand, proposed that the Chicago Convention be amended to incorporate the obligations under The Hague and Montreal Conventions relating to offenders as well as those under the Tokyo Convention requiring the release of passengers and crew and the return of the aircraft. Sanctions would be applied under Article 87 in the form of a suspension of air services to a state that the Council decided had not complied with these obligations. This provision was subsequently watered down and abandoned altogether, but to no avail, since the final text failed to be adopted by only two votes.

These proposals had the merit of imposing sanctions under the Chicago Convention as the only practical way of securing effective action by states rather than initiating a new instrument that would present insurmountable obstacles. A major objection was the time required since an amendment to the Chicago Convention could come into force only after ratification by two-thirds of all contracting states.

Among other controversial proposals was that of an independent fact-finding body put forward by Belgium and one by the Nordic states which would have the Council assume such responsibilities and recommend appropriate measures against a state found to be violating its obligations.[19] A Greek proposal to amend the Montreal Convention to include certain acts of violence at airports failed to pass by only five votes. Thirteen years later, after at least 36 attacks at international airports, the question, as discussed further on, came up again in the form of a protocol to the Montreal Convention.

The Rome Conference ended in dismal failure. The terse final paragraph in the report noted that 'none of the draft protocols presented for consideration by the Conference obtained the required majority when presented to final vote. No draft convention was presented to a vote. Consequently, the Conference terminated without having adopted any instrument'. The delegate of Zaire summed up the general frustration, saying: 'There is not the shadow of a doubt that some governments were not willing . . . to make mutual concessions to reach an acceptable compromise'.[20] In the end, as Gerald Fitzgerald has pointed out, what was remarkable was not that the proposed solutions failed, but that they did so by narrow margins.[21]

Significant as the ICAO conventions are in the codification of international air law, it was clearly perceived at the time that they fell short in some respects.[22] Nevertheless they represented the best that could be achieved in practice. All through the preliminary stages and the actual diplomatic conference at The Hague, the United States, the Soviet Union, and Israel (for varying reasons) pressed for the unconditional extradition of offenders while African and Arab states balked at the prospect of having to send alleged offenders to face trial in South Africa or Israel. For the sake of broad consensus, strongly worded provisions requiring extradition in all cases or at least the prosecution of offenders were gradually watered down in response to threats from individual countries or groups of countries to pull out of the negotiating sessions on The Hague Convention. The final version did not even require a state to prosecute if it did not extradite the offender, but only 'to submit the case to its competent authorities for the purpose of prosecution'. Each state is required to make the offence of hijacking punishable by 'severe penalties', but under national laws, this punishment can vary from a minimum of two years' imprisonment to the death penalty, depending on where the offender is prosecuted, as is shown in a report prepared by ICAO on national legislation for the punishment of acts of unlawful interference with civil aviation.[23]

REPORTING OR COVERING UP THE FACTS

ICAO's responses to hijacking incidents have now become fairly predictable. Hardly a Council or Assembly session takes place without exhortations for strict compliance with the Tokyo, The Hague, and Montreal Conventions. Whenever an incident takes place involving a signatory state, the Council President reminds authorities of their obligations, in particular that of providing as promptly as possible relevant information on the legal proceedings undertaken against offenders. Admittedly, the reporting system is deficient. Without an impartial fact-finding mechanism, the Council must accept reports by states at face value. Considering that at a minimum a state is bound only 'to submit a criminal act against civil aviation authorities for the purpose of prosecution' and to submit a report to ICAO 'as promptly as possible', it cannot be faulted for taking its time or doing so only *pro forma*.

The rationale behind the reporting system is that disclosures of relevant facts will prompt governments to take their obligations seriously for fear of world public opinion. Yet, it is a sad fact of international life that no attempt is made by the Council to scrutinise the reports or assess the action of the states concerned.

ICAO's exhortations have had little sway over the few states which have seen fit not to respond. Of 28 incidents of hijackings in the three-year period 1984–6 there were ten cases for which no report was received at all. These cases concerned Lebanon (four incidents), Saudi Arabia, Iran and Ethiopia (one incident each) and Iraq (three incidents, including two in which the offenders were given political asylum).[24]

The height of frustration and futility must have been reached with telegrams sent during the 1985 TWA hostage crisis by the President of the Council to Lebanon's minister of Justice, Nabih Berri, the leader of the Amal faction holding the passengers, and to the Druse leader, Walid Jumblatt, the Minister of Transport. Jumblatt had openly welcomed the members of a group that had hijacked and blown up a Jordanian airliner in Beirut just a few days before and was quite happy to wash his hands of the TWA incident. The telegrams calling for 'the safe release of passengers, crew and aircraft' were not even acknowledged. Obviously, compliance with international obligations assumes the existence of a government able to exercise authority, which was hardly the case in Lebanon. The Beirut hostage crisis which unfolded for 17 days in front of the television cameras was a unique case. When the drama was over the hijackers simply vanished. Yet even when it is in full control of the situation, a government for fear of retribution may not reveal or report all the facts.

As Alona Evans has shown, there are sufficient grounds to be sceptical of a state which has custody of a terrorist and refuses extradition or deportation while announcing that it will prosecute the offender. As examples, Evans cited a French court's acceptance of a political defence in the Holder-Kerkow case, followed by prosecution on the relatively minor charge of passport fraud (even while the two American black activists involved were wanted in the US after being indicted for the 1972 hijacking of a commercial flight to Algiers); the release by a Pakistani court in 1976 of six hijackers of an Indian aircraft, and Libya's failure to charge two Arab terrorists expelled after being sentenced to death in Greece for their attack on Athens airport in 1973.[25]

States will often use legal technicalities to justify political expediency. The case of Abu Daoud, who led the massacre of Israeli athletes at the 1982 Olympics in Munich is a prime example. He was arrested in France and expelled in January 1977 after France spurned extradition requests from both West Germany and Israel. More recently, Abu Abbas, the mastermind behind the *Achille Lauro* attack, was captured in 1986 when the US intercepted an Egyptian airliner in the Mediterranean. He was then handed over to the Italian authorities who, much to the chagrin of the US Government, allowed him to flee to Yugoslavia the same day that the United States issued an arrest warrant. In other well-publicised cases, Greece 'deported' to Libya a terrorist wanted in Italy and was holding a Palestinian wanted in the United States for involvement in two mid-air bomb attacks. Fears were expressed that he too would be expelled to a country of his choice in the face of threats against the judiciary.

Terrorist suspects who have been arrested use every legal means to fight prosecution or extradition. Thus, it took Canada two years to build a watertight case in Britain to have a Sikh extremist extradited to face charges in connection with the Narita Airport attack and Air India bomb explosion in 1985. Ironically, Canada was facing legal complications of its own in efforts to deport a convicted Palestinian hijacker whom it had inadvertently accepted as an immigrant in 1987. (The man had been convicted in Greece for his participation in the attack on an El Al airliner at Athens Airport but was freed after serving only five months of a 17-year sentence.)

THE LIMITATIONS OF ICAO CONVENTIONS

Without strict enforcement provisions, what can one say about the effectiveness of the present international legal system in dealing with hijackings and other criminal acts against civil aviation? In the view of Assad Kotaite, President of the ICAO Council:

> The Hague and Montreal Conventions now belong to the most widely accepted codifications of international law. The acts against security of aviation are now considered to be criminal offenses against the penal law virtually in all contracting states, regardless of the motive for such an act; the perpetrators of such acts cannot expect a 'hero's welcome' in any contracting state. Only on a few isolated but regrettable recent occasions, certain

states appear to have failed to exercise their duties under these Conventions, have not brought the offenders to justice and have not returned the aircraft to their lawful owners.[26]

Others, like Professor Bin Cheng, acknowledge that insofar as the punitive aspect is concerned, the ICAO conventions appear to have gone as far as is feasible. He notes, however, that despite the wider acceptance of the Tokyo, The Hague, and Montreal Conventions since 1970, some states still fail to comply with their obligations under the treaties, either by inflicting nominal penalties or by making little or no effort to prosecute following refusals to extradite.[27] There is no denying an improvement over the early days when states could deliberately hold passengers and crew to ransom for political demands.

Some analysts have noted that political asylum and the broader concept of national sovereignty are the central obstacles to developing a truly effective legal approach to terrorism. They play a particularly important role in any attempt to reach an agreement on the extradition of terrorist offenders. As Grant Wardlaw has observed, this problem is of more than academic importance because it is the main reason for the timid response of most states to terrorism and for the failure of the international community to launch effective multilateral initiatives to combat the problem.[28] In Wardlaw's words:

> the [ICAO] Conventions are effectively no more than collections of high statements of principle devoid of any real impact. It is quite obvious that political terrorists have not been deterred by the existence of the Conventions . . . because they reasonably believe that their actions will not be subject to the written restrictions.[29]

In a scathing article in *Foreign Affairs*, Abraham Sofaer, the legal adviser of the United States Department of State, wrote that the law as formulated 'cannot reasonably be expected effectively to repress international terrorism'. Sofaer contends that 'international terrorism is still supported by many nations as a legitimate means of struggle against regimes deemed by them to be colonial, alien or racist. At the behest of these states, and by the acquiescence of others, international law has been systematically and intentionally fashioned to give special treatment to, or to leave unregulated, those activities that cause and are the source of most acts of international terror'. Thus the 'extradition or prosecution' provisions of The Hague and Montreal Conventions implicitly allow states to refuse, on political grounds, to extradite suspects in crimes of hijacking and sabotage.[30]

Sofaer noted that the stock response to complaints about the law's failure to deal effectively with terrorism is to devise new laws rather than enforce those that already exist. His assertion is confirmed by the latest ICAO instrument for the suppression of unlawful acts of violence at airports serving international air transportation. A Canadian initiative led to a protocol to the Montreal Convention (signed on 24 February 1988) making a criminal attack in an airport terminal or ticket counter liable to the prosecution/extradition regime existing in The Hague and Montreal Conventions. Considering the number of incidents of violence at various airports since 1972 which were not covered by existing conventions, a supplementary protocol to deal with the matter was felt to be in order. Yet, one is left to wonder whether the new instrument, which suffers the same deficiencies as regards extradition and prosecution of offenders as the previous ones, is an improvement in international law. Under present conditions, justice might be better served by having terrorists who kill innocent travellers at airports tried under the criminal laws of the country in which they commit their crimes. The redeeming feature of the protocol is that it would subject the suspected offender to a regime of universal jurisdiction. However, as a report by ICAO on the matter pointedly noted: 'the international civil aviation community should not have any false illusions about the effectiveness of an international penal system regarding crimes against civil aviation when there is no international agreement on the necessity of a watertight national security system in this field'.[31]

Faced with the limitations of a collective approach based on treaties, countries like the United States which strike out on their own are in a quandary. As Geoffrey Levitt puts it: 'the weaker the collective approach appears, the greater the temptation for those states that have the requisite capability to resort to unilateral means. But the more such means are employed, the greater the danger of undermining the legal and political bases of the collective approach'.[32]

Sofaer has advanced cogent arguments for abducting terrorists wherever they can be found so they will be forced to stand trial. For him, the fundamental rule of the territorial integrity has already been bent by moral and practical considerations, for example in the hot pursuit of pirates. In this context, according to Sofaer:

> the territorial principle is only one of the many norms that states are obliged to respect. States also have the duty to avoid aiding pirates and other international criminals, the duty to capture and hold them when possible and the duty to prosecute or extradite them to other states with jurisdiction to prosecute. When a state fails to fulfill these duties, whether it is through unwillingness or inability, the moral and legal case for an adversely affected state to use the necessary and proportionate means to rectify the effects of violations of international law increases.[33]

This rationale led the United States to enact legislation in 1984 extending its jurisdiction over offences committed outside the United States in which Americans are taken hostage. President Reagan signed an intelligence order in 1986 giving FBI agents authorisation to seize suspects in foreign countries. The first offender convicted under this 'long arm of the law' statute was a Lebanese captured in September 1987 in an elaborate sting operation so that he could be arrested in international waters off Cyprus and be flown to American soil.[34] As to why the FBI settled for this particular bit-player is a mystery.

If this first abduction represents a radical challenge to accepted norms it also points to the problems of pressing charges years after the offence was committed. In this case, Fawaz Yunis was charged with taking part in the hijacking of the Jordanian airliner in 1985 in which two Americans were among the hostages. Even when terrorists can be identified and indicted, their pursuit and eventual capture take place in circumstances far removed from the orderly procedures and statutes of American law. Despite the difficulties in applying the broad powers given under the 1986 intelligence order, American officials remain convinced that the capture and trial of one hijacker will make others more insecure and demonstrate that the United States is resolved to go it alone in the absence of effective international countermeasures.[35]

THE EUROPEAN CONVENTION AND SUMMIT RHETORIC

When it seemed evident that there would be no further prospects of effectively dealing with acts of terrorism on a global level, the

Council of Europe initiated a multilateral regional convention with a view to taking 'effective measures to ensure that the perpetrators of such acts do not escape prosecution and punishment'. The crucial point in the preamble is the statement that 'extradition is a particularly effective measure for achieving this result . . .'.

The general aim of the European Convention for the Suppression of Terrorism signed in 1976 is to combat terrorism in general rather than acts against civil aviation. By depoliticising terrorist acts and including among them offences within the scope of The Hague and the Montreal conventions, the European Convention on Terrorism effectively assures that, at least for the European signatories, hijackings and other acts against civil aviation cannot be considered political offences for the purpose of avoiding extradition. However, under Article 5 of the Convention, states retain the right to refuse extradition of an offender if there are 'substantial grounds for believing that the request for extradition . . . has been made for the purpose of prosecuting or punishing a person on account of his race, religion, nationality or political opinion'. Article 13 also allows the consenting parties to refuse extradition on the basis that the offence is of a political character 'notwithstanding the fact that it is one of the offences listed in Article 1'. Therefore the Convention allows for a political loophole and does not effectively restrict the troubling concept of political asylum.[36]

Because the Convention is binding only on states in the Council of Europe which have ratified it, it does not provide a common position with respect to other states, as for instance in the case of a suspect who finds a safe haven in Syria or elsewhere. It did not help the United States secure custody of Abu Abbas who was released by Italian authorities before he could be served an arrest warrant issued by a US court.

This is precisely the kind of scenario the seven Western club members including Italy had tried to avoid when they agreed on ways to deal with terrorism. They have never come closer, at least on paper, than at their Bonn meeting in 1978 when, apparently without preparation, they issued what became known as the Bonn Declaration. They pledged to intensify their efforts and to apply sanctions against countries which refuse to extradite or prosecute hijackers by banning all flights to and from any such countries. The Western leaders further urged other governments to join them in their commitment.

At their Ottawa summit meeting in July 1981, the same heads of government expressed concern about the active support given to international terrorism through the supply of money, arms, training, and logistic and diplomatic assistance. At their meeting in Tokyo in 1986, the summit leaders once more pledged 'maximum efforts' to fight terrorism and agreed under pressure from the United States, to a limited package of measures against Libya. As for civil aviation, they also urged other countries to collaborate within ICAO and other international organisations to extend counter-measures against terrorism and those who sponsor or support it.

Conflicting responses of western nations on hostage-taking combined with the violations by the United States of its own arms embargo to Iran, revealed the fragility of a cohesive strategy on sanctions among otherwise like-minded partners. The only country against which effective action has been taken under the Bonn Declaration is Afghanistan for its alleged lack of cooperation following the hijacking of a Pakistani airliner in 1981. The boycott was one in which none of the partners in fact had much to lose.

The Bonn Declaration was also invoked in 1981 against South Africa in a bizarre hijacking following a foiled attempt by a group of South African mercenaries to overthrow the Seychelles government. These mercenaries had landed on the island posing as tourists, but when they were detected with their arms, they went no further than the airport and escaped by seizing an Air India jet and forced it to land in Durban. They were taken into custody and formally charged under The Hague Convention which South Africa had ratified in 1972. The manner in which South Africa dithered over their case led to warnings of sanctions by the Bonn signatories and a condemnation of South Africa by the United Nations and the ICAO Council, although it was never made clear whether the government was implicated in the aborted coup.[37] In the end, the mercenaries and their leader, Mike Hoare, were sentenced to various terms of prison. Since justice was served, it is a moot point whether the sanctions would actually have been carried out.

BOYCOTTS AND BILATERAL AGREEMENTS

Not surprisingly, the staunchest advocates of strong measures have been the pilots since along with their passengers, they are the first victims of hijackings and sabotage. Their tactics and boycotts have not always been welcomed by their airlines and governments but they have in the past forced action when others means seemed too slow.

The effectiveness of IFALPA in this field was demonstrated in July–August 1968, when it called on three European airlines – Air France, Alitalia and Swissair – to boycott Algerian routes because of that country's refusal to release a hijacked El Al airliner, the Israeli crew and some passengers. The boycott was called off, however, after IFALPA officials were personally assured by the Algerian Foreign Minister that this would be done as soon as Algeria completed its investigation. A French crew flew the airplane, crew and passengers to Rome. In another incident, IFALPA threatened to call a pilots' strike, this time against Syria, over the detention in Damascus of two Israeli civilians who were taken off the hijacked TWA airliner in August 1969. IFALPA was prevailed upon by the Secretary General of the United Nations to withdraw the strike threat. Syria released the Israelis after detaining them for four months. In August 1970, IFALPA also protested against the arrest of two Algerian passengers at the Tel Aviv Airport when a BOAC airliner made a scheduled stop there en route from Karachi to London. The two Algerians were released, although it is difficult to determine whether this release was due to IFALPA.[38]

Subsequently, IFALPA's efforts have concentrated on exerting pressure on the United Nations, ICAO, and governments, particularly in securing better preventive measures at airports. As a last resort, IFALPA will impose a 24-hour worldwide cessation of services to 'highlight official inaction and stressing that hijacking is not primarily a technical and safety problem but one for international law and united action by all governments'.[39]

In recent years, as in the case of Syria, IFALPA has threatened but stopped short of calling a boycott either because of pressure on individual IFALPA members by their own governments or airline companies or because of doubt on the limits of their personal liability.[40] It is doubtful whether IFALPA could in fact sustain continued pressure on any country unless it could muster the support of all airlines servicing that country. Effective sanctions would necessarily mean not only a boycott of states that harbour terrorists but also of states that refused to join the boycott.[41]

Betsy Gidwitz has rightly pointed out that the potential impact of IFALPA on the issue of unlawful interference in aviation is blunted by two conditions. First, pilots of airlines registered in states whose governments condone criminal acts for political reasons are unable to support IFALPA, however strongly they might wish to do so on a personal basis. Pilots in some other states may be prevented from striking or participating in other IFALPA action by legal procedures unrelated to politics. The absence of both groups from an IFALPA consensus reduces the impact of any IFALPA initiatives. Second, in common with IATA, IFALPA has only limited power to exercise control in criminal attacks. Only governments have final authority.[42]

Andreas Lowenfeld has offered an intriguing proposal to have sanctions against offending nations coordinated by a committee similar to the multinational CoCom which oversees technology transfers to the Warsaw Pact. Action by the most important industrialised Western nations could be tailored to the gravity of the circumstances and could include refusal to sell aircraft, services and supplies as well as denial of landing rights. Such sanctions, according to Lowenfeld, would be almost as effective as a complete boycott and easier to agree on.[43]

Since bilateral agreements are the backbone of international air transport, states can use them to secure compliance with international obligations. The fact that the United States and Cuba as well as the United States and the USSR have such agreements shows that even unlikely partners can agree on aviation security. There is no question but that the stiff penalties awaiting hijackers in Cuba have practically eliminated that country as a destination after the rash of incidents in the mid-1960s.

A review of bilateral agreements registered with ICAO shows that more than 80 treaties have been amended to include new or stronger security provisions. These clauses generally reconfirm and reinforce on a bilateral basis the obligations accepted by the parties on a multilateral level at Tokyo, The Hague, and Montreal, or require such obligations on the part of states not parties to the Conventions. Finally, these clauses may also provide for the termination of the agreement should one of the parties not comply with the aviation security provisions.[44]

Although ICAO did not pursue the subject after it had first been proposed by Canada in 1970, a model clause on aviation security was put on the agenda of the ICAO Council in 1985 with strong support by the USSR. In due course, after being amended several times by the Committee on Unlawful Interference, a final draft was approved in June 1986 without reference to the eventual consequences of a breach of agreement. The deleted paragraph was the subject of much debate in which some of the arguments against sanctions aired in Rome in 1973 re-surfaced, both in the Committee on Unlawful Interference and in the Council.

Most Council members felt that ICAO should not encourage sanctions after the concept was rejected at the Rome meetings and failed to get the support of the ICAO membership. Some members were prepared to accept denunciation of an agreement in case of violation of security arrangements, while others would have accepted a reference to consultations and possible arbitration as part of bilateral agreements. Since the model clause offers only guidance, states are free, of course, to add whatever enforcement provisions are mutually acceptable.

CONCLUSION

At least on the surface, the wave of terrorist attacks against aviation targets has abated. ICAO lists nine hijackings in 1989 and ten in 1988, including one in the Soviet Union in which nine people were killed. There were two acts of sabotage in each of these two years, including the destruction of Pan American Flight 103. None of these incidents, however, seemed to have been perpetrated by terrorists identified with previous attacks. It may well be that these groups and their state sponsors have now concluded that nothing can be gained from staging hijackings in which they can be easily unmasked.

The lull can also be attributed to stricter security measures, better intelligence work and a firmer if belated stand taken by Western countries against the sponsors of international terrorism. Paul Wilkinson, an authority on terrorism at Aberdeen University, contends that it was this concerted American and Western European action and the threat of further diplomatic and economic moves which were decisive in persuading Libya and possibly Syria to pull back.[45]

Few specialists in terrorism, however, are willing to call the lull anything but a temporary situation. There is always the possibility of a revenge attack of the kind that may have downed Pan American Flight 103. There are also too many unpredictable elements in what has been called 'a new kaleidoscope age' in Middle East terrorism in which no less than 33 separate organisations have claimed responsibility for terrorist operations carried out or planned in Lebanon alone in the past four years.[46] This was demonstrated with the mid-air explosion of a French airliner on 19 September 1989, the very day the 27th session of the ICAO Assembly opened. The suspected sabotage of the UTA DC–10 which was claimed by a Shiite Muslim extremist group moved the subject of terrorism once again to the top of the Assembly's agenda. The sad fact was that nine months after Lockerbie the international community was no closer to stopping criminal attacks against civil aviation. It probably never will be until states which finance and abet these attacks and provide a safe haven for their perpetrators, are made to account for their actions.[47]

Deregulation Dilemmas: Air Transport and European Integration

. . . at long last the problems are starting.

Jacques Delors, President of the European Commission

Politics and economics rarely blend well in national aviation policies. Flag-carriers are not operated in the public interest like the state-owned railway, nor can they be managed entirely like commercial enterprises geared to market and consumers' demands. Running an airline is an expensive business. This has been particularly true in Europe where subsidised carriers have operated for a long time under conditions that minimised competition and cost-savings and as a consequence allowed them to charge exorbitant fares. As a result of liberalisation policies, airlines and their governments are facing a number of intriguing problems in Europe which are peculiar to that continent.[1]

THE NATIONAL AND PUBLIC INTEREST

Every country wants to show the flag around the world and what better symbol of power is there than an airline that can be readily identified through its name or national colours? The very existence of a flag-carrier indicates that the nation is distinctive, efficient and progressive and that it is also contributing to the progress of mankind.

The political literature is of little help in understanding this basic concept in aviation. Scholars who have tried to clarify the national interest appear to be at a loss in finding a substantive definition. Yet, for all its vagueness, this concept is important if for no other reason that it is perceived as being so by policy makers. The lack of a general definition, however, has not discouraged the few scholars who have analysed the political underpinnings of civil aviation.

182

A central element in an analysis of the national interest is the role of the state in shaping aviation policies. This role was never in question when states controlled and, if necessary, subsidised their airlines in pursuit of national objectives. It follows that an international regulatory system based on protectionism admirably suited the national interest of most states. As one authority put it: 'in order to start an airline and to make it survive in a market which was or still is in an early stage of its development, one easily finds arguments justifying protective measures'.[2] Airlines have always been dependent on their state patrons because international routes are negotiated between states. This holds true even for the United States, leading one author to observe that the government and American carriers have been engaged in a 'peculiar love–hate relationship' resulting from private companies being used as explicit instruments of national policy.[3]

In a pungent critique of this state of affairs, Michael Bishop, the outspoken chief executive of British Midland, observed that 'airlines have mainly been founded and expanded as a clone of the government – an unassailable symbol of prestige and sovereign virility . . . The intimacy of these airlines with their governments developed a longstanding acknowledgement that consumer and commercial considerations have been subordinated to national interest and political interference'.[4]

In view of the difficulty of defining the national interest in international aviation, some theorists have focused their attention on the notion of the public interest. However, except for safety considerations, one looks in vain for this concept as a guiding principle in international air transport. One faces here the same predicament as with the national interest. How does one ascertain the public interest in a concrete case when different claims can be backed by a variety of reasons?[5] Yet, the concept cannot be ignored because it also figures prominently in the political discourse. The US, for instance, has justified its deregulation policies in aviation in terms of consumer benefits through lower prices brought about by increased competition.

The public interest in national aviation is usually defined as the need to provide regular and reliable flights to all parts of the country at the lowest cost consistent with a reasonable return to the carriers. On the other hand, one could argue that the public interest can best be served by increasing competition and allowing foreign carriers to operate on domestic routes. In any case, the notion of public interest is meaningless in an international system which features so many competitive restraints such as revenue pools, rate-fixing and other agreements between airlines. It has been argued, however, that such agreements benefit the consumer because unfettered competition creates too much instability. These arguments have been made most convincingly in Europe where domestic markets are too small for competition.

Not surprisingly, antitrust and consumer protection laws have rarely been used in air transport because governments have generally shielded their flag-carriers and exempted IATA tariffs from government action. While governments have taken consumer complaints more seriously in recent years, antitrust laws have been applied very sparingly in air transport.[6] It was not until 1986, when the European Court of Justice ruled that the competition rules in the Treaty of Rome applied to air transport, that charges could be filed in a national court against airlines for the kind of collusive practices which had been sanctioned by governments.

The reaction to another European Court's ruling three years later extending competition rules within the Community to international flights between EC members and other states is particularly instructive. Leon Brittan, the EC's Commissioner in charge of competition policy, hailed the decision as 'a landmark judgment with far-reaching implications for consumers and airlines alike'. IATA termed it another blow to national sovereignty which would do away with the last protective barriers in the bilateral agreements.

The European Commission has given notice that the public interest is no longer an idle notion. It has ample powers to ensure that airlines do not by restrictive agreements and mergers cause passengers to lose the benefits of competition. In 1986, for instance, the Commission formally charged ten airlines with infringement of competition rules. It also forced British Airways to give up certain routes after it acquired British Caledonian and could do the same in the case of other takeovers.

A key test of how the Commission defines the public interest will come when it decides what to do about airline alliances that threaten to undermine its competition policies. British Airways, KLM (Royal Dutch) and Sabena are planning a global partnership, and Air France, Lufthansa, and possibly Iberia another. To top it all, Air France took control of UTA (Union des Transports Aériens), its hapless rival for government benefactions. Since each carrier owned one-third of Air Inter, Air France also won majority control of the French domestic airline and a virtual monopoly of French domestic routes. Such a dominant position flies in the face of Commission policies. Particularly galling was the fact that a bid by Air France to acquire Air Inter had previously been denied by the Commission, leading observers to conclude that Air France simply circumvented that decision. The Commission quickly arrived at the same conclusion.

For the French Government, allowing Air France to become the leading European carrier was clearly in the national interest. As the Director of French Civil Aviation commented: 'When we look at the national flag, we cannot build on a micro airline'.[7] Industry analysts, however, view the link-ups as small cartels intent on defeating the Commission's policies before they are implemented. Under the guise of efficiency and better services, flag-carriers are in fact signing non-aggression pacts and protecting their markets. Like most observers, the *Financial Times* (16 January 1990) doubts that 'such arrangements will bring reduced costs or improved services; more likely, they will encourage collusion between champion carriers at the consumer's expense'.

One may very well ask whether the existence of state-owned airlines are compatible with EC rules. The dilemma for some states is that they are expected as members of the Community to enforce competition rules while as major stockholders they are not likely to encourage competition against their flag-carriers.

As shown with Air France, governments cannot be relied on to defend the public interest in air transport. They have even encouraged their carriers to pursue anti-competitive policies when faced with legal challenges in foreign courts. The uncertainty as to whether these courts had jurisdiction prompted several governments to pass their own 'blocking' legislation to prevent the enforcement of claims and punitive damages. The tribulations of Laker Airways became a classic example of how a court case escalated into a major diplomatic row after the liquidator of the maverick airline brought a suit in the US courts in 1982 against a number of other European and US carriers alleging a predatory pricing conspiracy. The Laker case was ultimately settled out of court after the UK enacted 'blocking' legislation. The case will also remain a classic example of how major airlines bowed to consumer demands and lowered their fares to compete with Laker only to put up prices again after they drove him out of business.

As for international regulators, it is difficult to find a reference to the public interest in the ICAO documentation on air transport. This is hardly surprising; as an intergovernmental agency, ICAO reflects the interests of government-owned airlines. It looks at economic issues more from the point of view of the carriers than that of the public. It can be argued that this is precisely what the governments had in mind when they created ICAO. K.G.P. Pillai, an early advocate of consumer rights, dismisses the argument, contending that ICAO was created to deal with all the problems of commercial aviation and if it does not have full authority to deal with economic issues then it should be given that authority.[8]

Evan Luard has suggested that a new body comparable to the former US Civil Aeronautics Board or the Civil Aviation Authority in the UK could attempt to strike a desirable balance between the conflicting interests.[9] This suggestion can only be considered utopian because governments, in the words of R.O. Keohane, 'cannot be counted on to behave benignly toward one another on a vague sense of global public interest'.[10]

CIVIL AVIATION IN EUROPE: THE 'HARD CORE' PROBLEM

The debate over the future shape of civil aviation in Europe brings into sharp focus national aeronautical and political ambitions which have mingled since the early days of commercial aviation. These interests explain the futile attempts in the past to bring civil aviation into the political integration process in Europe. Michel Folliot has researched no less than six stillborn projects in the EEC alone.[11] The lessons from past failures also explain the caution shown towards current integration efforts and their uncertain outcome.

In the distinctive integration process following the postwar dislocations in Europe, civil aviation was to have constituted an important element for both the 'federalists' who gave priority to the political institutions and the 'functionalists' who favoured the gradual integration of economic activities. It became clear as time went by, that states would not be so easily persuaded to give up sovereignty over their airspace and control over their airlines as they did in other fields of economic life.

These obstacles led Walter Hallstein, the first EC Commission President, to comment on the paradoxical nature of transport in Europe. By its very nature, it should have been the driving force in the unification of Europe by freeing its peoples of the constraint of distances. However, Hallstein was forced to conclude that the Community's policy on transportation constituted one of the least glorious pages in its history. In fact it was, as he recalled, one of the 'hard core' problems left to be negotiated in the preparatory discussions leading to the Treaty of Rome which established the EC in 1957.[12]

Since nearly all states operate a national airline, intra-European air transport is characterised by a large number of carriers for the area involved. In the words of Simone Veil, the first President of the European Parliament, 'Europe has inherited a star-shaped network of air routes which forms a rigid, meandering and costly structure with obvious disadvantages to both users and carriers'.[13] European airlines share problems of high operating costs compared with American carriers. They also face the stiff competition of subsidised rail services. Carriers have traditionally tried to reduce their operating costs through government subsidies and through bilateral agreements which divide traffic and revenues.

There are therefore strong economic as well as political arguments in favour of European solutions in civil aviation. The movement toward European unity, which led to the establishment of the Council of Europe in 1949, gave rise to discussions within that body on the need for regional cooperation in the field of air transport. Similar sentiments had been expressed before. Ivor Thomas, a one-time Parliamentary Secretary of Civil Aviation in Britain, had even proposed some sort of European airline authority 'as a practical garment with which to begin the move toward European political unity'.[14]

Ever since, proponents of European solutions in civil aviation have had a hectic time devising a politically-acceptable formula. In 1951, the Consultative Assembly of Europe tabled several proposals dealing with air transport, notably those presented by the French (the Bonnefous Plan), the Dutch (the Van de Kieft Plan) and the Italians (the Sforza Plan). The Bonnefous Plan would have created a High Authority for European Transport, not merely air transport, along the lines of the European Coal and Steel Community. Presumably, this would have meant the continued existence of separate airlines subject to a regulatory body with extensive controls over fares and routes. The Sforza Plan sought to establish a single authority in which each national airline would play a role determined by such factors as the country's population and geographical position. The Van de Kieft Plan aimed at a single European carrier or a consortium of existing airlines.[15]

As for the political implications, both the Bonnefous and Sforza plans would have meant abandoning to a common authority the sovereignty which every state exercises over its own airspace. Moreover, this common authority would have wielded a great deal of power over domestic transport.[16] In the face of strong objections by the airlines, the Consultative Assembly watered down the proposals when it made its recommendations to the Committee of Ministers of the Council of Europe. It recommended instead a conference of governments and airlines to consider the creation of 'an association of airline companies to take charge of communications between member states'. The Committee of Ministers, in fact, did not take any action until two years later in 1953 when it agreed in principle to hold such a conference, but required that no consideration be given to a single European airline or common authority for air transport. The Ministers declined even to call the conference of their own accord and instead asked ICAO to do so.

This historic conference, officially entitled the Conference on Coordination of Air Transport in Europe, met in Strasbourg in the latter part of April 1954. The main outcome was the establishment of a permanent regional body called the European Civil Aviation Conference (ECAC).[17] The creation of ECAC spelled the end of efforts to coordinate civil aviation beyond the wider geographical framework of the Council of Europe. It also brought to an end the hopes of the early 'functionalists' to devise supranational entities in civil aviation based on existing political models.

There was, however, another aborted attempt in the late 1950s within the EEC to establish a consortium of airlines so as to improve their competitive position against US carriers. This 'Little Europe' scheme known as 'Air Union' was to have been imposed on the airlines by the governments concerned. Like the previous projects, the idea was abandoned in 1965 because of conflicting national interests and because the airlines were unwilling to sacrifice their markets and accept an imposed distribution of international traffic.

The winds of change brought about by the free market and consumers' demands have forced states to put economic realities before other considerations in developing their aviation policies. Perhaps the most important consequence has been the boost given to the construction of a single European air market after years of uncertainty as to whether EC rules applied to air transport or not. Since the airlines concerned had always felt that they were exempt, the question lay dormant until deregulatory pressures started to build up in Europe. The European Commission, strengthened by a 1986 ruling from the European Court of Justice, finally obtained the power it needed to break down the protective barriers which made scheduled fares in Europe among the highest in the world.

Following up on the Commission's proposals, the Council of Ministers adopted on 14 December 1987 the first package of measures designed to increase competition in air transport. These measures which took effect on 1 January 1988 comprise Council regulations 3975/87 and 3976/87 on the application of competition in air transport, a Council directive on fares and a Council decision on capacity. In short, these measures provide for greater flexibility in tariffs, a reduction in the control of capacity and greater market access for Community airlines. New rules permit EC airlines to start some new routes within the Community without a preliminary bilateral accord and allow for more than one airline to fly a route which is also serviced by a national carrier.

In December 1989, after only two days of debate, the Council adopted in principle a second and more ambitious set of measures. If and when implemented, these measures would do away with many of the exemptions and national barriers in air transport within the Community, including those pertaining to competition on domestic routes and ownership of carriers. It would also create a cabotage area in the Community meaning that all traffic within and between member states is considered domestic and in principle reserved for Community carriers. These measures are the last step towards the completion of the single air market by the end of 1992. Their swift, albeit tentative approval, was seen as a desire by the Council to hasten the integration process in the Community in view of what was happening in Eastern Europe.

Until the single market becomes a reality, the EEC states remain competent for their bilateral relations in air transport and retain control over market access although the scope of their sovereignty has been substantially reduced. There will be little left of this sovereignty once the Commission starts negotiating Community agreements with third countries.

Whatever the final outcome of liberalisation policies in Europe, states and their flag-carriers are no longer independent actors in defining the national interest. Some have started privatising their flag-carriers, without however giving up complete control, to give them more leeway in devising their own strategies. Although doubts have been expressed as to whether the 1992 target for the single market can be achieved given the slow pace of implementation, the airlines are not taking any chances, as seen in the way they are tightening their grip on the market, more often than not with their government's blessing.

THE ORGANISATIONAL ASPECTS OF CIVIL AVIATION

The EC's commitment to create a single air market has sparked renewed interest in the organisational aspects of civil aviation in Europe. There are a number of issues to be dealt with. First, Community members do not present a unified stand on aviation. The most liberal positions are usually advocated by Britain and the Benelux countries while the go-slow states are Italy, Greece, Denmark and to a varying degree France and West Germany.

Next comes relations between EC countries and the non-EC states in Europe. Will the EC and the larger European Civil Aviation Conference (ECAC) coordinate their policies to create a European-wide market, or will they merely co-exist and split the continent into two separate markets? One difficulty that was not anticipated when the single market was created concerns future relations with the Eastern European countries eager for a new status in the 'common European house'.

The next set of issues involves the countries outside of Europe. Several questions come to mind. How will the Community negotiate traffic rights as a single entity with countries like the United States? Will the single market be considered as a cabotage zone which might necessitate a revision of the Chicago Convention? There are also particular issues facing European carriers as they restructure their operations and join forces in the globalisation of the industry. What kind of cross-border mergers and foreign ownership rules will apply that will satisfy the individual states, the airlines and the EC Commission?

Finally, beyond the commercial issues, there are a host of problems related to the management of the airspace and the flow of traffic in a continent which is already bursting at the seams. As the demand for travel increases faster than planners could have forecast some years ago, the overriding question is whether European states will agree on continent-wide solutions to solve continent-wide problems.

In considering the organisational structure of air transport in Europe, one is immediately confronted with territorial groupings that complicate the search for solutions. The organisation of civil aviation in Europe can be depicted in four concentric circles. The widest circle takes in all the states of the European region of ICAO which cooperate in technical matters and the management of the airspace. The second circle comprises the 23 members of the European Civil Aviation Conference (ECAC). The third circle groups the EC members which are now engaged in the most radical restructuring of civil aviation. The smallest circle consists of a nucleus of states belonging to EUROCONTROL, the multinational agency which controls air navigation services over a small segment of European airspace. All these groupings will be analysed separately.[18]

The European Office of ICAO encompasses the widest geographical area stretching from the Atlantic to the Asian republics of the USSR. It offers in theory the widest possible structural organisation for European cooperation but it is also the least cohesive. Yet in the absence of a coordinating mechanism, ICAO was the only agency that could devise practical solutions to cope with traffic delays that threatened a collapse of the air transport system in Europe as far back as the 1970s. ICAO convened the first Europe-wide flow control meeting in 1970 which gave air traffic controllers the possibility to assess for the first time needs and solutions on a continent-wide basis. These periodic meetings which covered the entire European region, from France to the Soviet Union and from Scandinavia to the Mediterranean, eventually resulted in the creation by the ICAO Council in 1972 of a permanent European Air Navigation Group to oversee this cooperative planning. Thanks to continuous collaboration, these states have come to recognise the fact that their air navigation systems are interdependent and cannot be allowed to be disrupted by unilateral interventions.

Since ECAC takes in 23 European states and may soon also include the east bloc countries, including the Soviet Union, it is for all practical purposes the broadest forum for collective action in civil aviation. ECAC has provided a common approach on several contentious issues such as noise limits and aviation security. Its most significant achievements have been the adoption of a code of conduct for its members on the use of computerised reservation systems (CRS) and two international agreements covering tariffs and capacity. As a result, ECAC states have agreed to apply amongst themselves liberal provisions in their bilateral agreements and to negotiate with the United States as a group. The resulting ECAC–US Memorandum of Understanding has been a turning point in US–European relations by preventing tariff issues from becoming major crises between individual ECAC members and the United States. ECAC therefore combines a dual system of liberalisation with respect to its own members and a more restrictive regulated approach toward outsiders.

ECAC is a purely consultative body. It works through resolutions and recommendations and its success depends on the willingness of its members to transpose these recommendations into their national rules and policies. A former ECAC President has remarked that this state of affairs represents both a strength and a weakness because:

> Cooperation and discussion can take place more freely and openly, even about initially controversial issues, without dramatic political overtones or political commitments. On the other hand, no European unity in rules or regulations or in policy can be achieved by compulsion. It has been suggested that this is a weakness, but perhaps there is something over-ambitious in such a notion as far as ECAC is concerned.[19]

One could speculate as to whether ECAC will ever become the focal point for a regional approach toward negotiating air agreements. Folliot doubts it. In his mind any further integration would have to proceed within the European Community itself where 'states have closer interests and are animated by a political will which can do away with nationalistic reflexes in a progressive but irreversible way'.[20]

As of now, ECAC has probably achieved the maximum in the regional integration of aviation policies. Any extension of the kind of liberalisation now in progress within the EC would require the consent of the go-slow states – the same countries which reluctantly accepted the first package in 1987 after obtaining suitable concessions. These states are likely to oppose any widening of liberal policies within ECAC while the others would not be prepared to extend them EC privileges without imposing the obligations of membership.

THE EUROPEAN COMMISSION AND AVIATION

The extent of the external competence of the Commission in respect of air transport has been a matter of debate among scholars in Community law. It has been argued that the Treaty of Rome does not contain a specific attribution of power to that effect and that the Council of Ministers is therefore the paramount body to exercise the Community's external competence. The debate is bound to go on as the Community's institutions, that is the Commission, the Council and the European Parliament, test their power in the evolving process of European integration.

The argument has also been made that the competence of EC states in conceding landing rights are concessionary powers subject to the Chicago Convention.[21] As far as the Commission is concerned, there is no conflict between the Treaty of Rome and the Chicago Convention because the Convention does not prevent states from exercising their sovereignty jointly through international agreements, if they wish to do so.[22] The Commission has already asked the Council for authorisation to conclude air agreements with third partners, starting with the countries of the European Free Trade Association (EFTA). It also wants to speak for the Community in international organisations and has requested and been granted observer status in ICAO.

The Commission asserts that the 'common commercial policy' as laid down in Article 113 of the Treaty of Rome affects various aspects of air transport and requires exclusive Community competence to negotiate with third states. The single market, jointly-owned computerised reservation systems and cross-border airline mergers give EC states no choice but to apply a common policy on commercial aspects of aviation. Mindful of the fact that each EC state has about 80 agreements with third parties, the Commission does not want to rush into a whole series of negotiations. While it wants exclusive competence, it would allow for a transition period during which EC states negotiate agreements within Community guidelines.

Whatever the legal arguments, implementation of a common air transport policy requires that the Commission takes over national competence in negotiating aviation agreements. This would mean that the 12 EC countries no longer appear as separate entities but as one negotiating partner within the European Civil Aviation Conference and with the rest of the world. The Council of Ministers has yet to approve such a transfer of power and a way to apportion the concessions obtained in future Community negotiations. To do so in a way acceptable to the Community carriers will not be easy. There is no indication that these carriers or the governments are more inclined to accept an imposed distribution of traffic rights now than in the days of 'Air Union'.

The 12 states represented on the Council of Ministers have differing positions, depending on their economic weight and geographical location. As indicated before, some countries want to moderate the pace of change while others want to push the process further and faster. Britain has espoused the most liberal position and proposes a system with airlines flying wherever they wish and at whatever fares they care to charge.[23]

States are bound to be influenced by the financial health of their carriers and will resist sweeping changes which threaten their survival. Thus, whatever the Commission's position on state subsidies, Olympic Airways, the Greek flag-carrier, has accumulated such heavy losses that it will need continued state help to fly out of trouble. Carriers such as British Airways, Aer Lingus and KLM (Royal Dutch) are pushing hard for a more liberal regime while Alitalia and some other airlines are not ready for it. There is also a lack of unity on bilateral agreements. France, for example, has always held that such agreements are the best means by which states can protect their interests. The Netherlands, on the other hand, finds these agreements unnecessary and irreconcilable with economic realities.

The international community faces a dilemma as to how to reconcile EC policies in air transport with bilateralism and the principles of sovereignty, national territory and nationality of airlines which are at the core of the regulatory system. As P.D. Sutherland saw the situation when he was Commissioner for Competition 'the logic of 1992 requires us to move away from the network of bilateral air service agreements and to develop instead the concept of a Community air space in which all carriers established within the Community will be free to compete in the Community domestic market'.[24] Yet, while the EC members can dispense with bilateral agreements among themselves, they will still collectively need to maintain control of entry to the market through agreements with third parties. The Commission has already started negotiations with the European Free Trade Association, which groups six non-EC states in order to replace bilateral with Community agreements.

There is even the intriguing possibility that faced with a concentration of power between the major flag-carriers the Commission will want to grant limited cabotage rights in these agreements to ensure more competition within the Community.

Even though their acquired rights are protected under the Treaty of Rome (Article 234), third parties which have agreements with individual EEC states are understandably apprehensive about future negotiations with the Community on such sensitive issues as the designation of airlines to fly certain routes, the use of airports and last, but not least, fifth freedom routes in Europe (for instance Pan Am's London–Frankfurt, TWA's Brussels–Berlin or Air Canada's London–Nice segments of overseas flights). The US alone has 18 such routes in the Community.

Community cabotage, as called for in the Commission's second package, may very well become a hot issue and a source of dispute. Canada's chief negotiator has already evoked the possibility of making use of the judicial mechanism of the ICAO Council and possibly that of the International Court of Justice.[25] Besides problems of interpreting Article 7 of the Chicago Convention, banning cabotage on an exclusive basis (see next chapter), there are also difficult questions of the extraterritorial jurisdiction of EC regulations which might be detrimental to outside carriers.

A leading member of the European Parliament who raised the possibility of conflict between the EC and the international aviation community did not have the answer. He did, however, conclude that 'from the European viewpoint [it] must not be for us now to adapt the facts to the requirements of the Chicago Convention', leaving open the question as to whether it should be the Convention that should be adapted to fit the new realities.[26]

The European Commission is not unaware that its policies have wide repercussions on the international system. This may be one of the reasons why air transport policy made little headway during the first two decades. At the same time, the Commission executive in charge of air transport pointed out the need to establish a Community approach to civil aviation consistent with the Chicago Convention as far back as 1980.[27]

ICAO has already pinpointed some potentially adverse effects of the single European market. One consequence could be that fifth freedom rights within the Community will be more difficult to negotiate for carriers based outside the region. This could be particularly damaging for the carriers operating long and low-volume routes which need to pick up traffic along the way. ICAO also foresees problems if new European mega-carriers threaten 'existing balances of fair and equal opportunity'.[28]

Whatever common policies are agreed upon, the Community is bound to face a tough response from the United States if, as expected, it insists on reciprocity in all areas of trade relations. The United States has already given notice that it will not automatically combine traffic rights if any of the proposed European airline partnerships come to fruition. These are crucial issues since American carriers now have access to all the main European gateways whereas European airlines have a limited number of destinations in the United States and few fifth-freedom rights. They are not allowed to carry domestic traffic within the country since the US does not allow cabotage.

The US Department of Transport has set the stage for future negotiations in a cautious way. It announced that international flights would be permitted without bilateral negotiations to cities which do not now have international services. As proposed, the new flights would be granted only to airlines from countries which already have liberal agreements with the US.[29] Because of the restrictions, it is difficult to assess whether the DOT proposal means a significant shift of policy or an opening gambit.

Assuming a transfer of power to the Community, negotiations of commercial rights with the EC as a unit will be complex and lengthy. One authority, the past-President of ECAC, provided a mind-boggling scenario: the Commission would require a mandate and specific instructions from the Council of Ministers. Before the Council of Ministers could consider granting such a mandate, the Commission, according to Article 84 of the EEC Treaty, would have to obtain the views of the European Parliament. Under such conditions, negotiations on traffic rights or tariffs which could require three years of preparation before they even begin, would be totally unrealistic.[30]

The statutory constraints and the fact that the Community, however unified, will never speak for the whole of Europe, makes ECAC the only body capable of devising regional policies in civil aviation. ECAC officials are comforted by the fact that the ECAC agreements on tariffs and capacity and part of its code of conduct on the use of CRSs have served as a model for the Community rules. In assessing the institutional aspects of European air transport, Stephen Wheatcroft and Geoffrey Lipman see no other alternative but for a Europe-wide approach that incorporates the EC and ECAC policy developments. Failing that, they fear that over time the emergence of Community policies and the activities of the Community institutions could reduce ECAC to a secondary advisory role and leave Europe divided.[31]

The uncertainties surrounding the final phase of the single aviation market is causing concern to airline executives who would just as soon see the Commission handle aviation matters on behalf of all EC states to avoid what one of them calls 'another agricultural disaster'. He shudders at the prospect of 'a continuous flow of regulations and directives valid only for a part of the Community irrespective of what is happening in other member states'.[32]

One overriding concern on the part of aviation policy makers is the absence of a supranational European civil aviation office, comparable to the US Federal Aviation Administration, which would deal with Europe's critical air-traffic congestion. Without urgent action, there is little hope of staving off paralysing problems for Europe's air industry in the 1990s. In 1987 a total of 150 000 flying hours were lost through delays, 70 per cent of which were the result of inadequate air traffic control. By the end of the century, according to a ECAC task force, the number of flights is expected to increase by 150 per cent compared to 1987.[33]

Obviously, the air traffic system as organised at present is hopelessly inadequate. All told there are 42 air traffic control centres, more than twice the number in the continental United States which covers an area double the size of Europe. Those centres operating as individual units will need to be integrated as part of a central authority comparable to the FAA. Under present procedures, for instance, a flight from Frankfurt to Madrid must be directed through eleven different air traffic control zones.

The problem is compounded by congestion at airports which lack sufficient runway and terminal facilities. Many of these airports will be fully utilised by the time the single market comes into effect. As a result, some countries may be tempted to use congestion at certain airports as an excuse to keep new airlines out of the market.[34] Small carriers, especially the newcomers, have complained that the present system of slot allocations at congested airports is discriminatory in that it favours those airlines which already have a slot (the so-called grandfather right). The Commission wants some of these slots allocated to new carriers and is also considering other proposals to deal with congestion in the sky and on the ground.

Even though the situation has improved, the traffic flow management system which ICAO put into effect was meant to cope with seasonal delays and not as a permanent answer to Europe's congested airways. The solution would require a supranational agency with sufficient power to manage the airspace. A start has been made with EUROCONTROL. It remains to be seen how far states will go in yielding some of their sovereign rights over the airspace to allow the agency to accomplish what it was set up to do. In raising the issue, the Secretary General of the European Airlines Association (Karl Heinz Neumeister) warned that 'sovereignty is now threatening to kill the airline industry in Europe'.[35]

Instead of political decisions, it would seem that some states have opted for functional approaches which would have the same effect. The Benelux countries and West Germany, which originally agreed to a broad integration of their air traffic control (ATC) systems when EUROCONTROL was created, have now embarked on a project to integrate five civilian and three military control centres. The agency hopes that this preliminary project will provide the 'systems concept' for a single European ATC network.[36]

As noted in Chapter 6, EUROCONTROL has been hampered by military restrictions and by its limited membership. Lately, more countries have joined in, but to gain wider membership, EUROCONTROL has had to give ground on its authority and amend its constitutional charter. It has now become an agency whose advisory role cannot be thought to impinge on the sovereignty of individual states. It is a far cry from the expectation of full supranational management of air traffic, but a realistic acceptance of the fact that states are not yet ready to give up control over their airspace. Nevertheless, whatever its shortcomings, EUROCONTROL is at present the only operational agency which can manage the airspace in Europe.

EUROPE'S NEW ENTREPRENEURS

As the pressures build up for Europe's privatised carriers to restructure and seek strategic alliances to meet challenges from the United States and the Far East, these airlines also view with concern new competition emerging on their own turf. Unlike Sir Freddie Laker who ultimately came to grief trying to outsmart the large carriers, the new entrepreneurs are working within the rules, such as they exist, and establishing themselves on the continent before the single market takes final shape. The most visible of these newcomers – Air Europe – is also the most ambitious, as its name implies. Working within existing regulatory constraints on airline ownership, Air Europe is assembling a low-priced pan-European network of local carriers. As an upstart undercutting its competitors, Air Europe has had problems finding other carriers willing to accept its tickets for travel on connecting flights. Even so, Air Europe is aiming for wider horizons and has asked the CAA for rights to serve the US, Canada, Mexico and the Caribbean.

To get round the obstacle that nationals must hold the majority control of an airline in the country where it is registered, Air Europe has created minority-owned companies in Spain and Norway and is planning to do the same in France and Italy. It has also bought minority control of a regional airline in West Germany. All these clone-companies as well as the UK flagship will operate charter and scheduled flights to and from their 'home' markets as well as to vacation destinations outside Europe. A Dutch-registered holding company, Airlines of Europe BV, has been set up to oversee the empire and lease aircraft to the local carriers.

The concept of a multinational airline group operating with a decentralised management and using local franchises or partnerships is gaining favour with the new entrepreneurs. The Australian tycoons Rupert Murdoch and Sir Peter Abeles, joint owners of the Ansett/TNT empire, are successfully using this concept to expand freight and package operations across Europe.

Several pan-European groupings of passenger airlines, charter and scheduled, are on the drawing board.[37] As planned, these carriers will be local companies managed and substantially-owned by nationals of the country in which they are registered. They are, however, part of a larger grouping and benefit from the financial, marketing and organisational power of a centralised 'umbrella' company. Ansett/TNT's use of the franchise system is in the different freight market. The company is part of a number of carriers like Federal Express, United Parcel Service and Emery Air Freight which fly their own aircraft across the Atlantic, setting up hub and spoke operations across Europe. All these companies are motivated by the same drive: to thrive in the lucrative shipment of parcels and high technology products in the single market. They are helped by the fact that European carriers are not yet geared for door to door service. In the absence of regulatory provisions, they are allowed to operate to the limit of the law, as far as postal regulations are concerned.[38]

These developments in the use of air transport go beyond the European context. They are part of the strategies being developed by newcomers and established carriers to face the global challenges of free trade. The globalisation of the industry with all its implications also raises questions as to whether the international regulatory system based on sovereignty principles, national control and ownership of airlines and the trading of traffic rights can still be relied on to govern the orderly development of civil aviation into the twenty-first century.

12 Deregulation Dilemmas: Flying the Flag in the Global Market

For business purposes the boundaries that separate one nation from another are no more real than the equator.

J. Maisonrouge, President of IBM in 1971

If any single word epitomises changes in most industries and services during the last decade it is 'globalisation'. The global market has reached a new dimension in the sky. Global strategies in air transport may be less conspicuous than in other industries, but they are nevertheless evident in every phase of civil aviation. Aircraft are built by international consortia, marketing has become a component of computerised reservation systems which are themselves part of conglomerates. A significant aspect of the global trend in air transport is international ownership and affiliation of airlines. There is scarcely a major airline that has not entered into some kind of partnership, affiliation or marketing agreement with another carrier.

Major changes in the airline industry have already affected operations beyond the predictions of policy makers and academics.[1] In the United States, the consolidation process has produced a group of four mega-carriers which in 1989 shared 90 per cent of the profits. Many of the smaller and medium-sized feeder carriers are dependent on these larger carriers for their survival. It is still unclear to what extent the American experience will be repeated in Europe but a consolidation of European carriers seems inevitable. Some analysts go as far as predicting that about five major European airlines – efficient and truly international – will emerge by the mid 1990s. The others will be essentially regional and feeder carriers, bringing passengers to high traffic hub airports where the major airlines will pick them up for transcontinental flights.

For the airline strategists like Louis Gialloreto of Air Canada, a ruthless global war has already begun and he makes this clear in the sub-title of a book addressed to his fellow industry managers. He advises them to start planning their global strategies now if they want to be around to participate in the coming technological revolution. 'We stand on the horizon of exciting times as did the Wright Brothers or Juan Trippe or Lindbergh', writes Gialloreto.[2]

He sees a four-stage evolution in the formation of a multinational mega-carrier. The first involves the consolidation of air carriers within a country. This has already occurred in the US, in Britain, West Germany and France. The second phase involves the building of conventional agreements between airlines of different countries, the marketing partnership between British Airways and United Airlines being a good example. The third phase is more complex, involving full and partial equity exchanges, such as those between KLM (Royal Dutch) and Air UK or between SAS (Scandinavian), the Texas Air Corporation and British Midland.[3]

The final phase of this global consolidation may very well do away with the world aviation system as we have known it for the past forty years. The erosion of existing barriers could result in a relatively small group of multinational airlines competing in markets around the world. According to one authority 'these airlines will operate far-flung networks of hubs, each supported by extensive services. The nerve centres of these airlines will be highly sophisticated computer systems that handle reservations, fares and seating, schedule aircraft and crews, track operations, monitor maintenance and generally provide all the operational data to control a global enterprise'.[4]

The way these mega-carriers will interact on the market will determine the economic environment of air transport in the years to come. One could argue that an oligopoly has always existed, at least within IATA. There is, however, a big difference between a cartel of government-owned airlines and a cartel of carriers responsible only to their managers and shareholders. Under deregulation, as noted by Knut Hammarskjöld, the long-time Director General of IATA, the dominant carriers are essentially the same core carriers which formed the oligopoly of pre-deregulation days, albeit with some restructuring and name changes. In his view, deregulation, which was meant to do away with a regulated oligopoly of airlines, has permitted the industry to form a privately-controlled oligopoly because antitrust laws were not adequately enforced.[5]

One might conceive that these carriers in an anarchic system will act according to Mancur Olson's theory of 'exclusive groups' to keep new firms from coming in to share the market and force those already in to shrink until there is preferably only one left.[6] No transport analyst would go so far as to forecast such a drastic scenario. Most probably, the resulting conglomerates would run afoul of even the most lenient regulators.

Hammarskjöld cited another scenario in which five airlines are depicted sitting around a poker table with a sixth waiting to play. The ante was defined as market power, cash, low labour cost and entrepreneurial management.[7] Pierre Jeanniot, the chief executive of Air Canada, remarked that in such a competitive environment 'the winners will always be those who can offer the best product at the lowest cost'. Hammarskjöld doubts that the poker game can continue for long even in a most liberal trade environment because a mega-carrier beyond a certain size can no longer operate efficiently and cost-effectively without being forced at some point to give up some of its gains.[8]

Most airline executives agree with this assessment, unable to imagine a hybrid mastodon surviving in the peculiar environment of aviation. In the words of Sir Colin Marshall, the chief executive of British Airways, 'to fly the globe is one thing, to be a true global airline is quite another'.[9] In his view there will never be a true global airline with equal penetration and marketing power all over the world.

Judging from their actions, rather than their pronouncements, the airline executives are engaged in a curious courting game of cross-border partnerships as they get ready for an inevitable consolidation of the industry. Some nostalgic airline chiefs, who have been used to flying for so long under their national flag, hope that sovereign interests in air transport will somehow retard the evolution. To be sure, major obstacles remain to block multi-national mega-carriers, not the least of which is pride in the flag. Strong national loyalties still exist in many countries with respect to flag-carriers.

While there have been some successful airline mergers, those which have aroused too many protests have been spurned or held in abeyance. SAS (Scandinavian), a perennial suitor, ran into a brick wall in 1987 when it tried to merge with Sabena, the Belgian flag carrier. It was likewise rebuffed when it tried to take over British Caledonian which finally merged with British Airways to stay in 'British hands'. SAS has cast its net as far afield as Argentina where its bid to acquire 40 per cent of the privatised Aerolineas provoked an angry outcry of a 'national sellout'. SAS, itself the product of a successful merger, is especially interesting in that its ownership structure is a mixture of governmental and private interests in three states. Successful mergers have taken place in neighbouring states whose airlines needed to reach a viable size to operate internationally. The best examples are Air Afrique jointly owned by a number of African francophone states and Gulf Air, a profitable carrier jointly owned by Bahrain, Oman, Qatar and Abu Dhabi.

A major obstacle in the way of cross-borders mergers is the nationality rule in bilateral agreements which requires that each party's designated carrier be substantially owned and effectively operated by its nationals. In the United States, the Federal Aviation Act of 1958 bars foreigners from owning more than 25 per cent of an airline. Since similar provisions exist in other countries, it is unlikely that the airline industry will go the way of many industries in losing control to foreign interests. Even countries which are privatising their flag-carriers are careful to spell out the extent to which foreign buyers can purchase shares.

These national regulatory restraints do not apply as yet to jointly-owned computerised reservation systems which can give an airline a decided advantage over its competitors. An airline with a dominant grip on disseminating market information has the means not only of influencing that market but also of distorting it.[10] This explains the open warfare between major airlines, or groups of airlines, all scrambling to extend the reach of their various systems. This battle is fought with financial resources which reflect the prize. Investments committed to data-processing capacity over the last couple of years run to hundreds of millions of dollars. The US hold on the market has already tested the resolve of European governments and their airlines to override national rivalries and accept certain risks between themselves in order to combat greater ones from outside.

Beyond cross-border amalgamations and global alliances, there looms the danger that the marketing system may run amok and escape any control. No government can claim sovereignty to stop Amadeus, Galileo, Abacus and Fantasia from linking together. These global systems, if they come about, are bound to influence the way air transport will develop in the future. Yet, it is a matter largely out of the hands of ICAO. Some fears have already been expressed that the airlines might lose control of their marketing and that the distribution systems may become divorced from the economics of air transport.[11]

Unfair practices in the use of computerised reservation systems have already provoked an international row. Three US carriers (Northwest, TWA and Pan American) filed a complaint in 1986 against Lufthansa under the US International Air Transportation Fair Competition Practices Act. The US complaints generated counter-claims by European carriers that the US rules were not good enough because they allowed discrimination against foreign airlines. At issue is the fact that because foreign carriers are not allowed to operate domestic US services, passengers using a foreign airline on a transatlantic crossing and making a connection in the US must inevitably transfer to a US carrier while those travelling on a US airline will usually have the option of making an online connection.[12]

European airlines and governments have voiced their complaints (thus far in vain) bilaterally and at the multilateral level at ICAO and ECAC. The US has pointed out that its rules may not be perfect, but at least it did have rules while no European country had attempted to regulate the use of computerised reservation systems.

How well the airlines will abide by codes of conduct remains to be seen, as carriers become more and more dependent on these systems for their global marketing. The airlines will want to ensure the best code-sharing arrangements as part of their marketing strategies and alliances. Before long, the American mega-carriers will hook up with their counterparts overseas. The international carriers that fail to woo the right partner may be left to fend for themselves in a system which no longer recognises 'fair and equal opportunity'. In this global context, a single country or a group of countries would hardly be able to enforce its own set of rules. The solution would be an international code of conduct acceptable to all countries, but one would still be faced with the need to enforce the rules.

THE NEW GLOBAL OPERATORS

The new global business environment has given rise to a new breed of operators who stay clear of bilateral constraints and move quickly to take advantage of market opportunities anywhere in the world. Their carriers operating on the fringe of the international system are global in the sense that they fly anywhere and that they do not respond to national objectives. The most notable example is Ansett Transportation Industries, an Australian company that Rupert Murdoch's News Corporation Ltd owns equally with Sir Peter Abeles's TNT Ltd, another Australian company. Ansett has avoided a competitive dogfight with Qantas, Australia's national carrier. It has instead been flying in all directions, expanding through subsidiaries and commercial alliances with other companies.[13]

In addition to its high-profile publishing and other activities, the Ansett/TNT empire now encompasses a major international leasing operation which has helped the parent company purchase minority stakes in various airlines using its leased aircraft. Ansett has become the part owner of the US regional carrier America West and of a Chilean carrier. Its foray in the European market is part of its global strategy. Foregoing the use of older second-hand aircraft for courier express services, it plans to use the latest BAC 146 Quiet Trader to circumvent noise curfews and move intra-European freight by air rather than by road.

Ansett at one point was close to dominating the South Pacific through its control of various national airlines as flags of convenience. It had agreements to operate Polynesian Airlines and Cook Islands International as well the airline of Vanuatu (formerly New Hebrides) and almost bought a share of Fiji's Air Pacific. This would have given the Australian carrier a dominant position within the region with its aircraft flying for various governments, changing logos along the way. There was also the alluring possibility of opening international routes to Australia, New Zealand, Japan, Singapore and points as far away as Canada and the United States. Ansett's strategy, however, went sour when Qantas ended up buying part of Air Pacific and poor financial returns forced Ansett to pull out from its agreements with Cook Islands and Vanuatu.

Ansett activities in the South Pacific did not occur without creating frictions. Its management of Air Vanuatu at one point caused New Zealand to object that the Australian-owned company competed unfairly with New Zealand carriers. Its activities at home look even more alarming from its competitors' point of view. In addition to interlocking interests in restaurant chains, credit cards and resorts, it has built up a local empire of subsidiaries and affiliated airlines and is positioning these companies to take up a major slice of a booming tourist market. Ansett leaves no doubts as to its global objectives. According to Sir Peter Abeles: 'Ansett is a potential mega and we are aware that others are paranoid in case we become one'. If there is a strategy that applies to the whole conglomerate, he adds, it is 'to become the biggest transport group in the world'.[14]

The new partnerships and alliances in the airline industry have been greatly facilitated by the wide use of leasing even for short terms, thus relieving the new companies from assuming the burden of heavy capital costs. The lease agreements run across political boundaries with lessor, lessee, lender and guarantor all domiciled in separate countries. Aircraft leasing is not a new phenomenon as witnessed by the need for an amendment to the Chicago Convention (Article 83 *bis* not yet in force) to enable the transfer of legal responsibility of the aircraft from the state of registry to the operator. But few people at the time could have predicted the demand. Inevitably a new kind of intermediary has come onto the scene to supply this demand. These suppliers now own some of the world's largest fleets of aircraft. One aviation consultant expects that by the turn of the century all aircraft operated by Latin American and Caribbean airlines will be owned by the major leasing companies.[15] These include the GPA Group based in Shannon, Ireland; the California-based International Lease Finance Corporation (ILF) and the Worldwide Aviation Service owned by the ubiquitous Ansett/TNT empire.

Ireland is not normally perceived as being a major aeronautical power, yet the GPA Group may soon boast the world's largest fleet of aeroplanes even if none will ever display the shamrock. The Group not only leases its aircraft, it arranges for their financing and maintenance. The leasing companies finance their own operations through various financial and investment institutions, many of them Japanese. GPA's biggest competitor is the ILF. Together they placed orders in 1989 for aircraft worth well over $20 billion. In doing this well ahead of the airlines, the leasing companies may have in fact cornered the market for some types of aircraft and left the airlines no choice but to lease their aircraft. 'You have to secure the merchandise ahead of time when the demand is strong', explained Leslie Gonda, the chairman of ILF when he announced that his firm had placed $1 billion worth of jetliners with nine foreign airlines, including five first-time customers.[16]

THE PRESSURES ON INTERNATIONAL REGULATORS

Looking at the last 10 years, one cannot help but wonder at the radical transformations that have taken place in what has been the most regulated and least competitive industry in the world. The debate no longer centres on how much needs to be protected but on how few safeguards need to be preserved. The regulatory system established at the 1944 Chicago Conference is so full of leaks that one may well ask how long it can withstand further storms and still function.

The most visible loser in the new global era is IATA whose tariff coordinating conferences were a mainstay of the system. In the past, governments readily approved IATA's decisions, not because the fares were necessarily in the best interests of the airlines and consumers, but because governments generally had no wider objectives than the welfare of their flag carrier. After waging a losing battle against deregulation, IATA has restructured itself into a trade organisation, gradually dropping its cartel practices and rescinding its tariff enforcement programmes.

The last blow to the fare-fixing arrangements between airlines was the Ahmed Saeed case in which the European Court of Justice confirmed that the competition rules of the Treaty of Rome applied to domestic as well as to international routes between EC and non-Community states.[17] The ruling was also a signal that henceforth cases could be brought before national courts against airlines which infringed these rules, whether on domestic routes or international routes between the European Community and third states.

The various rulings and directives concerning the application of competition rules in the European Community are but the latest indications that the bilateral regime for the exchange of commercial rights in air transport is in serious trouble. The model used for more than 40 years was the Bermuda Agreement between the US and the UK which defines the conditions for entry, capacity, routes and pricing. These Bermuda rules are out of date in a deregulated environment. The rumbles of discontent were first heard in 1977 when the US and the UK renegotiated the Bermuda II Agreement which left both parties equally dissatisfied with the outcome. As a result both countries have held repeated and longdrawn negotiations on various contentious issues such as the number of gateways and fifth-freedom rights to be enjoyed by each party.

A number of countries besides the UK have expressed their

discontent with bilateral arrangements concluded with the US at a time when that country was in a dominant position and could force the issue. The United States must now deal with countries which are in no mood to accept further restraints and have threatened to denounce their agreements. There is particular resentment in South-East Asia and the Pacific, a booming market into which the US wants increased access for a number of its carriers, but offers insufficient concessions. Thus Australia held out for two years in arduous negotiations until it extracted improved access to the US market for its own carriers. The rising demand for business and leisure travel in South-East Asia has persuaded governments and airlines in that region to adopt a tougher stance in their bilateral negotiations, not only with the US but also with the UK. The outlook is no better in Europe where bilateral talks between the US and the UK, West Germany and France have either broken down or been postponed until after 1992. These EC states do not want further imbalances caused by the existence of several American carriers competing against their sole flag carrier. A number of countries are at a loss to reconcile the US actions with its free-trade pronouncements. For example, Canada, which signed a Free Trade Agreement that should benefit both countries, has been seeking in vain limited cabotage rights into the US while Scandinavian negotiators who tried to promote a similar proposal returned home empty-handed. The case of Canada is particularly troublesome because it is such a close neighbour. Yet, negotiations to improve the transborder air-route system have been deadlocked since 1979.[18]

Some analysts believe that the United States has reached an impasse in bilateral negotiations and finds itself caught between the interests of new carriers seeking to expand internationally and those of incumbent carriers which want to consolidate their position. The top US air transport negotiator put it this way:

> We face . . . an important dilemma. An anachronistic, highly regulatory system of bilateral agreements has actually worked to the advantage of the US airline industry to such an extent that we are beginning to deny ourselves the widely acknowledged benefits of an expanding, dynamic, international transport market.[19]

Another unexpected outcome of deregulation which is causing concern at the US Department of Transport is that competition on international routes may be curtailed if airlines as part of the industry's consolidation sell off their traffic rights. At issue is whether airlines designated to operate these routes can claim them as their exclusive property and sell them like other assets. Thus, American Airlines in a relentless expansion of its overseas network was able in one huge shopping spree to acquire Latin American and some Canadian routes from a financially-troubled Eastern Airlines, as well as the lucrative Chicago–London route from TWA. Pan Am opposed the deal as being anticompetitive. Oddly enough, Pan Am's bid to acquire the same Latin American routes from Braniff in the mid 1980s had been blocked for the same reasons.

In some instances, carriers might be acquired for the potential sale value of their routes. As an indication of how valuable such routes can be, Pan Am sold its Pacific routes along with the aircraft that fly them to United Airlines in 1985 for $750 million. These routes now account for some $2 billion in annual revenues.[20]

Beyond this American phenomenon, regulators will need to face up to another dilemma resulting from the emergence of new global airlines: can 'substantive ownership' and 'effective control' rules rest with more than one 'nationality'? These rules, which were devised at the Chicago Conference to bar the flags of convenience prevalent in the maritime industry, are part of every bilateral agreement. No country has yet shown any inclination to relax these rules, least of all the United States where the 25 per cent limitation of foreign ownership of a US carrier is made even more restrictive by another provision in the Federal Aviation Act setting at 10 per cent the level at which control is presumed and therefore subject to government review.

There is also the anomaly of the 'nationality' of the aircraft which must be that of the state of registry, whether or not the aircraft is actually owned by foreign interests. A recent survey indicates that while financially-strong airlines still own the majority of their aircraft, a number of important carriers like Pan Am own considerably less than half of their fleets. Even the airlines with strong capital assets have said publicly that they will need to lease more aircraft in the future.[21] As governments deregulate the markets which provide much of the financing needed in such a capital-intensive industry as air transport, it is a matter of time before foreign investors will want to exercise more control over their investments. They would certainly want to do so at the first signs of a global recession.

The globalisation of air transport clearly runs counter to a bilateral regime based on the 'nationality' of airlines designated to use traffic rights. H.A. Wassenbergh has observed that: 'under the prevailing bilateral system the only way to introduce an "international airline" into the international air traffic market is to create a new nationality out of different nationalities of the merging airlines as was done for SAS (a Scandinavian nationality)'.[22] The question therefore is whether existing bilateral agreements can accommodate the consolidation and cross-border mergers of airlines or whether the boilerplate clauses on 'nationality' and 'substantial ownership' will need to be reformulated.

The catalyst for change may well come from the European Community as it puts in shape its single market. The European Commission is pressing member states to drop national ownership clauses from their bilateral agreements and national laws and replace them with a Community clause. As a consequence, EC states may well have no choice but to give carriers from other member states the same traffic rights as those enjoyed by their own airlines. For the time being, however, the airlines are mapping their strategies according to national laws. The logical outcome of the EC integration process would be to 'denationalise' the airlines and to designate a 'Euro' flag which will do away with the traditional concept of the carrier's nationality.

TOWARDS A REFORM OF THE SYSTEM

Since the international regulatory system is in such disarray, perhaps a Chicago II Conference would be in order to reassess concepts formulated 50 years ago. This conference could re-examine such notions as 'national sovereignty', 'substantial ownership' and 'effective control' of an airline and consider whether they are as essential today to the development of civil aviation as when they were proclaimed at the 1944 Chicago Conference. What would happen, for example, if a number of 'Euro' airlines were granted exclusive rights to operate cabotage routes in the Community? Since Article 7 of the Chicago Convention declares that each state 'undertakes not to enter into any arrangements which specifically grant [cabotage] privilege on an exclusive basis to any other state' the ambiguity over what constitutes exclusive rights needs to be resolved.

The single market may force states to grapple once more with the whole issue of cabotage rights. In 1968 Sweden proposed an amendment to Article 7 which would drop the restriction of exclusive rights, thus leaving states free to grant or refuse cabotage rights as they see fit.[23] It may be a proposal whose time has come.

Another notion requiring rethinking is that of control and ownership of an airline. The 'nationality' of future mega-carriers may be open to questions. How would country A react if country B designated as its national carrier a 'franchise' airline owned by country C or by a global entrepreneur? If, for instance, Murdoch were tempted to buy an American carrier would he still be considered an Australian even though he took out US citizenship papers to buy into the regulated US broadcasting industry?

The success of an eventual Chicago II Conference depends on whether states find it possible to mesh commercial interests in aviation as they have done in technical matters. A reform of the system poses formidable problems which cannot be resolved by simply analysing conflicting national interests. The national interest in air transport today is interlocked not so much with foreign policy and prestige considerations as it is with trade in services, consumer demands, the forces of the market and the global strategies of the carriers.

A Chicago II Conference could map the broad outlines of the development of civil aviation based on new realities. This will be a daunting task. The participants would be confronted with the same vexing problem as their predecessors on the disposition of national property rights. However, the options proposed at the time when air transport was a budding industry are no longer available. The major aeronautical states arrived at a compromise in 1944 but they would now have to face the demands of Third World states which were absent the first time around. Having in theory at least gained equal access to international aviation through what Stephen Krasner calls 'authoritative rather than market allocation', these states would want to keep as many protective barriers as possible.[24]

Regimes rise and fall in response to their own dynamics, or as the result of a changing political and economic environment. Which way will the international regulatory system in civil aviation evolve? Two theoretical possibilities can be readily ruled out, that of complete freedom of the air and, at the other extreme, that of an international authority to operate a global airline.[25] Both proposals were rejected at the Chicago Conference in 1944. There is nothing to indicate that five decades later they stand a better chance to be acceptable on political or economic grounds.

One possibility is that air transport will follow the general trend towards regionalism in trade and other matters. National economic regulation would be replaced by group regulation as states within the same region coordinate their interests in international air transport. Wassenbergh foresees that besides the EC, regional groupings are in the offing in North America (the US and Canada) and in the Far East with the ASEAN countries. To a lesser extent a regional approach would prevail among African, Arab, Caribbean and Latin American states. The international regulatory system would evolve into a new form of 'bilateralism' as these regional entities negotiate among themselves and also with individual states that are not part of a regional grouping. The negotiators would then automatically have to choose whether to trade on a basis of the greatest possible freedom or utmost protection.[26]

There is nothing in the Chicago Convention to stop states from choosing such a regional approach if Article 1 can be interpreted as allowing states full discretion on how they wish to exercise their sovereign rights. In legal terms the Convention in Chapter XVI gives a regional grouping of states considerable scope in pooling their air services on any routes or in any regions. The difficulties would arise in sharing or apportioning the traffic rights presently held by individual states.

While there is a growing trend to pool civil aviation facilities on a regional basis, this has not as yet involved the touchy issue of traffic rights. Conceivably the various regional commissions which coordinate policies at the regional level could become the focal point of new regional policies but so far none of them have sought a mandate. They remain a forum for regional consultations. The three instances in which a group of states has designated a multinational carrier to exercise their traffic rights are exceptional (SAS, Gulf Air and Air Afrique). It is worth noting that in the latter case the African states which agreed on exclusive cabotage amongst themselves continue to negotiate bilaterally with third states and hand over the traffic rights obtained for common exploitation by their designated carrier (Air Afrique).

A major development in the joint exercise of traffic rights was a resolution submitted by a number of Caribbean states to the ICAO Assembly in 1983 (Resolution A24–12). The Assembly agreed that a carrier's substantial ownership and effective control could be detrimental to the developing states. It therefore endorsed the concept of a 'community of economic interests' in designating an airline controlled by one or more developing states within the same group to exercise traffic rights negotiated bilaterally.

APPLYING THE GATT RULES TO AIR TRANSPORT

A more radical approach would bring air transport under the rules of GATT (the General Agreement on Tariffs and Trade). Proponents of this idea point out that, inasmuch as the question of reciprocity is a major issue in air transport, GATT allows a good deal of flexibility. The US, however, is reluctant to open up its lucrative domestic market unless it can obtain similar concessions abroad. GATT would allow a trade-off between cabotage rights in the US in exchange, for instance, for access to a major telecommunications market at present under state control.[27] This kind of trade-off, of course, presupposes that if governments privatise their airlines, they will allow air transport to be treated like any other industry.

It is ironic that multilateral negotiations are being advocated as a novel solution to replace bilateralism considering that the idea was rejected in 1944. In order to bring air transport within GATT's multilateral framework, it will be necessary to reconcile two antithetical approaches. The protectionist system which evolved from the Chicago Conference was based on a compromise between national interests. Market participation was to be controlled by the regulation of commercial air services through bilateral agreements. The national interest was respected since the system provided for the survival of flag carriers regardless of cost factors or economic efficiency. GATT, which designates both a Free Trade Agreement and the Geneva-based international agency created to implement it, aims for open, expanding multilateral trading based on the progressive reduction of protectionist barriers and other measures which distort competition. As one proponent of GATT writes:

> Chicago is directed to the regulation of producers (national airlines) and is by definition discriminatory as it is based on nationality. GATT aims to regulate the import of products, regardless of the nationality of the producer. Thus the application of GATT principles would facilitate airlines to become global multinationals and could rule out discrimination on the basis of nationality.[28]

States have held preliminary negotiations under the auspices of

GATT for the last ten years to conclude an agreement in the trade in services covering banking, insurance, telecommunications and transportation, including air transport. However, it was not until the Uruguay round of trade negotiations in September 1986 that aviation officials became aware of the eventual consequences for air transport. At present, GATT principles apply only to trade in goods. Efforts by the GATT negotiators to transfer these rules to the trade in services have been thwarted by the nature of the different services and the way these are being regulated nationally and internationally. With respect to air transport there are almost insuperable obstacles which will be analysed further on in this chapter.

As a matter of principle, to apply the same GATT rules to air and surface transport, and other activities such as banking or insurance, would deny the specific characteristics of international aviation. From a practical standpoint, GATT's membership comprises only about two-thirds that of ICAO. Even if a deal covering air transport were reached, it would not be worldwide and would have to be extended to the other countries.

To get round these problems, it has been suggested that instead of bringing air transport into GATT, GATT rules should be applied to the present regulatory system. The International Chamber of Commerce (ICC) has championed this idea through its standing Commission on Air Transport, a group chaired by H.A. Wassenbergh. The ICC approach would involve the inclusion of GATT trading principles in bilateral agreements and in the form of a multilateral framework for international economic air transport regulation. The ICC-Wassenbergh proposal addressed to 'international organisations in civil aviation' looks toward a new regulatory regime governing the economic side of international transport.[29] In other words, the specific characteristics of air transport would be preserved if the GATT rules were administered by existing specialised aviation bodies. The problem with the ICC proposal is that states have steadfastly resisted giving ICAO regulatory authority over economic matters. At best, ICAO could develop guidance material and a model agreement to promote GATT principles in air transport.

A major drawback in applying GATT principles to air transport is that states would have to abide by norms which run counter to several provisions of the Chicago Convention. The GATT norms will therefore require major revisions in the Convention and this in turn will require states to reconcile their conflicting trade and aviation policies.[30]

The key GATT principle in any agreement is the Most Favoured Nation treatment (usually designated as MFN). It requires that any benefits, privileges or concessions by one signatory are automatically and unconditionally extended to all signatories to the agreement. This principle is associated with that of non-discrimination under which any trade restrictions applied by one signatory must also be applied equally to all the others. At their Montreal meeting in 1988, the GATT ministers agreed that the MFN-non discrimination principle should be part of the trade in services agreement but they left open the form and nature of the clause.

The MFN principle is completely alien to air transport. Something similar had been inserted in the Chicago Convention in one of the working drafts in connection with provisions to govern landing fees, airport access and charges, but it was discarded in favour of a non-discrimination provision on airports and similar charges (Article 15) and an exemption provision for customs duties (Article 24). A related principle of non-discrimination between contracting states was written into the objectives of the Organisation (Article 44g). It also governs the International Air Services Transit Agreement with respect to the first two freedoms (non-commercial stopovers). Except for these two freedoms, most impediments to trade in air services stem from regulatory practices which are essentially discriminatory in nature. Bilateral agreements based on reciprocity between two countries may be highly discriminatory towards third-country airlines.[31]

Another GATT principle crucial to the debate is that of National Treatment (NT) which is fairly well understood in a services context. It means that foreign suppliers of services shall be accorded a treatment no less favourable than that accorded to domestic suppliers in the same market. That rule is a familiar one in air transport with respect to airport and other charges (Article 9 of the Chicago Convention) as well as in the way airlines conduct their commercial operations. It certainly does not extend to market access. Given that foreign airlines are normally precluded by law from providing domestic services in virtually all countries, the application of national treatment to domestic markets would entail far-reaching legislative and policy changes.

Another important GATT principle is that of Market Access which relates to offering services in a foreign market affected by entry barriers or special requirements. Market access runs counter to a basic provision in the Chicago Convention under which states must ask each other for permission to operate scheduled services (Article 6). This principle cannot easily be reconciled with bilateral air agreements which define and limit market access in air transport. Limitations on entry and routes to be served, as well as on the type and volume of traffic that may be carried, would be viewed as protectionist barriers for GATT negotiators. As in other industries, there are also important ancillary factors in the way of market access. These include currency conversions, repatriation of funds, access to local distribution channels, ground handling facilities and airport user charges. The biggest impediments to market access are found in the computer reservation systems jointly owned by large airlines.

Finally, as GATT itself recognises, market access is threatened by the scarcity of airports and facilities which, unlike the regulatory constraints governing entry and capacity, cannot be dealt with in the GATT context. Faced with a finite number of airport slots and gates and given the perpetual rights of incumbent airlines to existing facilities, new airlines may find it difficult to gain access to the most attractive foreign markets.[32]

Daniel Kasper points out that the application of GATT principles to air services is fraught with problems that would exacerbate rather than help the bargaining process because of difficulties in extending across the board the commercial rights gained in bilateral negotiations.[33] He brings out the fact that foreign carriers would be granted access to domestic markets on the same terms as local carriers under the National Treatment principle. This would essentially benefit nations with closed domestic markets without expanding access for airlines whose domestic markets have already been deregulated.

The principles of Most Favoured Nation treatment and National Treatment would need to be strictly defined or limited so that liberal trade benefits would not automatically extend to protectionist countries, regardless of how restrictive their markets might be. In effect if GATT rules were to be applied in air transport without restrictions, nations with a closed market would gain access to a deregulated domestic market without having to give up anything in return. Kasper suggests instead a 'conditional MFN' principle which would define a liberal regime and extend it only to those nations prepared to abide by its terms.[34]

It has been suggested that as a start the GATT principles should apply only to so-called 'soft rights', that is the freedom to price, service, communicate and market the services in foreign countries, and that these multilateral rules should become annexes to the Chicago Convention. The more contentious 'hard rights', that is the route and commercial rights, would move gradually from the bilateral to a multilateral framework.[35] The suggestion is a tempting one even if the difficulties in separating such 'soft rights' as computerised reservation systems from the 'hard rights' could complicate and even scuttle the negotiations.

An important principle in GATT is that of transparency. It requires that all trade laws, regulations and administrative guidelines be published and made available to all interested parties. To the extent that states publish their national laws and regulations in air transport and are required, under Article 81 of the Chicago Convention, to register their bilateral agreements with ICAO, one might think that this GATT principle is already applicable. This is not so, because not all agreements are registered. Furthermore, registered bilateral agreements may have been counteracted by confidential arrangements between governments.

While GATT recognises the special needs of the Third World, this is not so much a principle as an acceptance of the fact that the participation of developing countries in the free trade process requires special or preferential treatment. In air transport, such participation is not dealt with by means of preferential market access. If past performance is any indication, there is no reason to expect major aeronautical states to be more generous in their multilateral than in their bilateral negotiations.[36]

GATT allows various safeguards and exemptions under which a signatory, whose producers are severely hit by imports can impose restrictions or suspend a concession. With respect to air transport, a country can only suspend its obligations under the Chicago Convention in case of war or national emergency (Article 89). Other national defence safeguards can be found in bilateral agreements. Many countries consider air transport critical to their national security and require as a condition of licensing that an airline's aircraft be subject to requisition in time of war.

Other concepts could cause concern such as the GATT's dispute settlement mechanism which includes panels of independent experts for consultation and conciliation.[37] It has been found slow and sometimes ineffective and might not be much of an improvement over the bilateral consultation procedures used in air transport.[38]

Outside of the GATT framework, other approaches have been suggested, one being a 'plurilateral' solution which would combine the liberal bilateral air agreements into one multilateral agreement. Wassenbergh, acting as chief negotiator for the Dutch flag carrier KLM, first floated this idea as a 'Bermuda III' agreement in 1980 but without success. He thinks that the plurilateral solution is still a possible alternative but seems more inclined to favour a GATT approach that would do away with the traditional distinction of traffic rights (that is third, fourth and fifth freedom rights).[39]

In the final analysis, a combined multilateral/bilateral framework would seem to be the most logical approach. It would bring the states committed to deregulation into a single market and allow each to deal bilaterally with the other states. Essentially, this would mean reviving and revamping the International Air Transport Agreement which calls for the reciprocal exchange of the five freedoms. This agreement was accepted at the 1944 Chicago Conference but was never given a chance after the US denounced it two years later rather than place its carriers in jeopardy over fifth freedom rights.[40]

Conclusion

The velocity of change is so great in all aspects of science, technology, economics and politics that the tectonic plates of national sovereignty have begun to shift.

Walter Wriston, 'Technology and Sovereignty', *Foreign Affairs*, 67 (2), 1988

As we look beyond the first 50 years in the aviation system, we are faced with many unanswered questions concerning the future of civil aviation. What shall we see by the turn of the century? Will we travel in thousand-ton flying ships and globe-circling hypersonic transport planes? Or will the future airliner be another larger version of the familiar jumbo jet packing more people to more destinations?

Will these aircraft of the future be built by national or multinational corporations? Which of today's airlines will become the mega-carriers of tomorrow? Will they devise their global strategies solely on the basis of profitability or will states be able to enforce rules of competition that take into account the public interest?

How long will the system be able to cope with saturated airways and congested airports? Will the inexorable growth in air travel result in new forms of cooperation leading to the international management of the airspace?

Finally, how will the regulatory system that was instituted some 50 years ago, when there were barely two million passengers, be adapted to the needs of the two billion passengers expected by the end of the century? How will the growth of traffic affect safety? Can the airline industry maintain its enviable record in the face of an overloaded system and the structural and economic changes taking place in air transport? Will financially hard-pressed carriers be tempted to compromise on safety to protect profits? Since safety controls are the responsibility of national authorities, will they be able to keep track of the growing interchange and leasing of aircraft?

While technological developments can be visualised in their broad outline, the political and economic conditions in which air transport will have to operate cannot fit easily in a model. Theoretical models

220

might at best provide some understanding of the interplay of conflicting interests and competing forces but they yield few answers.

Some trends, however, are unmistakable. More and more airlines will become part of conglomerates of interlocking companies owning hotels, car transportation, related services and all-inclusive reservation systems. Mega-carriers will form alliances to improve market penetration and link up with global networks to deny market opportunities to their competitors. These alliances will take the form of joint marketing agreements, shared facilities, code-sharing and equity exchanges. This could lead to an oligopolistic situation in which the largest carriers will carry an increasing share of the total traffic at the expense of smaller airlines, notably those of the developing countries.

There will be fewer flag-carriers operating in this highly competitive environment. Private ownership of airlines will expand although governments will try to retain some influence in management decisions through majority or minority shareholdings. In such diversified multinational ownership, foreign interests, but not necessarily foreign control of airlines, will become commonplace.

Capital markets can be expected to have a growing influence on the way air transport will develop, from the kind of aircraft that will be built to the way they will be sold or leased. Capital markets could also have a growing influence in airline management decisions and strategies. The smaller airlines, particularly those of developing countries, will be hard pressed unless they become part of regional groupings that can pool airline operations and negotiate traffic rights.

Advanced automation technology will play a larger role in all aspects of airline operations and the marketing of services. The most efficient airlines will be those that can use this technology to best advantage to compete effectively around the world. As airport and airways congestion constrains flight operations in the most travelled regions of the world, governments will be forced to take concerted action to manage the flow of traffic. Bilateral agreements will give way to regional and multilateral negotiations on the disposition of commercial rights and the opening of new international routes.

Looking to the immediate future, air transport will require new forms of international cooperation. Whether ICAO's contracting states will respond to the challenge depends on their willingness to sacrifice some of their sacred sovereign rights. The expansion of air transport on the global scale with ever-increasing traffic densities has brought about problems which must be solved through new multilateral mechanisms. As a first step, states must decide on the management of a global navigation system that meets the needs of the aviation community without restrictions. In the longer term, states will be facing responsibilities of much greater political significance involving the allocation of sovereign rights in the control and management of the airspace.

This will be a daunting challenge since international agencies are not geared to assume activities that impinge on national sovereignty. Air transport by its very nature should have been a counterforce to nationalism. Yet, the regulatory system in civil aviation is still as firmly rooted in the principle of national sovereignty as when it was first proclaimed at the Paris Convention of 1919 and reaffirmed in the Chicago Convention. Sovereignty over the airspace has remained the cornerstone of relations between states in all aspects of air transport.

Article 1 of the Convention has also been responsible for restricting the authority of ICAO as an intergovernmental regulatory agency. For all its extensive activities, the Organisation has only limited authority. It sets standards but cannot enforce them. It devises solutions but cannot impose them. It has drafted conventions but is powerless to deal with states that fail to live up to their provisions. To implement its rules ICAO must rely on the goodwill of states rather than legal requirements. A major restriction on its activities is the fact that it is not allowed to exercise any kind of regulatory authority in the field of economics which remains the sole prerogative of sovereign states.

This book has concentrated on ICAO as the centrepiece of the international system, and on various issues which affect its regulatory tasks. Aside from summations in the previous chapters, one can draw some overall conclusions. First, whatever the expectations its founders may have had on its role as a functional agency, ICAO is a political body. It could not be otherwise given the nature of civil aviation. ICAO was created as the result of a political act. It reflects the policies and objectives of the large aeronautical states which control its decision-making process. The important decisions of its governing body may be justified on technical, economic or legal grounds. They are nevertheless political decisions which cannot be separated from their political context.

ICAO has shown that it can deal pragmatically with conflicts within areas of its competence but it is ill-equipped to resolve issues which are outside its mandate. Unlike the United Nations, it does not have the necessary constitutional safeguards to avoid being manoeuvred into impossible situations. Fortunately, the Organisation has been spared the ideological conflicts which have disrupted the work and threatened the very existence of other agencies in the UN system. But international agencies are not stable political bodies. As long as states bring extraneous political issues before ICAO's governing bodies, there is always the danger that the Organisation may be overwhelmed by problems which belong to the political organs of the United Nations. Political wisdom dictates a policy of restraint to avoid unnecessary dissension that would erode ICAO's usefulness and risk in the long run to undermine its credibility.

Secondly, although ICAO was created to oversee the orderly development of civil aviation, it cannot live up to the task because it was never granted authority commensurate with its responsibility. As a result, it cannot provide leadership on the critical issues affecting the future of air transport, and its voice is too faint to be heard. The most important developments in air transport are taking place outside the sway of ICAO in such a way that it cannot shape their outcome.

While ICAO has been successful in its field of technical competence precisely because of its limited assignment, the major challenges facing the Organisation will come as the result of the gradual breakdown of the regulatory system. Global issues in air transport can no longer be dealt with at the bilateral level. ICAO therefore remains the only viable institutional framework in which states can work out new rules.

While ICAO does not have a specific mandate to regulate the economic aspects of air transport, nothing in the Chicago Convention prevents it from assuming such a role. ICAO's mandate, according to Article 44, is to 'insure the safe and orderly growth of international civil aviation throughout the world'; to 'meet the needs of the peoples of the world for safe, regular, efficient and economical air transport' and to 'prevent economic waste caused by unreasonable competition'. Based on a broad interpretation of these objectives, the Organisation cannot fulfil its mission without addressing the economic and regulatory issues which stand in the way of the efficient and economic use of air transport.

When substantive economic issues were raised in the past, the majority view held that such matters should be left to IATA and bilateral negotiations. These arguments are no longer valid. The Chicago Conference left the door open for ICAO's involvement in such issues; the various unsuccessful efforts to put them on ICAO's agenda do not alter that fact. According to Article 66 of the Chicago Convention, it was even foreseen that ICAO would carry out 'the functions placed upon it by the International Air Transport Agreement' if it came ever into force.

It makes little sense to assert that economic problems will embroil ICAO in national policies. This is already the case for certain issues such as noise restrictions. As part of a broad mandate, the Organisation would be concerned with political issues which fall within its purview. Admittedly, this will require a drastic reversal in the attitude of states towards ICAO. As a start, ICAO's contracting states will need to give the Organisation a new sense of purpose. ICAO has been relegated to the back seat for so long that it cannot be thrust overnight into the driver's seat without being given a clear sense of direction.

Like other agencies of the same generation, ICAO's effectiveness has also been hampered by bureaucratic reflexes and by its set ways. It reacts to situations rather than anticipates them. It lacks the tools and the staff to study problems in depth. But what ICAO needs above all is a compelling vision of the future and where it fits into the new aviation environment.

It is almost 50 years since the international community set the foundation of the international system in civil aviation. Profound political, economic and technological changes have taken place in air transport. Throughout that time, the development of international aviation has been sustained by the strong commitment of states in building a global network of routes and facilities. The Chicago Convention is living proof that states can work together to make air transport a safe mode of travel. They must now show the same determination in solving the more contentious issues so that the airline which has long served the exclusive interests of states can become 'the chosen instrument' of their common interests.

Notes and References

INTRODUCTION

1. Andreas Lowenfeld, 'A New Take-off for International Air Transport', *Foreign Affairs*, 54(4), October 1975, p. 47.
2. A simple definition of a system is that offered by Robert Gregg and Michael Bakin: 'a political system is simply presumed to exist . . . wherever and whenever a group of actors are caught up in a nexus of relationships, both conflictual and cooperative, generated by common problems and the need to deal with them'. *The United Nations System and its Functions* (Princeton: D. Van Nostrand, 1968) p. 4. Systems and regimes are often used interchangeably. In this book, however, a regime refers more specifically to 'a set of principles, norms, rules and decision-making procedures around which actors' expectations converge in a given issue-area', as defined in Stephen Krasner (ed.), *International Regimes* (Ithaca: Cornell University Press, 1983) p. 2.
3. This is borne out in an extensive analysis by James Rosenau of textbooks in international relations used in the US. Of 29 institutions listed, those most frequently mentioned are the United Nations, UNESCO, WHO, ILO, FAO and the IAEA. ICAO, ITU, IMO and OMM are not mentioned once. *The Study of Global Institutions* (New York: Nichols Publishing, 1980) pp. 289–92.
4. John C. Garnett, *Common Sense and the Theory of International Politics* (London: Macmillan, 1984) p. 1.
5. Inis Claude, *Swords into Plowshares* (New York: Random House, 1956) p. 7.

1: THE CHICAGO CONFERENCE REVISITED

1. For an authoritative analysis of early conventions, see Duane Freer (at the time Director of ICAO's Air Navigation Bureau) in the *ICAO Bulletin*, April, May, June 1986.
2. Christer Jönsson, 'Sphere of Flying: The Politics of International Aviation', *International Organization*, 35 (2), 1981, p. 281.
3. For all practical purposes, Pan American Airways had become the dominant American flag carrier as the result of the exclusive concessions which Juan Trippe, Pan Am's chief executive, had wrangled from various countries, substituting private contracts for bilateral agreements with Washington's acquiescence. By 1939, Pan Am had become the largest international carrier, covering 38 countries.

(Jacqueline Dutheil de la Rochère, *La Politique des Etats-Unis en matière d'aviation civile* (Paris: Librairie de Droit et de Jurisprudence, 1971) pp. 30–6.

4. Henry Wallace, 'What Will We get out of the War', *American Magazine*, February 1943, and Wendell Willkie, *One World* (New York: Simon & Schuster, 1943).

5. Thirty-First Wilbur Wright Memorial Lecture, London, 1943. Warner Papers, ICAO.

6. Adolf A. Berle, *Navigating the Rapids: From the Papers of Adolf A. Berle*, edited by Bishop Berle and Travis Beal Jacobs (New York: Harcourt, Brace Jovanovich, 1973) p. 510.

7. Ibid., p. 481.

8. *Foreign Relations of the United States* (1943 Conferences at Washington and Quebec) pp. 679–81. Hereafter cited as *FRUS* with year, volume and page.

9. *FRUS* (1944), 2:360–2.

10. Warren F. Kimball (ed.), *Churchill and Roosevelt: The Complete Correspondence*, 3 vols (Princeton: Princeton University Press, 1984), vol. 2, p. 451.

11. *FRUS* (1944), 2:403–4 and 420.

12. Winston Churchill, *Triumph and Tragedy* (Boston: Houghton, Mifflin, 1953) p. 702.

13. Berle, op. cit., p. 496.

14. *Great Britain Parliament*, 'International Air Transport', Command 6561, October 1944 (London: HMSO).

15. Editorial, *Aeroplane*, 22 December 1944.

16. *FRUS* (1944), 2:571–2. The Soviet Union formally ratified the Chicago Convention in 1970 although it had always abided by international aviation rules.

17. Steven Eli Shanes, *International Cooperation in Civil Aviation 1945–1947*, doctoral thesis, Cornell University, 1949, p. 5.

18. *US Department of State: Proceedings of the International Civil Aviation Conference*, Chicago, November-December 1944, 2 vols (Washington: 1948). Vol. 1, pp. 42–3 and pp. 55–62. Hereafter cited as *Proceedings*.

19. 'Chicago Bargaining', 2 December 1944.

20. Betsy Gidwitz, *The Politics of International Air Transport* (Lexington, Mass.: D.C. Heath, 1980) pp. 48–9.

21. Berle, op. cit., pp. 501–2.

22. Ibid., p. 503.

23. According to Anthony Sampson, the concession was the result of 'a historic British muddle'. Sir Peter Masefield, an adviser to Lord Beaverbrook, who later became minister of civil aviation, recalled that conflicting instructions were sent to Chicago. Anthony Sampson, *Empires of the Sky: The Politics, Contests and Cartels of World Airlines* (London: Hodder & Stoughton, 1984) p. 68.

24. *FRUS* (1944), 2:584.

25. Ibid., pp. 585–6.

26. Ibid., p. 589 and Kimball, op. cit., vol. 3, p. 407.

27. *FRUS* (1944), 2:590–2.

28. *Proceedings*, 1:445ff.
29. *FRUS* (1944), 2:594–5.
30. As cited by Duane Freer (formerly Director of the ICAO Air Navigation Bureau), *ICAO Bulletin*, September 1986.
31. *FRUS* (1944), 2:597.
32. Kimball, op. cit., vol. 3, p. 428.
33. Berle's report to the President, *FRUS* (1944), 2:608.
34. Berle had been under intense pressure from the media for giving away too much. The strongest critic was the *Chicago Tribune* which supported Trippe's views.
35. Berle, op. cit., p. 510.
36. *FRUS* (1944), 2:612.
37. *IATA: The First Three Decades*, IATA publication, Montreal 1949.
38. Telegram dated 6 December 1944, *FRUS* (1944), 2:598. The Germans were putting up a stiff resistance in Italy at the time and blocking Canadian and British troops approaching the Rhine.
39. R.L. Thornton, *International Airlines and Politics: A Study in Adaptation to Change* (Ann Arbor: Michigan International Business Studies No. 13, 1970), p. 34.
40. Dutheil de la Rochère, op. cit., p. 312.
41. Kimball, op. cit., vol. 3, pp. 519–20 and pp. 566–7.
42. *An Introduction to Airline Economics*, 4th edn (New York: Praeger, 1989) p. 43.
43. ICAO Doc. AT-WP/772.
44. K.G.J. Pillai, *The Air Net: The Case Against World Aviation Cartel* (New York: Grossman, 1949) p. 125.
45. Ibid.
46. ICAO Doc. AR-WP/Min LI 5, 20 April 1964.
47. Response by ICAO to a questionnaire from the Group of Negotiations on Services (GATT), 1988.
48. See Chapter 2.
49. Christer Jönsson, *International Aviation and the Politics of Regime Change*, (London: Frances Pinter, 1987) p. 121.
50. Pillai, op. cit., p. 36.
51. Gidwitz, op. cit., p. 96.
52. ICAO Circular 215-AT/85, 1989.
53. Joan Feldman, 'IATA Moves from Controversy toward Trade Association', *Air Transport World*, December 1987. See also Chapter 11.
54. The state was Franco's Spain. See Chapter 3.
55. Michael Milde, 'The Chicago Convention after 40 Years', *The Annals of Air and Space Law*, IX, 1984.
56. See Chapter 7.

2: FROM THE DC-3 TO HYPERSONIC FLIGHT

1. Because of different requirements in various parts of the world, ICAO convenes meetings periodically in each of its nine regions to plan the facilities and services which are essential for the safety of civil aviation. The regional plans are reviewed by the Air Navigation Commission and adopted by the Council to be implemented by the states concerned in each region. The regional plans when taken together constitute an integrated worldwide air navigation system.

2. Twenty-two governments are parties to these joint agreements which cover air traffic control, communications and meteorological services for flights over the North Atlantic.

3. R.R. Shaw, 'Are We Investing in Our Intellect for the Future?', *IATA Review*, July-September 1987, p. 3.

4. For an analysis of technological changes on the airlines, see Doganis Regas, *Flying Off Course: the Economics of International Airlines* (London: Allen & Unwin, 1985) pp. 3–5.

5. States and airport operators were fearful that many of their newly laid runways and ramps would become obsolete for jumbo jets the same way as the facilities built in the 1950s for prop-driven aircraft became inadequate when the first jets entered service.

6. The ILS (instrument landing system) has been the standard landing aid since the 1950s. Its main handicap is that its single narrow approach forces aircraft to line up, single file, and land in turn. The MLS (microwave landing system) provides a wider approach and operates on much higher frequencies than the ILS.

7. It had been estimated that the capital required for satellite systems would be in the order of $5 to $6 billion and that nearly half of it would have to be borne by the aircraft operators. Dr R.R. Shaw, 'Satellite Technology and Civil Aviation', *IATA Review*, April-June 1984, p. 8.

8. INMARSAT was created in 1976 as an intergovernmental, commercially-orientated organisation to provide maritime satellite communications. It amended its charter in 1985 to provide satellite services to aeronautical as well as maritime users.

9. A short summary of the agreement is contained in ICAO Doc. FANS (Paris) WG/2 WP/19, 7 April 1989.

10. Andrew H. Malcolm, 'Aviation Experts Warn of Gridlock at U.S. Airports', *The New York Times*, 19 June 1988.

11. See 'Airport Congestion – A Special Report', *ICAO Bulletin*, January 1989.

12. *The Economic Situation in Air Transport – 1978 to the Year 2000*, ICAO Circular 222-AT/90, 1989, p. 42.

13. State of the Air Transport Industry 1988, presentation of the annual report by the Director General of IATA, Montreal, 31 October–1 November 1988.

14. As cited by Marion Cotter, 'Traffic May Cripple European Decontrol', *The Journal of Commerce*, 21 June 1988.

15. Various meetings to map new routes have been held at the Bangkok regional office of ICAO. The most direct route for the B747–400 would be across the Soviet Union and Mongolia.

16. Airlines would be charged hefty fees for the use of Soviet airspace since the USSR is not a signatory to the International Air Services Transit Agreement.

17. Changes in the separation minima are being considered by a special ICAO panel based on studies and evaluations being carried out in Canada, Western Europe, the US and the USSR. *Annual Report of the Council – 1988*, p. 46.

18. Pilots have been at odds with the airlines over this issue since 1966 when IFALPA successfully delayed the introduction of reduced separation standards over the North Atlantic until proven operationally safe. It has insisted on thorough statistical research every time the question has come up.

19. Richard Witkin, 'Airlines Ordered to Install Devices to Avert Collisions', *The New York Times*, 6 January 1989, and 'Testing Urged for Airliner Safety Device', *The New York Times*, 24 February 1989; Susan Carey, 'Europeans Perturbed by US Pressure to Install Aircraft-Collision Protection', *Wall Street Journal*, 28 June 1989. The FAA concedes that its rule has ruffled some feathers. 'Some countries have raised arguments that the US is jumping ahead by unilaterally imposing this regulation on foreign carriers', says Joseph Del Balzo, the FAA's executive director of system development. But he says that argument pales before the system's safety advantages. (Carey, ibid.).

20. The US government already heavily committed in spending $16 billion to complete the National Airspace System Plan designed to modernise air traffic control opposes efforts by the airline industry to use the $5.6 billion surplus in the Airport and Airways Trust Fund for airport expansion. The fund, financed largely by the eight per cent tax on tickets, has been allowed to accumulate in order not to increase the federal deficit. 'FAA Seeks More Airports to Lessen Congestion', *Wall Street Journal*, 26 August 1987.

21. Report of the President of the Council, ICAO Doc. WP/7960, 18 February 1985; *Interavia Airletter* no. 11,274, 25 June 1987, reports that pilots have had to cope with unchecked beacons and malfunctioning approach radars at Nigerian airports and that this probably accounts for the fact that there are on average two near-misses a day.

22. 'The Airport Straitjacket', *Airline Business*, April 1988, p. 25.

23. The overall coordination will be managed by EUROCONTROL, the agency originally set up in 1963 to oversee air traffic control in Western Europe. However, the agency will not be able to control European airspace as a single entity since each country retains national sovereignty over its airspace.

24. The commercial jet era started in May 1952 when the British-designed Comet 1 was introduced on the London-Johannesburg route. In 1954, disaster struck when two Comets went down. The aircraft was with-

drawn from service. Investigation revealed that the accidents had been caused by metal fatigue.

25. Address to the 21st Technical Conference of IATA, in Montreal (September 1987).

26. LaFond, *The Shape of Things to Come*, ICAO Public Information Office.

27. *Fleet Renewal and Investment in Airport Infrastructure*, ICAO Doc. A27-WP/48, p. 2 (7 July 1989).

28. See R. Daley, *An American Saga: Juan Trippe and His Pan Am Empire* (New York: Random House, 1980) p. 432. Trippe's biggest contribution to aviation was the support he gave to the development of the 747 jumbo jet in the mid-1960s when Pan American was still the most influential airline in the world. Flushed with the success of his 707, Bill Allen, then president of Boeing, was thinking of a larger version. Trippe persuaded Allen to build the 747 by agreeing that Pan American would buy and operate twenty-five of the aircraft.

29. See S. Wheatcroft, *Air Transport Policy* (London: Michael Joseph, 1984) p. 50. In this pioneering study of the aviation industry, Wheatcroft has shown the strong linkage between government-subsidised manufacturers and government-owned airlines. He quotes a British airline executive to the effect that less frequent replacements of transport aircraft by new and more advanced designs is likely to help rather than hinder the healthy economic progress of the airlines.

30. These statistics from the US Department of Commerce and Dow Jones News Service are cited in Helen V. Milner and David B. Yoffie, 'Strategic Trade Policy and Corporate Trade Demands', *International Organization*, 43 (2), 1989, p. 257.

31. See 'The National Interest', *Flight International*, 14 August 1982. Frank Borman, the chairman of Eastern, was quoted as telling his employees: 'If you do not kiss the French flag every time you see it, at least salute it. The export financing on our Airbus deal subsidized this airline by more than $100 million'.

32. See generally 'Europe Forging New Alliances for Civil Aircraft Production', *Aviation Week & Space Technology*, 27 July 1987, and 'Competitive Gambit', editorial in the same publication, 3 August 1987.

33. Editorial, *Aviation Week & Space Technology*, 3 August 1987.

34. The report was prepared by the Center for High Speed Commercial Flight at Battelle, Ohio. See *Aviation Week & Space Technology*, 21 November 1988.

35. Deborah Wise, 'Europe Looks Beyond the Concorde', *The New York Times*, 12 September 1988.

36. *Annual Report of the Council–1988* (ICAO Doc. 9530), p. 38.

37. Between 1979 and 1983 the financial losses of IATA members amounted to over $6 billion. (ICAO Doc. A–26 WP/73)

38. Knut Hammarskjöld (former IATA Director General), Lloyds of London Press International Civil Aviation Conference, New York, April 1980.

39. Special Air Transport Conference, Information Paper 3, 1977.

40. See Howard Banks, *The Rise and Fall of Freddie Laker* (London: Faber & Faber, 1982).
41. Hammarskjöld, Address to Freight Seminar, Gothenburg, March 1977.
42. Andreas F. Lowenfeld, 'A New Take-Off for International Air Transport', *Foreign Affairs*, October 1975, p. 44.
43. Christer Jönsson, *International Aviation and the Politics of Regime Change* (London: Frances Pinter, 1987) p. 36.
44. John F. Brindley, 'U.S. Air Transport Policy', *INTERAVIA*, 5/1979, p. 428.
45. The last time ICAO dealt with regulatory issues in air transport pursuant of a resolution of the first ICAO Interim Assembly was in Geneva in 1947.
46. 'First International Air Transport Meeting in Three Decades Sought Multilateral Solutions for Critical Areas', *ICAO Bulletin*, July 1977.
47. Brindley, above, note 44.
48. Jönsson, op. cit., p. 124.
49. Lowenfeld, *Aviation Law* (New York: Matthew Bender, 1981) Section 5–111.
50. Ibid.
51. See paper presented by the Secretary General *Unilateral Measures which Affect Air Transport* AT-Conf/3 WP/3. Several airlines were particularly concerned about the application of US antitrust laws to the way they could conduct business as the result of a Show Cause Order which would have lifted antitrust immunity for all IATA-approved tariffs. See Jönsson, op. cit., Chapter 7. As a result IATA tariff conferences had been paralysed and some of them had to be cancelled at the last minute. After a lengthy review, the Department of Transport issued an order saying it would accept procedural changes made by IATA as satisfactory to maintain antitrust immunity and clarifying under what conditions the DOT would retroactively rescind such immunity in cases of specific violations of an IATA agreement (DOT Order 88–6–9 of 9 June 1988).
52. Paul Stephen Dempsey, 'The Role of the International Civil Aviation Organization on Deregulation, Discrimination and Dispute Resolution', *Journal of Air Law and Commerce*, (52) 1987, p. 541. The report of the Conference is contained in ICAO Doc. 9470 (1985).
53. See *Developments on Trade in Services*, ICAO Doc. AT-WP/1543, June 1988.
54. Chris Lyle, 'Computer-Age Vulnerability in the International Airline Industry', *Journal of Air Law and Commerce*, (54) 1988, p. 177. On the ICAO study see ICAO Doc. A27-WP/50 EC/11 and Circular 214-AT/84- *Guidance Material on the Regulation of Computer Reservation Systems*. See also Vladimir D. Zubkov (Director of the ICAO Air Transport Bureau), 'The Development of Computer Reservation Systems: the ICAO Viewpoint', *ITA Magazine*, March/April 1987.
55. Lyle, above, note 54.
56. ICAO Doc. AT-WP/1543. GATT designates both the General Agreement on Tariffs and Trade which governs the trade in goods and

the Geneva-based organisation which oversees the GATT rules. The negotiations on trade in services are separate from those on the trade in goods. See Chapter 12 for GATT and air transport issues.

57. ICAO Doc. A27-Min EC/3, 28 September 1989.
58. Duane Freer, 'New Problems Arise, Old Ones Return', *ICAO Bulletin*, January 1987. Freer was Director of the Air Navigation Bureau at ICAO at the time of the article.
59. Lowenfeld, *Aviation Law*, Section 5–111.

3: ICAO IN THE UNITED NATIONS CONTEXT

1. Inis L. Claude, *Swords Into Plowshares* (London: University of London Press, 1966) p. ix.
2. Leland M. Goodrich and David A. Kay (eds), *International Organization: Politics and Process* (Madison: University of Wisconsin Press, 1973) p. xx.
3. As expressed in the introduction to a volume of essays by David Pitt and Thomas G. Weiss (eds), *The Nature of United Nations Bureaucracies* (London: Croom Helm, 1986), p. xi.
4. Paul Taylor and A.J.R. Groom (eds), *International Organization* (London: Frances Pinter, 1978), especially Chapter II by Anthony J.N. Judge which deals specifically with problems of classifying international organisations. It is usual to distinguish between three types of international organisation, namely intergovernmental organisations, international non-governmental organisations and multinational enterprises. Intergovernmental organisations with which we are concerned are basically defined as: (a) being based on a formal agreement between governments of nation-states; (b) including three or more states parties to the agreement; and (c) possessing a permanent secretariat performing ongoing tasks.

    A concrete and comprehensive definition of the term 'international organisation' was given some 40 years ago by Sir Gerald Fitzmaurice: 'The term international organisation means a collectivity of states established by treaty, with a constitution and common organs, having a personality distinct from that of its member states, and being a subject of international law with treaty-making capacity'. (Fitzmaurice, *Report on the Law of Treaties*, UN Doc. A/CN.4/101, page 104.
5. Mahdi Elmandjra, *The United Nations System: An Analysis* (London: Faber & Faber, 1973) p. 34.
6. Leon Gordenker (ed.), *The United Nations in International Politics* (New Jersey: Princeton University Press, 1971) p. 152.
7. Ibid.
8. This realist view has been expressed among others by Hans J. Morgenthau, 'The Yardstick of National Interest', *The Annals of the Amer-*

ican Academy of Political and Social Science, 296 (November 1954) p. 79.

9. Claude, op. cit., p. 373.
10. James A. Caparaso, *Functionalism and Regional Integration* (Beverly Hills: Sage Publications, 1972) p. 25.
11. Elmandjra, op. cit., p. 319.
12. Gerald Fitzgerald, Lecture notes, McGill University Air and Space Law Institute.
13. Jacob Schenkman, *International Civil Aviation Organization* (Geneva: Librairie E. Droz, 1955) pp. 5–6. Claims that travel contributes to peace still crop up in ICAO statements and speeches on special observances like UN Day.
14. Quincy Wright, *Problems of Stability and Progress in International Relations* (Berkeley: University of California Press, 1954) p. 302. A similar opinion was expressed in more pungent terms by Sir William Hildred (late Director General of IATA): 'I can't say that aviation has done anything to promote friendship and understanding. The nations still compete as much as ever, and I'll tell you why: when human beings are crowded like rats, they fight like rats'. As quoted in Anthony Sampson, *Empires of the Sky: The Politics, Contests and Cartels of World Airlines* (London: Hodder & Stoughton, 1984) p. 229.
15. Claude, op. cit., p. 396.
16. ECOSOC Document E/183, 27 September 1946.
17. From a legal point of view, it was by no means easy for ICAO to comply with the conditions imposed by the UN General Assembly because Spain had already ratified the Convention. The ICAO Assembly might conceivably have invalidated the Spanish instrument of ratification. The Assembly did not take this step. Instead, it proceeded on the assumption that Spain had become a contracting state and that an amendment to the Convention was necessary to comply with the condition imposed by the General Assembly. Thomas Buergenthal, *Lawmaking in the International Civil Aviation Organization* (Syracuse: Syracuse University Press, 1969) p. 40.
18. ICAO Doc. 7325 (C/852) Resolution A1–3.
19. As cited in Schenkman, op. cit., p. 136.
20. For the text of the amendment see the appendixes (Chicago Convention).
21. R.Y. Jennings, 'Some Aspects of the International Law of the Air', *Recueil des Cours de l'Académie de Droit International de La Haye*, 1949, II, vol. 75, p. 509. Actually, there has been no instance of a rejection by the General Assembly of a membership application to ICAO.
22. Ibid.
23. ICAO Doc. A1-CP/17, 8 May 1947.
24. Statement by the Spanish Delegation, ICAO Document 7325 (C/852), p. 127.
25. Resolution 386 (V), UN Resolutions.
26. Schenkman, op. cit., p. 140.

27. Buergenthal, op. cit., p. 42.
28. Strictly speaking, according to Peter Calvacoressi, it is doubtful whether the measures envisaged in these articles ought properly to be called sanctions since it has been argued that the only true sanctions prescribed by the Charter are expulsion from the Organisation (Article 6) and loss of voting rights (Article 19). Peter Calvacoressi, 'The Politics of Sanctions: The League and the United Nations' in *Sanctions Against South Africa, Report of an International Conference on Economic Sanctions Against South Africa*, London, 1964 (Baltimore, Md: Penguin Books, 1964) p. 53.
29. Ibid., p. 57.
30. Letter of 30 March 1966 to the UN Secretary General (UN Doc.A/6294, 1966). Under Article 5 of the Chicago Convention, each contracting state accords to aircraft engaged in non-scheduled services of other states, rights of transit and stops for non-traffic purposes without prior permission.
31. Malcolm Fraser and Olesegun Obosanjo (co-chairmen of the Commonwealth Group of Eminent Persons), 'What to Do about South Africa', *Foreign Affairs*, 65, 1, (Fall 1986) pp. 158–9.
32. ICAO Doc. A–26-MIN EX/10.
33. ICAO Doc. 8522 (A15-EX/43) and ICAO Doc. 8516 (A15 P/5).
34. Resolution A18–4 (18th Session of the Assembly).
35. Resolution A21–6 (21st Session of the Assembly).
36. It has been argued that, since Article 93 *bis* calls for the 'termination of membership' of the Organisation only, a state expelled in accordance with its provisions could still continue to be a party to the remainder of the Convention, thereby maintaining the rights accorded to it by Article 5. Since South Africa has not ratified the amendment which introduced Article 93 *bis*, it could also be argued that, at least as regards her international aviation relationships with other states which similarly refrain from ratifying the amendment, the terms of the Convention will still be considered to be applicable *per se*. Elizabeth R. Dutkiewicz, 'Applicability and Effect of International Civil Aviation Conventions in Southern Africa', *South African Yearbook of International Law*, vol. 4, (1978) p. 82.
37. Major airlines flying to Johannesburg include British Airways, UTA, KLM, Lufthansa, Iberia, Olympic, Alitalia, Sabena and Swissair. Many flights between Europe and Johannesburg are routed via Nairobi, Kenya, a nation that bars overflights or landing rights by SAA but tolerates en-route flights by European carriers. Other such African countries allowing air services to South Africa include Cape Verde, Comoros, Congo, Gabon, Malawi, Mauritius, Mozambique, Zaire, Zambia, Zimbabwe and the Ivory Coast which is the latest country to be linked by direct air flights. South Africa has built a flourishing trade with these countries.
38. Thornton has argued that had the African states bargained for traffic rights for their own airlines rather than limiting their efforts to political gains, they would have gained substantial advantages and traffic rights since South Africa would have had to pay a high price to

overfly the continent. Robert L. Thornton, *International Airlines and Politics – A Study in Adaptation to Change* (Ann Arbor, Mich., 1970) p. 118.

39. James Brooke, 'Pretoria Lends Helping Hand to Friends with Big Airstrips', *The New York Times*, 21 October 1987, p. A12.
40. ICAO Country Files (Lesotho).
41. ICAO Doc. C-WP/5469, 74th Session of the Council.
42. Ibid.
43. The problem was a real Chinese puzzle. If the People's Republic of China is the only party to the Chicago Convention, the second instrument of ratification deposited by the Republic of China would have to be considered as 'accession' by a new state which was not a signatory of the Chicago Convention; thus both the People's Republic of China and the Republic of China would be parties to the Chicago Convention. If on the other hand, the Republic of China is the only party and has effectively exercised the rights and duties of its membership in ICAO, then the People's Republic of China would have to accede to the Chicago Convention as a new member of ICAO.
44. ICAO was one of the first specialised agencies to act. There were some delays in other agencies because procedures vary and because China was selective in its choice of institutions. In a number of cases, China simply refused to follow up on the action taken by the agencies (ILO, IAEA and GATT).
45. For all the formality of the occasion, the protest was handwritten on paper without a letterhead.
46. ICAO Registry Files.
47. Donald E. Fink, 'Diplomatic Status Poses ICAO Dilemma', *Aviation Week & Space Technology*, 3 July 1978.
48. At the same time, the People's Republic of China notified ICAO that it recognised the signature of the Chicago Convention in 1944 and the ratification of that Convention in 1946 by the then Government of China. It also came to an agreement with ICAO on the level of its assessment taking into account the accumulated arrears.
49. Houshang Ameri, *Politics and Process in the Specialized Agencies of the United Nations* (Aldershot: Gower, 1982) p. 53.
50. Elmandjra, op. cit., p. 116.
51. Ibid., p. 115.
52. The two most important studies are those of Robert Jackson. 'A Study of the Capacity of the United Nations Development System', vol. 1, (Geneva: United Nations, 1969); Madhi Elmandjra, op. cit. and Maurice Bertrand, 'Some Reflections on Reform of the United Nations', (JIU/REP/85/9, 1985). See also Victor-Yves Ghébali, 'Réflections sur les activités opérationnelles des Nations Unies', *Etudes Internationales* 17 (4), 1985, and with respect to ICAO, E. Sochor, 'International Civil Aviation and the Third World: How Fair is the System?', *Third World Quarterly* 10, Summer 1988.
53. Milton J. Esman and Daniel J. Cleever, *The Common Aid Effort* (Ohio State University Press, 1967) p. 29.

54. ICAO's relations with other agencies are reviewed in E. Sochor, 'The United Nations After 40 Years', *ICAO Bulletin*, October 1985.
55. See the issue of the *International Journal* on 'The Politics of International Communications', XLII, 2, Spring 1987.
56. Thomas L. McPhail and Brenda McPhail, 'The International Politics of Telecommunications: Resolving the North-South Dilemma', ibid.
57. Ameri, op. cit., pp. 83–4.
58. See Chapters 7 and 8.
59. Claude, op. cit., p. 396.
60. Abba Eban, *The New Diplomacy* (New York: Random House, 1983) pp. 277–8.
61. ICAO Doc. 8516, A/15 P5, Appendix, p. 17.
62. As cited by the United Kingdom delegate at the 26th Session of the ICAO Assembly (A26/MIN EX/10, pp. 148–9).
63. Gordenker, op. cit., p. 153.

4: DECISION-MAKING IN ICAO

1. Robert W. Cox and Harold K. Jacobson, *The Anatomy of Influence: Decision-Making in International Organization* (New Haven: Yale University Press, 1973) pp. 5–6.
2. Ibid., p. 371.
3. Christopher T. Tourtellot, 'Membership Criteria for the ICAO Council: A Proposal for Reform', *Denver Journal of International Law and Policy*, 11 (1), Fall 1982, p. 56.
4. According to the Instrument for the amendment of the Constitution of the ILO adopted by the IL Conference on 24 June 1986, subject to ratifications, the ILO Director General will be appointed by the Governing Body, subject to approval by the IL Conference.
5. Whatever the criteria, these states also rank as major powers on the basis of indicators used by Cox and Jacobson (that is, Gross National Product, per capita GNP, population, nuclear capability and prestige). Cox and Jacobson, op. cit. Appendix A, pp. 437–43.
6. Tourtellot, op. cit., p. 62.
7. Tourtellot, op. cit., p. 63.
8. Although the rules relating to the elections of the Council were modified in 1962, the following have been applied since the Organisation came into being: (i) the election is held in three parts corresponding to the three categories of states described in Article 50(b); (ii) before every election the Assembly decides the maximum number of states to be elected in each part; (iii) the candidate decides in which part to run and if unsuccessful is allowed to run in the second and, if again unsuccessful, in the last part (iv) voting in each part of the election is by secret ballot and a majority of the votes cast is required.
9. Tourtellot, op. cit., p. 61.

10. *Verbatim Minutes of Final Plenary Session, December 7, Proceedings of the International Civil Aviation Conference,* Chicago, 1944, vol. 1 (Washington: US Government Printing Office, 1948, pp. 104–11).
11. Tourtellot, op. cit., p. 59.
12. Tourtellot, op. cit., p. 74. He advocates the abolition of the seats in Category 2 to make more room for representation in the other categories without increasing the size of the Council. Category 1 would remain more or less as it is, except that it would comprise two subdivisions: states pre-eminent in the aeronautical industry and those in air transport. The other category of states would reflect geographic diversity.
13. Thomas Buergenthal, *Law Making in International Civil Aviation Organization* (Syracuse: Syracuse University Press, 1969) p. 9.
14. See Chapter 7.
15. ICAO Doc. 3088, C/382, 1947, p. 2.
16. ICAO Doc. A10-WP/5.
17. Paul Koring, 'Vote Ends Western Domination: Indian to Head U.N. Aviation Group', *Toronto Globe and Mail,* 9 March 1988. Actually, Yves Lambert lost by only one vote and might have made it were it not that Argentina switched its position in the last balloting. According to Argentinian press reports, Argentina, one of two Latin American countries which supported him, sent conflicting instructions to its Council member and in the end was swayed to vote for the Indian candidate because both countries belong to the Group of 16 for Peace and Nuclear Disarmament.
18. Denyse Harari and Jorge Garcia Bouza, *Permanence and Innovation: the Nature of United Nations Bureaucracy* (London: Croom Helm, 1986) p. 43.
19. See 'The Role of Personnel Policy in the Present Crisis of the Organizations of the U.N. System', paper prepared by Roger Barnes (executive secretary of the International Civil Service Commission) for the David Davies Memorial Institute in the UK, 1985.
20. Thomas F. Franck, *Nations Against Nation* (New York: Oxford University Press, 1985) p. 114.
21. Ibid., p. 115.
22. Council Minutes C-Min 124/13, 5 October 1988.
23. Ibid.
24. James Rosenau, *Interdependence and Transnational Relations* (New York: Nichols, 1980) p. 1.
25. Menachem Sheffy, 'The Air Navigation Commission of the International Civil Aviation Organization', *Journal of Air Law and Commerce,* 25(3), Summer 1958, p. 440.
26. Philip J. Klass, 'ICAO Group Picks U.S. Landing System', *Aviation Week & Space Technology,* 24 April 1978.
27. The secret ballot was proposed by France and defended strongly by the UK and other supporters of the Doppler system. Open balloting was favoured by the US, Canada and other backers of the American proposal.
28. Philip J. Klass, 'Lessons Found in Landing System Fight', *Aviation Week & Space Technology,* 8 May 1978.

29. Ibid.
30. L.F. Mortimer, 'New ICAO Rules Considered for Long-Range Twin-Engine Aeroplane Flights', *ICAO Bulletin*, April 1984.
31. 'Twins Over the Atlantic', *Airport Forum*, April 1985.
32. 'Twins Over the Oceans', *Flight International*, 2 July 1983.
33. 'FAA Broadens Inspection of the Wiring on Boeing Jets', *The New York Times*, 1 February 1989.

5: THE POLITICS OF EQUAL OPPORTUNITY

1. The concept of equality of opportunity originated in historical sequence from the achievement of individual liberty to independence by new states and logically progressed to liberal egalitarianism being applied to the emergent world society. (See V. Kubalkova and A.A. Cruickshank, *International Inequality* (New York: St. Martin's Press, 1981).)
2. Ronald Bickley, 'World Air Transport Development – 40 Years of Continuous Growth', *ICAO Bulletin*, November 1984, p. 16.
3. Stephen Krasner, 'Regimes and the Limits of Realism', *International Organization*, 36(2) 1982, p. 506. If one accepts Krasner's 'realist' position that the developing countries sought 'authoritative' over 'market-oriented' modes of power allocation, the evidence does not support his contention that the Third World did better in aviation than in shipping. Krasner, *Structural Conflict: The Third World Against Global Liberalism* (Berkeley, University of California Press, 1985).
4. Address to the 18th International Air Transport Public Relations Conference, Barcelona, Spain, June 1987.
5. Robert L. Rothstein, 'Dealing with Disequilibrium: Rising Pressures and Diminishing Resources in Third World Nations', *International Journal*, 34(3) 1984, pp. 554–5. See also Rothstein, 'Is the North-South Dialogue Worth Saving?', *Third World Quarterly* 6(1), 1984.
6. For statistics see *The Economic Situation of Air Transport – Review and Outlook 1978 to the Year 2000*, ICAO Circular 22-AT/90, 1989. With so many variables, classifications are out of order. The situation is different from country to country even in the same region. Ethiopia's Marxist government has allowed its national carrier EAL to operate as an efficient capitalist venture serving as a model to other countries. It presently flies to more than thirty countries. Neighbouring Kenya has capitalised on tourism but is losing this trade to foreign carriers because of governmental delays in modernising its airline. Nigeria Airways perhaps best illustrates the economic misfortunes besetting an airline. Previously one of the world's fastest growing air carriers during the country's oil boom, it has been consistently operating in the red and has been suspended from the IATA clearing

house for failing to settle its debts. James Brooke, 'Nigeria's Flying Elephant', *The New York Times*, 3 August 1987.

7. Until a route was recently started by Air Afrique and Ethiopian Airlines, between Abidjan and Addis Ababa with intermediate stops, it was easier to travel East–West via Paris and London.

8. David Woolley, 'Civil Aviation in Africa – Struggling Against Major Disadvantages', *Interavia*, September 1983, p. 918. See also *International Air Passenger and Freight Transport – Africa, 1984*, ICAO Circular 189-AT/73.

9. Christer Jönsson, 'Sphere of Flying: Politics of International Aviation', *International Organization*, 35(2) 1981, p. 299.

10. Ronald Bickley (then Director of ICAO's Air Transport Bureau), Lloyds of London Press International Civil Aviation Conference No. 6, Montreal, October 1984.

11. Robert L. Thornton, *International Airlines and Politics: A Study in Adaptation to Change* (Ann Arbor, Michigan International Business Series No. 13, 1970) p. 72.

12. Bickley, Lloyds of London Conference.

13. V.H.L. Dubourcq (of KLM) quoted in K.G.J. Pillai, *The Air Net* (New York: Grossman, 1969) p. 141. Thornton came to the same conclusion after canvassing US participants in the IATA Tariff Conferences. (See R.L. Thornton, 'Government and Airlines' in R.O. Keohane and J.S. Nye Jr. (eds), *Transnational Relations and World Politics* (Cambridge, Mass.: Harvard University Press, 1972).)

14. IATA statement to the 21st Session of the ICAO Assembly A21-Min EC/8, p. 73. In open-rate situations, fares are determined according to existing agreements or are maintained until a compromise is reached.

15. See Chapter 4.

16. See Chapter 1 (Legacy).

17. Betsy Gidwitz, *The Politics of International Air Transport* (Lexington, Mass.: Lexington Books, 1980) p. 86.

18. Krasner, *Structural Conflict*, pp. 196–226.

19. *The Effects of Discriminatory and Unfair Civil Aviation Practices on the Growth of Air Transport in Developing Countries*, UNCTAD Document TD/B/860 21 July 1981, p. 38.

20. To quote the Ethiopian delegate at ICAO's Special Air Transport Conference in 1977: 'The objective of such carriers is to monopolize major traffic routes, without due regard to users and to carriers from developing countries. The users and the small carriers are becoming victims of this attitude, which is being fostered by the new voting procedures in IATA (limited agreement). We know that small carriers have been exploited and will continue to be exploited unless governments save them from the consequence of this dangerous violation of IATA principles'. (ICAO Doc. SATC-WP/44.)

21. ICAO Doc. A27-WP/124 EC/18. The rapid spread of the CRS accessible to airlines and travel agents and potentially also to the public, has become a major cause of concern for airlines which are not participating in any of the systems controlled by the large carriers. See Vladimir Zubkov (Director of ICAO's Air Transport Bureau),

'The Development of Computer Reservation Systems: the ICAO Viewpoint', *ITA Magazine*, March-April 1987.

22. ICAO Doc. A27-WP/123 EX/40 and A27-WP/47 EX/12. See also *Economic Implications of Future Noise Restrictions on Subsonic Jet Aircraft*, ICAO Circular 218-AT/86, 1989.

23. Raúl Prebisch, *Towards a New Trade Policy for Development* (New York: United Nations, 1964). The 'prestige' factor which kept some airlines flying at great cost on uneconomic routes (for example Ghana under Kwame Nkrumah) cannot be discounted. Robert Mugabe, when he was chairman of the Non-Aligned Movement, was reported anxious to keep Air Zimbabwe flying on its intercontinental routes in spite of the airline's chronic inefficiency and drain on government resources. 'Air Zimbabwe – African Dilemmas', *Avmark Aviation Economist*, April 1987, pp. 4–5.

24. William E. O'Connor, *Economic Regulation of the World's Airlines: A Political Analysis* (New York: Praeger, 1971) p. 38.

25. Besides suffering from perennial deficits because of unpaid contributions, the carrier from its inception has been plagued by intense national rivalries between the twelve constituent countries for employment, service to their own capitals, location of regional headquarters, naming of aircraft after national capitals, and similar issues. The governments concerned have now put their differences aside and decided to accept a French rescue plan. They imposed restrictions on traffic rights to foreign carriers in order to give Air Afrique a chance to survive. Other multinational ventures in Africa are in the offing. Tanzania, Uganda, and Zambia have agreed on creating a joint regional carrier as have Guinea, Liberia and Sierra Leone. Five North African states (Algeria, Morocco, Tunisia, Mauritania and Libya) have held preliminary talks to do the same.

26. Ali Ghandour, address before the Salomon Brothers Second Annual Transportation Conference, Washington, DC (October 1987, as cited in *Aviation Daily*, 20 October 1987).

27. Address by Auxence Ickonga, International ITA Symposium, Marakech, October 1988. On paper at least, the African ministers responsible for civil aviation in a solemn declaration signed in Yamoussoukro (Ivory Coast) in October 1988 endorsed a plan to amalgamate their airlines and work towards the creation of airspace involving civil aviation operations and traffic rights. (See 'Why Yamoussoukro', *ITA Magazine* no. 52, November-December 1988.

28. See Assad Kotaite (President of the ICAO Council), 'The Wings of Progress', *Development Forum*, June 1981; see also 'Civil Aviation – A Force for Social Development', 31, *Impact of Science on Society* (UNESCO), 31(3) 1981 and a study by the World Bank, 'Aviation and Development', prepared by the World Bank Transportation, Water and Telecommunications Department, 1980.

29. 'Aviation: Crucible and Catalyst for Economic Growth', *IATA Review*, October-December 1983.

30. *Studies to Determine the Contribution that Civil Aviation Can Make*

to the Development of the National Economies of African States, Final Report, March 1977, UNDP/ICAO Project RAF 74/021.

31. ICAO's share of EPTA funds was fixed at one per cent, the remaining 99 per cent being earmarked for expenditure by the UN, ILO, FAO, UNESCO and WHO. As EPTA developed, certain distinctions were gradually drawn between small organisations such as ICAO, ITU, WMO, and major organisations such as the UN, ILO, FAO, UNESCO and WHO. Some advanced countries were against extending the activities of ICAO because of the high cost of airport facilities in developing countries. The underlying reason was to prevent ICAO from competing with the private sector and from eroding the advanced countries' control over air transport and related industries. See Mahyar Nashat, *National Interests and Bureaucracy versus Development Aid* (Geneva: Tribune Edition, 1978) pp. 41–2.

32. Robert Jackson, *A Study of the Capacity of the United Nations Development System*, vol. 1, United Nations, Geneva, 1969. See also Mahdi Elmandjra, *The United Nations System: An Analysis* (London: Faber & Faber, 1973).

33. Maurice Bertrand, 'Some Reflections on Reform of the United Nations', JIU/REP/85/9, 1985, pp. 31–2. Bertrand has been a persistent advocate of structural changes in the UN system.

34. Ibid., p. 32. See also Victor-Yves Ghebali, 'Réflexions sur les Activités Opérationnelles des Nations Unies', *Etudes Internationales*, 17(4) 1986.

35. Heritage Foundation, a conservative think-tank, has shaped critical attitudes toward the UN within the Reagan Administration. The indictment against the UNDP is developed in Richard E Bissell, *The UNDP, Failing the World's Poor*, Washington, DC.: Heritage Foundation, 1985. See also John Gerard Ruggie, 'The United States and the United Nations: toward a New Realism', *International Organization*, 39(2), 1985.

36. The level of ICAO's technical assistance funding declined from $39.8 million in 1981 to a low of $29.8 million in 1987. It has since increased to $38.1 million in 1988 and is expected to reach $46 million in 1989. (*Annual Report of the Council – 1988*, ICAO Doc. 9530.) In absolute purchasing power, the UNDP resources since 1970 have remained the same – up by over 300 per cent in 16 years, but with a dollar worth about only a third as much. In the same period, populations in the developing world have increased by 40 per cent so the UNDP has been doing less per capita in 1986 than in 1970. (Interview of William Draper III, UNDP Administrator, *Development Forum*, vol. XV, no. 2, March 1987.)

37. William Ascher, 'New Development Approaches and the Adaptability of International Agencies: the Case of the World Bank', *International Organization*, 37(3), 1983, p. 415.

38. The World Bank has provided loans and credits for airport projects and operations but has steadfastly resisted moves to provide financial assistance to purchase aircraft. The Bank's first loans for commercial aviation development were made between 1952 and 1957 to help

KLM, Qantas and Air India buy jet aircraft. Because funds were available from commercial sources for aircraft purchases, the Bank soon stopped making this type of loan. In recent years, states with aircraft-construction industries have offered help to buyers of aircraft made in their countries. Hence, no need was felt for World Bank participation. See Adele C. Schwartz, 'Airports in Developing Nations: World Bank Helps with Financing Expert Guidance', *Impact of Science on Society*, UNESCO, 31(3), 1981.

39. 'Implications of Greater or Lesser Competition in International Civil Aviation on the Economic Development of LDCs', 23, *ITA Bulletin*, June 1979, p. 523.

40. UNCTAD Report, p. 26. Referring to a statement by the Secretary-General of the African Civil Aviation Committee that African airlines will need 650 additional jets (including more than 100 widebodies) over the next twenty years to meet anticipated growth, Frank Kennedy, Director of the Equator Bank, conservatively estimated a total investment of $32.5 million or an average of $1.6 million per year, not taking into account turbo-props or replacement aircraft. He told an Air Finance Conference in New York that airlines and banks alike will need to learn new approaches. *Interavia Airletter* no. 11, 272, 23 June 1987.

41. Krasner, 'Power Structures and Regional Development Banks', *International Organization*, 35(2) 1981, p. 326. He notes that the independence of the African bank could only be purchased at the expense of limited financial resources, p. 322.

42. *Activities and Policy on Technical Assistance Provided Under the UNDP and Through Trust Fund (TF) Arrangements*, ICAO Doc. C-WP/8180.

43. K. Matohadinegoro, 'Report on Technical Cooperation Activities of the International Telecommunications Union', JIU/REP/86/4, p. 6.

44. A new resolution was subsequently adopted by the Council and by the 27th session of the Assembly in 1989. It urged the international community to increase financial and material assistance for aviation security particularly through ICAO's technical assistance programme. (ICAO Doc. A27-WP/39 EX/8).

45. See Chapter 4.

46. Raoul Lahogue, *l'Organisation de l'Aviation Civile Internationale (OACI) et les États du Tiers Monde*, doctoral thesis, Université de Paris I, 1976, p. 216.

47. Mathu, op. cit., p. 518.

48. Bertrand, op. cit., pp. 67–9.

6: CIVIL AND MILITARY AVIATION

1. I refer, among others, to R.O. Keohane and J.S. Nye, *Power and Interdependence* (Boston: Little, Brown, 1977); Harold K. Jacobson, *Networks of Interdependence: International Organizations and the Global Political System* (New York: Knopf, 1984) and James N. Rosenau, *Interdependence and Transnational Relations* (New York: Nichols, 1980).
2. The most influential book on the subject was Oliver J. Lissitzyn's *International Air Transport and National Policy* (New York: Council on Foreign Relations, 1942). His views carried much weight both in the United States and Europe at the time of the Chicago Conference. Another important book which came out on the eve of the Conference was *Civil Aviation and Peace* by J. Parker Van Zandt – the second volume of a series under the general title *America Faces the Air Age* published by the Brookings Institution (October 1944). In this slim volume, the author gives a geopolitical analysis of the postwar development of air transport. He concludes that: 'Security against aggression will be a primary objective in the post-war world. In considering civil aviation's future, it would be wholly unrealistic not to give full weight to its military implications, whatever this may be.'
3. R.L. Thornton, *International Airlines and Politics: A Study in Adaptation to Change* (Ann Arbor, Mich.: Michigan International Business Studies, no. 13, 1970) p. 80. Many delegates to the Conference were or had been part of their national military establishment. The civil aviation departments of France, Britain, Greece and Italy were parts of or subordinate to their respective military air ministries and several other directors of civil aviation or aeronautics at the time held military rank. The same situation still holds true today in many countries of Asia, Africa and Latin America.
4. *ICAO and Forty Years of Air Navigation in Europe*, published by the ICAO Regional Office in Paris, 1987, p. 13.
5. Commercial carriers in many countries are still expected to be available for military transport in times of national emergency.
6. I am indebted to Paul G. Berger, formerly with the ICAO Regional Office in Paris, for invaluable information on the postwar situation in Europe.
7. Resolution of the Assembly A10–19.
8. I am indebted to Leif Klette, the senior NATO official responsible for CEAC, for information on its activities and operations. See also his article 'Civil and Military Air Traffic Management and Control', *NATO's Sixteen Nations*, October-November 1983, pp. 39–44.
9. Since the ICAO Secretariat comprises staff from 75 countries (including the USSR) all files pertaining to ICAO/NATO coordination are highly confidential.
10. ICAO Registry Files (AN 13/4.2, vol. 18), and Air Navigation Commission Minutes, 115th Session, 1987 (AN Min. 115–7). See also Chapter 7.

11. See E.A.G. Verploeg, *The Road Towards a European Common Air Market*, Doctoral thesis, Utrecht, 1963 and Michel Folliot, *Le transport aérien international* (Paris: Librairie générale de droit et de jurisprudence, 1977) pp. 264–9.

12. Harry Hopkins, 'Eurocontrol: Taking a New Direction', *Flight International*, 9 March 1985.

13. *IATA Review*, January-March 1983, p. 10.

14. Ibid., p. 14.

15. *Activities of the Regional Offices, Implementation of Regional Plans*, ICAO Doc. AN-WP/5962.

16. President's Memoranda to the Council, 15 October 1979, 17 January 1980 and 15 July 1981.

17. ICAO Registry Files (AN 13/4.3, vol. 8). See also Chapter 7.

18. ICAO Doc. AN-WP/6289 and ICAO Doc. A27-WP/68 TE/3 (12 July 1989).

19. R.L. Thornton, 'Governments and Airlines' in R.O. Keohane and J.S. Nye (eds), *Trans-national Relations and World Politics, International Organization*, vol. 25, no. 3 (Summer 1971), p. 542.

20. Geo R. Besse (at the time Director General of the Institute of Air Transport), 'Aviation and Society', *Impact of Science on Society*, vol. 31, no. 3, 1981, p. 342.

21. Yet, Thornton has pointed up the doubtful values of an international airline's routes in such emergencies when KLM transported defence material and personnel to the Dutch East Indies at the time of the second Indonesian 'police action' in December 1948. Within a few days of the start of the action, the governments of Pakistan, India, Burma, Iraq, Saudi Arabia, and Ceylon had closed their territories and airports. Thornton, *International Airlines and Politics*, p. 82.

22. 26th Session of the Assembly, 1986, ICAO Doc. A26-WP/51.

23. Ibid.

24. Jay Tuck, *High-Tech Espionage* (London: Sidgwick & Jackson, 1986) p. 167.

25. Ibid.

26. The French Government subsequently issued a statement accepting the Soviet version that the mishap was not deliberate. 'Paris Calls Soviet Flight Over Base Unintentional', *The New York Times*, 17 April 1984.

27. Ever since the launching in February 1986 of an advanced French satellite called SPOT, which can photograph ground objects as small as 10 metres in length, civilians and military analysts have increasingly used space photos to peer at bases and other military facilities around the world.

28. Resolution 7, Third Air Transport Conference, 1985, ICAO Doc. 9470.

29. Walter Lacqueur, *A World of Secrets* (New York: Basic Books, 1985) p. 202.

30. Christopher Robbins, *Air America* (New York: Putnam's, 1979) p. 18. The most interesting of these carriers in the context of this study is Civil Air Transport (CAT) which originated in 1946 as an offshoot of the Flying Tigers. According to Marchette and Marks, a top-secret memorandum (no. 22) in *The Pentagon Papers* (New York: Bantam

Books, 1961) describes CAT as a 'commercial airline' engaged in scheduled and non-scheduled operations throughout the Far East. Its main
role was to provide logistical support 'under commercial cover' to most
CIA and the US government agencies' requirements as well as support
clandestine air operations. Among such operations were air-drops in
Indo-China and in Indonesia in support of the rebels fighting Sukarno
in 1958. The airline with headquarters in Taiwan was reorganized as a
Delaware Corporation under a CIA-proprietary holding company. It
eventually split into Air America which took over CAT's South East
operations and Air Asia which operated the maintenance facilities in
Taiwan. CAT itself continued to operate as a civil airline until the CIA
decided it no longer served its primary mission. It was then turned
over to China Air Lines but not until a spectacular accident of one of
its Boeing 727s at Taipei Airport in 1968, which resulted in 21 deaths,
caused a public uproar on the island. Victor Marchetti and John D.
Marks, *The CIA and the Cult of Intelligence* (New York: Dell, 1983)
pp. 121–30.
31. 'CIA Used Zaire as a Supply Base for Angola Rebels, Diplomats Say',
    Globe and Mail (Toronto), 2 February 1987.
32. See Clyde H. Farnsworth, 'The Company As Big Business', *The New
    York Times*, 4 January 1987. Actually from 1960 to 1973, Southern
    Air was a CIA proprietary owned outright by the agency which used
    it primarily on missions in Southeast Asia.
33. ICAO Doc. A24-MIN P/7.
34. The drafting history of this article according to Michael Milde indicates
    that the underlying intent of Article 4 was to prevent the use of civil
    aviation by states for purposes which might create a threat to the
    security of other nations. Article 4 originated in a Canadian draft which
    was inspired by the text of the 1928 Briand–Kellogg Pact in which the
    signatories renounced war 'as an instrument of national policy in their
    mutual relations'. The words 'purposes inconsistent with the aims of
    this Convention' in Article 4 therefore essentially mean 'threats to the
    general security'. M. Milde, 'Interception of Civil Aircraft vs Misuse
    of Civil Aviation', (Background of Amendment 27 to Annex 2) *Annals
    of Air and Space Law*, vol. XI, 1986, McGill University, Montreal,
    pp. 105–30.
35. See Chapter 8.
36. Anthony Sampson, *Empires of the Sky: the Politics, Contests and Car-
    tels of World Airlines* (London: Hodder & Stoughton, 1984) p. 119.
37. Bernard E. Trainor, 'U.S. Fears Soviet Use of New Nicaraguan Air-
    field', *The New York Times*, 26 July 1987.
38. Keesing's Contemporary Archives, 15 October 1982.
39. ICAO Doc. A24-MIN P/7.
40. *Final Report of Investigation presented by the Secretary General*, ICAO
    Doc. C-WP/7764.
41. See Chapter 8, note 36.
42. The issue has been raised most persistently by David Pearson, a Yale
    University scholar, who wrote an article in *The Nation*, 18–25 August
    1984, later expanded into a book. His evidence based on a taped

transcript purportedly showing that civil air traffic controllers knew of the deviation and failed to warn the aircraft, did not hold in court. A judge dismissed a negligence suit brought against the US Government by families of the passengers and concluded that there was nothing in the tape recording to support the assertion that the Air Force had contacted civil controllers to alert them that Flight 007 might be in peril. Richard Witkin, 'Judge Dismisses Suits in Downing of Korean Plane', *The New York Times*, 8 May 1986.

43. Murray Sayle 'KE007: a Conspiracy of Silence', *New York Review*, 25 April 1985, pp. 46–7.
44. ICAO Doc. AN-WP/5580.
45. ICAO Doc. C-MIN 116/5.
46. The amendment was adopted by 22 votes against 4 (US, USSR, Egypt and Czechoslovakia) with 6 abstentions (C-MIN 117/12). The various technical provisions became applicable on 20 November 1986.
47. Richard Witkin, 'New Pacific Air Pact Let Planes in Trouble Land in Soviet', *The New York Times*, 22 November 1985; Philip Taubman, 'Keeping the Air Lanes Free: Lessons of a Horror', *The New York Times*, 17 September 1987. See also Chapter 8.
48. This has already been demonstrated in a test flight by a Sabreliner travelling 9000 kilometres from Iowa to Paris in May 1983. The GPS navigation system performed flawlessly, providing navigation accuracy ranging from 80 to 14 metres during the entire flight. In comparison, inertial navigation system errors of 13 kilometres and VLF/Omega errors over 18 km were experienced during the flight. Upon arrival at Le Bourget, the aircraft was taxied along the taxiway to predetermined waypoints using GPS signals displayed on the co-pilot's horizontal situation indicator. The aircraft was stopped only 6.5 metres beyond and 3.8 metres to the left of the parking waypoint.
49. *Cooperation through ICAO: Defining the Future Air Navigation Infrastructure*, 1986 World Exposition Symposium Series, March 1985, Vancouver.
50. Keohane and Nye, op. cit., p. 19.
51. This article gives the ICAO Council the power to legislate with binding effect for all contracting states with respect to rules applicable over the high seas.
52. See Chapter 8 concerning the Israeli interception of a Libyan aircraft in 1986.
53. This substantive amendment adopted by unanimous consent at the 25th Session (Extraordinary) of the ICAO Assembly on 10 May 1984, is now in the process of ratification. See Chapter 8 (the KAL incident).
54. Major John T. Phelps III, 'Aerial Intrusions by Civil and Military Aircraft in Time of Peace', *Military Law Review*, vol. 17, (Winter 1985), p. 266.
55. Bjarne Gaustad, formerly Chief of the Rules of the Air and Traffic Section at ICAO, at the Lloyd's of London Press International Civil Aviation Conference, Montreal, 1984.

7: CONFLICTS AND THE SAFETY OF AIR TRAVEL

1. Article 89 of the Chicago Convention which gives states the right to suspend provisions of the Convention in case of war or emergency conditions upon due notification to the Council, raises several problems of interpretation since it applies equally to both circumstances. If, however, a state of war can be readily determined, this is not the case of a state of emergency. Fitzgerald has pointed out that such a declaration to the Council presumably would be based on military necessity or public safety. On that basis, he doubts that an international tribunal faced with this problem would accept a subjective determination and would need to review the conditions which led to the declaration. Gerald Fitzgerald, Lecture, Institute of Air and Space Law, McGill University, Montreal, 1986.

2. J. Schenkman, *International Civil Aviation Organization* (Geneva: H. Studer, 1955) p. 376.

3. M. Milde, 'Dispute Settlement in the Framework of the International Civil Aviation Organization (ICAO)' in *Studies in Air and Space Law* (Koln: Carl Heymanns, 1979) p. 91.

4. Paul Delaney, '283 Years Later, Dispute Over Gibraltar Persists', *The New York Times*, 30 July 1987. *Interavia Air Letter*, no. 11.277, 30 June 1987.

5. Milde, op. cit., p. 93. The Indian position is outlined in S.K. Agrawala, *Aircraft, Hijacking and International Law* (Dobbs Ferry, NY: Oceana Publications, 1973) Chapter 10.

6. Dr Edward Warner, the first Council President, wrote in 1945: 'No international agency composed of representatives of States could be expected to bring judicial detachment to the consideration of particular cases in which large national interests were involved'. 'The Chicago Air Conference', *Foreign Affairs*, April 1954. His two successors have expressed similar reservations.

7. Milde, op. cit., p. 90.

8. Hans J. Morgenthau, *Politics Among Nations* (New York: Knopf, 1973) p. 425. Morgenthau specifically refers to the Kashmir issue and Nehru's rejection of a resolution of the United Nations Security Council calling for arbitration of the India–Pakistan dispute. As Nehru put it: 'Great political questions – and this is a great political question – are not handed over in this way to arbitrators from foreign countries or any country'.

9. *Times of India*, New Delhi, 19 December 1984 and *Patriot*, New Delhi, 19 December 1984.

10. Milde, op. cit., p. 92.

11. Memorandum from the President to the Council, 1 February 1989.

12. *Good Offices of ICAO*, ICAO Doc., C-WP/5211, 71st Session of the Council, 1970.

13. Air Traffic Services, South East Asia Region, AN 13/4.5, vol. 3, ICAO Archives.

14. The area in question had been a matter of dispute since China in

1974 defeated a Vietnam naval force and reiterated its long standing claim over Hainan. (See Marwyn S. Samuels, *Contest for the South China Sea* (New York: Methuen, 1982).)

15. See Chapter 6, note 16.

16. President's Memorandum to the Council, 10 February 1983 and ICAO Press Release, PIO 9/83. To avoid signing a formal agreement, a Memorandum of understanding was signed by ICAO with each of the states concerned.

17. President's Memorandum to the Council, 10 February 1983. Report of the President of the Council, C-WP/7365, 11 November 1981.

18. As dramatically illustrated when South Korea formally charged North Korean agents with planting a bomb on a KAL Boeing 707 which went down in the Thai–Burmese jungle in November 1987 killing all 115 persons on board (ICAO Doc. PRES AK/152 with south Korea's findings of the investigation). South Korea brought the matter up before the Council under Article 54(n) of the Chicago Convention. The Council condemned the act of sabotage without, however, passing judgement on South Korea's charges. ICAO Doc. C-WP/8584, 22 March 1988.

19. President's Memorandum to the Council, 10 February 1983.

20. Statement by the Turkish observer to the Air Navigation Commission, AN Min 115–17, 10 June 1987. See also Council Doc. C-WP/8435, 12 June 1987 and AN-WP/6078, 15 May 1987.

21. Van Coufoudakis, 'Greek–Turkish Relations, 1973–1983: The View from Athens', *International Security*, 9(4), p. 199.

22. Andrew Wilson, 'The Aegean Dispute', Aldelphi Paper no. 155, London, *International Institute for Strategic Studies*, Winter 1979–1980, p. 7.

23. ICAO Registry Files AN13/4.2, vol. 17. The only international carrier using ERCAN is Turkish Airlines.

24. Ibid.

25. Memorandum from IFALPA to the Secretary General of ICAO, November 1984 (ICAO Registry Files AN13/4.2, vol. 8).

26. Statement by the Chief delegate of Cyrpus to the 24th Assembly, October 1983. In a letter to the Council President, he reported more than 120 incidents in 1982 and early 1983 in which aircraft were deliberately prevented from complying with instructions issued by the Nicosia FIR or were intentionally retained on the 'ERCAN' frequency and issued instructions not approved or coordinated by Nicosia.

27. The problem was further complicated when instructions were issued by the 'Turkish Republic of Northern Cyprus' in March 1987 designating a second international airport for the northern part of the island.

28. Air Traffic Services, Middle East Region, AN 13/4.3, vol. 6, ICAO Archives.

29. Idem. See also 'Iran Institutes Strict Control Over Its Airspace', *Aviation Week & Space Technology*, 3 December 1979.

30. Air Traffic Services, Middle East Region, vol. 6, ICAO Archives.

31. Ibid.

32. Ibid.

33. President's Memorandum to the Council, 19 March 1985.
34. Council Minutes, C-Min, Extraordinary, 1985, p. 194.
35. President's Memorandum to the Council, 26 March 1985. This assurance was repeated when he visited Baghdad two years later, Council Minutes 120/13.
36. Air Traffic Services, Middle East Region, AN 13/4.3, vol. 8, ICAO Archives.
37. Ibid.
38. ICAO Doc. C-WP/8644.
39. Specifically Assembly Resolution A26–8 (1986), Annex 11 of the Chicago Convention (Air Traffic Services) and the Recommendations of the Mideast Regional Air Navigation meeting MID/3 RAN 1984.
40. Steve Lohr, 'Gulf Patrols Give Jitters to Pilots and Controllers', *The New York Times*, 10 July 1988. See also Chapters 6 and 8.
41. ICAO Doc. C-WP/8644.
42. *Report of the FIR/SSR Emirates Implementing Meeting*, Paris, 21–23 January 1986.
43. Council Minutes C-Min Extraordinary 1988 and ICAO Press Release PIO 9/88. Some improvements were subsequently reported when Qatar confirmed its intention to open its airspace to international traffic.
44. See Chapter 6.
45. Letter to the Chairman of the State Organization for Iraqi Civil Aviation, Air Navigation Services, Middle East Region, AN 13/4.3, vol. 6, ICAO Archives.
46. Thomas Buergenthal, *Lawmaking in the International Civil Aviation Organization* (Syracuse: Syracuse University Press, 1969) p. 226.
47. Yves Beigbeder, 'Le Rôle politique, administratif et opérationnel du Secrétaire Général de l'Organisation des Nations Unies', *International Review of Administrative Sciences*, LI(4), 1985, p. 282.

8: ARMED ATTACKS AGAINST CIVIL AVIATION

1. Communication to the ICAO Regional Representative (2 July 1949), ICAO Registry Files.
2. Second Middle East Regional Air Navigation Meeting, Istanbul 1950. ICAO Doc. 7053. In recent years, such meetings have been held in Geneva or in Montreal to allow for Israeli participation.
3. Statement of the delegate of Israel to the Assembly's Executive Committee (A6-WP/36, 6 June 1952). L.C. Green argues that in the absence of specific provisions in the law of armed conflict, the Chicago Convention could be made to apply in wartime to protect civil aviation 'Aerial Considerations in the Law of Armed Conflict', *Annals of Air and Space Law*, 5 (Montreal: McGill University Press, 1980), pp. 89–117.

4. ICAO Registry Files.
5. U Thant, *A View from the U.N.* (Garden City: Doubleday, 1978) p. 302.
6. ICAO Doc. C-WP/4946, 15 January 1969. (In any case, Algeria never adhered to the Convention.)
7. Ibid.
8. U Thant cautiously avoided putting his feelings on paper. He conveyed his message through a personal representative, U Thant, op. cit., p. 306.
9. Ibid., p. 308.
10. ICAO Doc. C-WP/4946.
11. United Nations Security Council Official Records (no. 1460, 29 December 1968).
12. Minutes of the Council (22 January 1969) ICAO Doc. 8793–1, 13.
13. Ibid., pp. 8–12.
14. Ibid., p. 20.
15. 'Anti-Israel Move Fails – Air Piracy Curbs Urged', *Toronto Globe and Mail*, 22 January 1969.
16. Edward McWhinney, CBC-TV Viewpoint, unedited transcript (24 January 1969). Dr McWhinney at the time was Professor of Law and Director of the Institute of Air and Space Law at McGill University.
17. Israel found it ludicrous for the Assembly to condemn acts of air piracy and then 'welcome' an organisation which, it claimed, had been responsible for 54 attacks on airlines and airports. (ICAO Doc. A–22 Min P/12). See also 'PLO Terror: Data on the PLO Terrorist Organization' in Yonah Alexander (ed.), *The 1986 Annual Terrorism* (Dordrecht: Martinus Nyhoff, 1987); Yonah Alexander and Joshua Sinai, *Terrorism: the PLO Connection* (New York: Crane Russak, 1989).
18. Excerpts from the verbatim record of the Security Council debate are contained in William Stevenson, *90 Minutes at Entebbe* (New York: Bantam Books, 1976) and *United Nations Chronicle* 13 (8). See also John F. Murphy, 'State Self Help and Problems of Public International Law' in Alona E. Evans and John Murphy (eds), *Legal Aspects of International Terrorism* (Lexington, Mass.: Lexington Books, 1978) p. 556. Essentially Israel invoked the right of self-defence to protect its nationals where no other means of action are available.
19. Gregory V. Goodings, 'Fighting Terrorism in the 1980's: The Interception of the Achille Lauro hijackers', *The Yale Journal of International Law*, 12 (1), Winter 1987, p. 175. As shown by its air raid on Libya in 1986, the United States feels free to bend international law when dealing with terrorism. In an unprecedented action, the FBI arrested a Lebanese hijacker in international waters in the Mediterranean to face charges in the United States. (See Chapter 10.)
20. On 10 August 1973, Israeli jets intercepted a Lebanese aircraft over Beirut and forced it to land at a military base. The Israelis believed the aircraft was carrying George Habash, the leader of the Popular Front for the Liberation of Palestine. The action was condemned by

both the United Nations Security Council (Resolution 337, 1973) and
the ICAO Assembly (Resolution A–20–1).

21. United Nations Security Council, 2655th Meeting, S/PV 2655 (6 February 1986).

22. ICAO Doc. C-WP/8206, 28 February 1986.

23. ICAO Press Release PIO 14/85.

24. Oliver J. Lissitzyn, 'The Treatments of Aerial Intruders in Recent Practice and International Law', *American Journal of International Law*, 47 (1953), p. 559.

25. The listing includes the El Al, Libyan and KAL incidents described in this chapter. (Memorandum from IFALPA to the Secretary General of ICAO, 20 August 1986).

26. On the basis of skimpy press reports, James Oberg asserts that the chartered cargo aircraft inadvertently entered Soviet airspace in Azerbaijan on its way back to Cyprus after delivering weapons to Iran and was deliberately rammed by a Soviet interceptor aircraft when it ignored instructions to land. Argentina never acknowledged the incident. James Oberg, *Uncovering Soviet Disasters* (New York: Random House, 1988) pp. 32–9.

27. The report on the circumstances of the incident together with Bulgaria's response are contained in ICAO Circular 50-AN/45, 146–157 and *Aircraft Accident Digest no. 7* – Report 35. See also ICAO Doc. C-WP/2018, 13 November 1955.

28. ICAO Doc. C-WP/5734.

29. At its 78th Session, the Council instructed the Secretary General to institute a fact-finding investigation. A report was submitted to the 79th Session of the Council but was never made public. (ICAO Doc. C-WP/5764 Restricted.)

30. In that particular incident, a Korean Boeing 707, on a scheduled flight from Paris to Seoul, deviated some 1000 nautical miles off course and was intercepted by a Soviet fighter which opened fire. The aircraft experienced rapid decompression but managed to land on a frozen lake south of Murmansk. Two passengers were killed and ten injured. (*World Airline Accident Summary*; Memorandum to Council, 19 May 1978, Council Minutes 94/1.)

31. See Major John T. Phelps III, 'Aerial Intrusions by Civil and Military Aircraft in Time of Peace', *Military Law Review*, vol. 107, winter 1985. See also Chapter 6.

32. 'Soviet Says Order to Down Jet Came at a Local Level', *The New York Times*, 10 September 1983. At the ICAO Council Session, Soviet delegates used a map purporting to track the flight of the 'intruder plane' but were obviously unprepared when challenged by the United States delegate J. Lynn Helms. When Helms wanted to know how a Boeing 747 could fly 620 nm in 32 minutes at an average speed of 1140 knots (the Soviet version), the Soviet delegates quickly withdrew their charts and refused to turn them over to ICAO. (Minutes of the Council, Extraordinary Session, 15–16 September 1983, ICAO Doc. 9416-C/1077).

33. Hours after the tragedy, United States Secretary of State George

Shultz told a news conference: 'We can see no excuse whatsoever for this appalling act. . . . The aircraft that shot the commercial airliner down moved itself into a position with the aircraft so that with the eye you could inspect the aircraft and see what you are looking at'. United States intelligence officials subsequently indicated that the Soviets probably did not know what type of aircraft they were shooting down. 'Soviets Downed Jetliner in Error, Congress Told', *Toronto Globe and Mail*, 13 January 1988.

34. Council Minutes, ICAO Doc. 9416-C/1077.

35. Report of the ICAO Fact-Finding Investigation, C-WP/7764, p. 56. ICAO investigators were hampered by the absence of the black boxes and survivors. They had to proceed on the basis of limited hard evidence, limited facts, circumstantial evidence, assumptions and calculations. Some of their key findings were based on postulations which were then simulated to provide the most likely scenarios of what may have transpired. Gerald F. FitzGerald, 'The Use of Force Against Civil Aircraft: The Aftermath of the KAL Flight 007 Incident', *The Canadian Yearbook of International Law*, 22 (1984), pp. 295–6.

36. The most authoritative book on the KAL tragedy is a two-year study by Seymour Hersh: *The Target Is Destroyed* (New York: Random House, 1986) which vindicates the conclusions of the ICAO report and dismisses claims that KAL Flight 007 was on a spy mission. Hersh's evidence, based on a review of American intelligence data and interviews with Soviet officials, points to human error on the part of the crew of the KAL and a series of blunders which led Soviet military to mistake it for the RC–135 reconnaissance aircraft which was in the vicinity at the time. These blunders and the contention by Hersh that Soviet officials have actually no proof for their claim that the KAL 007 was on spy mission may explain their reluctance to make public their own version of events. As Hersh notes, those in Washington who chose to increase international tension, and their counterparts in Moscow who responded in kind, were acting in ignorance of the facts. Flight 007 was a crisis made far more dangerous by the extent of misunderstanding and anti-Soviet feeling it engendered. The ready acceptance of the Soviet claim and the various conspiracy theories are obscuring much deeper implications about attitudes of the superpowers which is the subject of a book by Alexander Dallin, *Black Box: KAL and the Superpowers* (Berkeley: University of California Press, 1985). The most persuasive case for the intelligence mission was made by R.W. Johnson in *Shootdown: The Verdict on KAL 007* (London: Chatto & Windus, 1986). His case, however, is built entirely on circumstantial data and offers no conclusive evidence. Unlike, Hersh, Johnson by his own admission did not seek or enjoy access to Soviet authorities. This did not deter them from publishing a carefully edited version of Johnson's arguments (as they first appeared in the *Guardian*) omitting all remarks critical of the USSR.

37. ICAO Press Release PIO 2/84 and *ICAO Bulletin*, November 1983.

38. The amendment will enter into force when ratified by 102 states. In

spite of its unanimous approval, Article 3 *bis* has been ratified by only 50 states (as of April 1989), a sure indication that the amendment process of the Chicago Convention is too slow and too cumbersome to be effective.

39. ICAO Press Release PIO 2/86 and ICAO Doc. C-WP/8628. See also Chapter 6.
40. Steven Erlanger, 'Similarities with KAL Flight Are Rejected by U.S. Admiral', *The New York Times*, 4 July 1988.
41. One such instance had come before the ICAO Council in 1986 when Iran accused Iraq of shooting down a civilian aircraft inside Iranian airspace resulting in the death of 40 passengers. Iraq claimed Iran was using commercial aircraft for military transport and confirmed it had shot down a F–27 Friendship attached to the Iranian Air Force. It claimed the aircraft was piloted by military personnel and was transporting a number of high-ranking personnel. (President's Memorandum to the Council AK/1061 of 10 March 1986)
42. Minutes of the Council C-MIN Extraordinary, 13–14 July 1988.
43. Security Council Resolution 616 (20 July 1988).
44. John F. Burns, 'Aviation Unit Rebuffs Iran's Bid Against U.S.', *The New York Times*, 13 July 1988.
45. Richard Halloran, 'Navy Is Not Monitoring Air Traffic Control in Gulf', *The New York Times*, 13 July 1988.
46. Bernard E. Trainor, 'Errors by a Tense US Crew led to Downing of Iran Jet', *The New York Times*, 3 August 1988.
47. ICAO Doc. C-WP/8708 (restricted), 7 November 1988.
48. ICAO Press Release PIO/5/88, 7 December 1988.
49. ICAO Doc. C-WP/8821, 16 March 1989.
50. Press Conference as reported in *La Presse* (Montreal), 18 March 1989.
51. While the US has not laid charges, there have been various press reports emanating from government sources blaming a radical Palestinian faction 'hired' by Iran.
52. 'International and National Law and Community Problem-solving on Aerial Piracy' in Y. Alexander and E. Sochor (eds), *Aerial Piracy and Aviation Security* (Dordrecht: Martinus Nyhoff) forthcoming. McWhinney draws an analogy with the *Dogger Bank* Incident of 1904, when the Imperial Russian Navy fired on and destroyed English fishing boats in the North Sea, some 60 miles off the coast of Great Britain, in the mistaken belief that they were Japanese Navy torpedo boats. Notwithstanding the fact that Russia was at war with Japan, a special international arbitral commission rejected Russian claims of self-defence and mistake, and ordered Russia to pay full financial compensation.
53. ICAO Doc. C-DEC 127/10, 9 June 1989; Paul Lewis, 'U.S. Lets World Court Try Iran Air Case', *The New York Times*, 15 August 1989. The United States has offered payments to the families of the victims but will not deal directly with the Iranian Government on the matter.

9: SETTING SECURITY STANDARDS

1. Robert G. Bell, 'The US Response to Terrorism Against International Civil Aviation', *ORBIS* 19(4) 1976, p. 195.
2. ICAO Doc. 8849-C/990/2. The Committee comprising eleven members chosen from the Council, was to develop preventive measures and procedures to safeguard international civil aviation, and, at the request of a contracting state, to assist the national authorities of that state in the adoption of such measures and procedures.
3. ICAO Doc. 8784–8 C/981–8 Council, Sixty-fifth (1968) and Doc. 8784–9 C/981–9, Council Sixty-fifth Session (1968).
4. Ibid.
5. The Council action was in pursuance of two resolutions adopted by the 17th Session of the Assembly (Extraordinary) in 1970:
   (a) Resolution A17–10 *Implementation by States of Security Specifications and Practices adopted by this Assembly and further work by ICAO related to such Specifications and Practices*. Paragraph 3 provides that the Assembly 'requests the Council with the assistance of other constituent bodies of the Organization, to develop and incorporate, as appropriate, the material in the Appendices to this Resolution as Standards and Recommended Practices and Procedures in existing or new Annexes or other regulatory documents or guidance material of the Organization'.
   (b) Resolution A18–10 *Additional Technical Measures for the Protection of Security of International Air Transport*. Paragraph 1 provides that the Assembly 'requests the Council to ensure, with respect to technical aspects of air transportation security, that (a) the subject of air transportation security continues to be given adequate attention by the Secretary General with a priority commensurate with the current threat to the security of air transportation'.
   It is interesting to note that the interpretation of the terms 'security', 'act of unlawful interference', 'security programme' and 'appropriate security' was left to the discretion of states, pending the development of definitions of such terms. The term 'security' in Annex 6 (Operation of Aircraft), however, is used in the sense of 'prevention of illicit acts against civil aviation'. Sakeus Akweenda, 'Prevention of Unlawful Interference with Aircraft: A Study of Standards and Recommended Practices', *International and Comparative Law Quarterly*, 35(2) April 1986, p. 437.
6. The first security measures instituted in the United States were largely optional. The intent of the programme was also thwarted by a certain casualness on the part of airports and carriers. See A.E. Evans, 'Aircraft Hijackings: What is being done', *American Journal of International Law*, 167:641, p. 649. See also Bell, above, note 1.
7. Edward McWhinney, *Aerial Piracy and International Terrorism* (Dordrecht: Martinus Nyhoff, 1987) p. 119.
8. Specific measures are contained in the Security Manual.

9. Akweenda, op. cit., p. 439.
10. Perhaps the most incredible aspect in the TWA incident, besides it being one of the longest hijacking (17 days), is the fact that the aircraft was forced to shuttle back and forth between Beirut and Algiers until the pilot finally landed in Beirut under harrowing conditions with practically no fuel left. Instead of taking action during refuelling, Algeria let the aircraft take off after the hijackers were allowed to exchange Greek passengers for one of their comrades arrested by the police at Athens Airport. Algeria could not be taken to task since it has not ratified any of the ICAO Conventions on unlawful interference, unlike Greece which was clearly in violation of The Hague Convention. It placed national interests over its international obligations which were to bring criminal proceedings against the suspect in its custody.
11. Council Minutes 115/14, 27 June 1985. Even while the Council was considering the amendments to Annex 17, in November 1985, air piracy took its bloodiest toll yet when hijackers took over an Egyptian airliner carrying 98 passengers and crew on a flight from Athens to Cairo and forced it to land in Malta. The hijackers released 11 women then began shooting US and Israeli passengers after Maltese authorities refused a request for refuelling. Egyptian commandos in a bungled attempt to free the remaining passengers set the aircraft on fire killing 56 people and bringing the death toll to 60.
12. *Program report on the Plan of Action.* C-WP/8079, 2 October 1985.
13. Department of Transportation Press Release DOT 128–85, 27 November 1985.
14. Council Minutes 115/14, pp. 15–16.
15. Aviation Security, working paper presented by Israel, A–26 WP/75.
16. Letter dated 5 January 1986 from Haim Corfu to the Ministers of Transport of ICAO member states, distributed at the 41st session of the United Nations General Assembly (UN Doc. A/41/81 S/17723, 8 January 1986). That Israel had indeed something to contribute was made clear when an El Al employee at Heathrow stopped the girlfriend of a Syrian intelligence officer from unwittingly carrying a bomb aboard an El Al flight bound for Tel Aviv in October 1986. Were it not for such vigilance, the El Al flight with 375 passengers on board would have exploded over the Atlantic the same way as the Air India jet. The security employee had simply detected a discrepancy in the weight of the hold-all bag in which the bomb was concealed. (See Chapter 10).
17. Presentation of IATA at the 26th session of the ICAO Assembly. (ICAO Doc. A26-WP/53).
18. C. Emanuelli, 'Legal Aspects of Aerial Terrorism: the Piecemeal vs the Comprehensive Approach', *Journal of International Law and Economics*, 10:503 (1975).
19. Council Minutes 116/29.
20. Council Minutes 122/4.
21. Richard Witkin, 'FAA to Toughen Check-in Security' *The New York Times*, 29 December 1989.

22. S. Fred Singer, 'Machines Won't End Air Terrorism', *Wall Street Journal*, 20 June 1989.
23. *Report of the Meeting of the Ad-Hoc Group of Specialists on the Detection of Explosives*, Montreal, 6–10 March 1989.
24. ICAO Doc. C-WP/8250, 28 May 1988.
25. 'Government Carriers Top Security Burden', *Financial Times*, 23 December 1986, p. 6; 'Accident Reveals Difficulties in Enforcing Airport Security', *Aviation Week & Space Technology*, 2 January 1989, p. 31.
26. 'US Airlines Ask Government to Take More Active Security Role', *Aviation Week & Space Technology*, 9 January 1989, p. 62.
27. *Travel Management Daily*, 9 January 1989. The mind-boggling task of collecting and disbursing these funds makes such proposal too unrealistic for practical consideration by ICAO. IFALPA has suggested that this could be done through IATA's clearing house activities.
28. Statement by Cuba, Council Minutes C-Min 126/3.
29. Ibid.
30. ICAO Doc. C-WP/8782 and C-WP/8754.
31. Council Minutes, C-Min 126/5 and 6.
32. The Germans countered with a press statement to the effect that the announcement was premature and that it could not be excluded that something was added to the container in London.
33. Council Minutes C-Min 127/6 and 126/7.
34. Revised work programme of the AVSEC panel as listed in ICAO Doc UI-WP/202, 9 January 1989. This latest amendment to Annex 17 was adopted in June 1989.
35. James Overton, 'INTERPOL: Its Perspective on Unlawful Interference with Civil Aviation', *ICAO Bulletin*, June 1988. The author notes that Interpol guidelines for assessing security threats are the same as those contained in the ICAO Security Manual.
36. Bin Cheng, *Aviation Security: Safeguarding International Civil Aviation Against Acts of Unlawful Interference*, Lloyds of London Press International Civil Aviation Conference, Montreal, October 1984.
37. Ibid.
38. ICAO Doc. UI-WP/196.
39. Ibid.
40. Evan Luard, *International Agencies: The Emerging Framework of Interdependence* (Dobbs Ferry, N.Y.: Oceana Publications 1977) p. 288.
41. Rodney Wallis (Director of Security of IATA), presentation to the *Financial Times* World Aerospace Conference, London, August 1986.
42. McWhinney, op. cit., p. 170.

10: LOOPHOLES IN THE LAW

1. Quoted by Eliane Sciolino, 'In Terrorism, it's Every Country for Itself', *The New York Times*, 15 February 1987.
2. Draft Interim Report of the Working Group on Terrorism of the North Atlantic Assembly's Political Committee, 1986, p. 23.
3. Robert Oakley, 'International Terrorism', *Foreign Affairs*, 65 (3), 1987, p. 618.
4. 'Smiting Syria with a Sponge', editorial in *The New York Times*, 30 October 1986.
5. Hans Morgenthau, *Dilemmas of Politics* (Chicago: Chicago University Press, 1958) p. 226.
6. All but ignored at the time was Britain's decision to cancel also its air agreement with Libya in retaliation for that country's alleged use of its national airline to smuggle arms for terrorist attacks. *Aviation Week & Space Technology*, 6 October 1986, p. 31.
7. The action on 9 December 1985 was described as 'historic' and 'a truly important achievement'. *U.N. Chronicle*, 23 (2), 1986. The gap between the pious condemnations of terrorism and the brutal realities was dramatically illustrated three weeks later when terrorists attacked airports in Rome and Vienna. For the UN record on terrorism, see Noemi Gal-Or, *International Cooperation to Suppress Terrorism* (New York: St. Martin's Press, 1985); L.C. Green, 'The Legalization of Terrorism', in Yonah Alexander, David Carlton and Paul Wilkinson (eds), *Terrorism: Theory and Practice* (Boulder, Colo.: Westview Press, 1979).
8. See Chapter 8.
9. See among others Flora Lewis, 'Response to Terrorism', *The New York Times*, 24 June 1985, who recommends a worldwide convention to prosecute persons guilty of terrorist acts; 'To Fight Terrorists', *Toronto Globe & Mail*, 25 June 1985, which calls for a convention to expose 'as international pariahs the states which harbour the marauders of innocents'; *The Times* (London), 10 September 1986, advocates the creation of an international commando unit within ICAO; 'There Must be Sanctions', *Washington Post*, 29 December 1988; 'No Hiding Place', *The Economist*, 7–13 January 1989.
10. Article 93 of the Chicago Convention provides that a state shall automatically cease to be a member of ICAO when it is expelled from the UN. Article 62 provides for the suspension of the voting power of a state that 'fails to discharge within a reasonable period its financial obligations'. This article has been used in the early years of ICAO and for the last time in 1971 against South Africa. (See Chapter 3).
11. J.L. Brierly, *The Law of Nations* (Oxford: Clarendon Press, 1955) pp. 98–9.
12. Edward McWhinney (ed.), *Aerial Piracy and International Law* (Dobbs Ferry, NY: Oceana Publications, 1971) pp. 21–2.

13. Charles Butler, 'The Path to International Legislation Against Hijacking', ibid., p. 32.
14. U Thant, *View from the U.N.* (Garden City, NY: Doubleday, 1978) p. 342.
15. Security Council Resolution 286 (9 September 1970).
16. ICAO Doc. 8912-C/997 C-Min LXXI/1.
17. L.C. Clark, 'Implementation of an International Enforcement System', *Aerial Piracy and International Law* (Dobbs Ferry, NY: Oceana Publications, 1971) pp. 94–6.
18. The various draft proposals and statements are contained in the minutes of the Assembly, A20 Min. ICAO Doc. 9087.
19. The need for an impartial fact-finding mechanism was shown in the Iran–Iraq conflict when both countries issued conflicting reports about civil aircraft being shot down. ('Iran reports Iraqis Attacked an Airliner', *The New York Times*, 16 October 1986.)
20. International Conference on Air Law, August-September 1973, Minutes and Documents, ICAO Doc. 9225 LC/178.
21. Gerald FitzGerald, 'Recent Proposals for Concerted Action against States in Respect of Unlawful Interference with International Civil Aviation', *Journal of Air Law and Commerce*, 40 (1974), p. 224.
22. FitzGerald, 'Air Hijacking: an International Perspective', *International Conciliation*, November 1971, p. 65; S.K. Agrawala, *Aircraft Hijacking and International Law* (Dobbs Ferry, NY: Oceana Publications, 1973); Edward McWhinney, *Aerial Piracy and International Terrorism* (Dordrecht: Martinus Nyhoff, 1987) Chapter 3.
23. ICAO Doc. C-WP/8540 (Appendix B), 22 January 1988.
24. ICAO Doc. A26-WP/29 EX/3, Appendix F.
25. Alona E. Evans and John Murphy (eds), *Legal Aspects of International Terrorism* (Lexington, Mass.: Lexington Books, 1978) p. 503.
26. Assad Kotaite, Aviation Security: Future Prospects, address to the IATA Aeropolitical Advisory Group, Montreal, September 1986.
27. Bin Cheng, presentation to the Sixth International Civil Aviation Conference of the Lloyds of London Press, Montreal, 1984.
28. Grant Wardlaw, *Political Terrorism: Theory, Tactics and Counter Measures* (Cambridge: Cambridge University Press, 1986) p. 4.
29. Ibid., p. 116.
30. Abraham Sofaer, 'Terrorism and the Law', *Foreign Affairs*, 64 (Summer 1986).
31. ICAO Doc. LC/SC-VIA WP/3.
32. 'Unilateral Actions and Sanctions', in Y. Alexander and E. Sochor (eds), *Aerial Piracy and Aviation Security* (Dordrecht: Martinus Nyhoff, 1990).
33. Letter to Editor, *The New York Times*, 28 January 1986.
34. Kenneth B. Noble, 'Lebanese Suspect in '85 Hijacking Arrested by FBI while at Sea', *The New York Times*, 18 September 1987.
35. Stephen Engelberg, 'Washington's War on Terrorism Captures Few Soldiers', *The New York Times*, 4 March 1989 and 'U.S. Convicts Arab in Jet's Hijacking', *The New York Times*, 15 March 1989.
36. North Atlantic Assembly Report, p. 34; Gal-Or, op. cit.

37. C-WP/7434, 7 December 1981 and Resolution 496 of the Security Council, 15 December 1981. See also ICAO Document 9369-C/1067, Minutes of the Council, 105th Session, 22 March 1982 and Doc 9372-C/1069, Minutes of the Council, 106th Session. Unlike their colleagues captured in Seychelles, those arrested and sentenced in South Africa were eventually freed.

38. Narunder Aggarwala, 'Political Aspects of Hijacking', *International Conciliation*, November 1971, p. 26.

39. Ira M. Shephard, 'Air Piracy: the Role of the International Federation of Airline Pilots Associations', *Cornell International Law Journal*, 3 (1), 1970; Evans and Murphy, op. cit., pp. 32–6.

40. IFALPA voted in 1983 to impose a boycott of flights to Moscow in protest against the Soviet destruction of the KAL Flight 007. Pilots from a dozen countries obeyed the order for about two weeks.

41. Andreas Lowenfeld, 'Why International Hijack Sanctions Don't Work', letter to the Editor, *The New York Times*, 5 July 1985.

42. Betsy Gidwitz, *The Politics of International Air Transport* (Lexington, Mass.: D.C. Heath, 1980) p. 102.

43. Presentation to the Aviation Security Conference, The Hague, January 1987, Conference Proceedings, International Institute of Air and Space Law, University of Leyden, pp. 120–35.

44. ICAO Doc. C-WP/8054.

45. James Markham, 'Europe's Anti-Terrorism Tied to U.S. Libya Raid', *The New York Times*, 14 April 1987.

46. Beau Grosscup, *The Explosion of Terrorism* (Far Hills, NJ: New Horizon Press, 1987) p. 276.

47. The airliner disappeared over the Niger desert on a flight from Chad to Paris. All 171 people on board were killed. A preliminary report confirmed that the explosion was caused by plastic explosives.

11: AIR TRANSPORT AND EUROPEAN INTEGRATION

1. The new liberal regime for air transport in the European Community is governed by (1) The Single European Act, 1986, which sets down the measures leading to a single market in the Community by 31 December 1992; (2) a package of Council decisions and directives, the most important being Council Regulation 3975/87, 14 December 1987, which lays down the procedure for the application of competition rules in air transport and Council Regulation 3976/87 on the application of Article 85(3) of the Treaty of Rome to certain categories of agreements and concerted practices in air transport; (3) the Commission's proposals of 19 July 1989 for a second package of measures to come into effect on 1 July 1990. For the text of 1986–7 decisions, see P.J. Slot and P.D. Dagtoglou (eds), *Toward a Community Air Transport Policy* (Deventer: Kluwer, 1989).

In addition they are two important judgements of the European Court of Justice, namely the Nouvelles Frontières case, April 1986, which held that competition rules apply for domestic and international services within the Community and the Ahmed Saeed case of April 1989 which extended these rules to services between EC states and third countries.

For basic policy statements see *Politique aérienne commune*. (Brussels, EC, Comité Economique et Social, 1985); *ECAC Policy Statement and Resolution on Intra-European Air Transport*, ICAO Doc. AT/Conf/–1P/2; *European air transport policy* (London: HMSO, 1985); *Air transport and the consumer: a need for change?* (London: National Consumer Council, HMSO, 1986).

2. Hans Raben (Director General Netherlands Civil Aviation Authority), 'Deregulation: A Critical Interrogation', in *International Air Transport in the Eighties*. A colloquium organised by the Netherlands Institute of Transport (Deventer: Kluwer, 1981) p. 4.

3. F.C. Thayer, 'A Microcosm in Need of New Approaches', *International Organization* 24 (Autumn 1971), p. 79.

4. As cited in *Airports International*, June 1989, p. 17.

5. F. Kratochwil, 'On the Notion of Interest in International Relations', *International Organization* 36 (Winter 1982), p. 6. See also F.J. Sorauf, 'The Conceptual Muddle', in C.J. Friedrich (ed.), *The Public Interest* (New York: Atherton Press, 1962).

6. *Deregulation and Airline Competition* (Paris: ICAO, 1988) pp. 38–53. The most obvious lack of enthusiasm is shown in the United States where the Department of Transport in the period 1985–7 approved six major mergers, three of which were opposed by the Justice Department as being anti-competitive. The mergers were allowed to proceed even when it was evident that they would restrict competition and result in higher fares. Even before deregulation, the CAB whose job it was to protect consumers when issuing licenses, was more interested in reducing competition and protecting 'incumbent market players'. Louis Gialloreto, *Strategic Airline Management: The Global War Begins* (London: Pitman, 1988) p. 11.

7. Barry James, 'Airlines are Weary after EC Imposes Ban on Fare Fixing', *International Herald Tribune*, 13 April 1989.

8. K.G.J. Pillai, *The Air Net* (New York: Grossman, 1969) p. 129.

9. Evan Luard, *International Agencies: The Emerging Framework of Interdependence* (Dobbs Ferry: Oceana, 1977) p. 78.

10. R.O. Keohane, 'Reciprocity in International Relations', *International Organization*, 40 (1), 1986, p. 20.

11. M. Folliot, 'Les voies et moyens de l'évolution règlementaire du transport aérien en Europe', *Revue française de droit aérien*, 57 (1), 1986.

12. Walter Hallstein, *Europe Inachevée* (Paris, 1970) pp. 225–30.

13. Address on the occasion of the 25th anniversary of ECAC, Paris, 4 December 1980.

14. O'Connor, op. cit., p. 72.

15. See E.A.G. Verploeg, *The Road Towards a European Common Air Market*, doctoral thesis, Utrecht, 1963, Chapter VII.

16. Ibid.

17. As a regional body, ECAC has a unique status quite unlike the other regional civil aviation commissions. It reports both to the ICAO Council and to the Council of Europe. Its plenary sessions are convened in Strasbourg while its secretariat is located in the ICAO Regional Office in Paris with which it works in close liaison.

18. Ernst Haas' pioneering work should be singled out in the abundant literature on regionalism and integration. He suggests three types of compromise, each indicative of certain measures of integration which would fit the pattern in civil aviation: (1) the least demanding common denominator among equal bargaining partners (as represented by the ICAO process); (2) accommodation by splitting the difference based by concessions of equal value which would fit the ECAC and (3) upgrading 'the common interest' of the parties which comes closest to the political process within the EC. 'International Integration: The European and the Universal Process', *International Organization*, 15 (Summer 1961).

19. Address by Eric Willoch at the 25th anniversary of ECAC.

20. Folliot, *Le Transport Aérien international*, p. 217 and pp. 241–2.

21. Bastiaan van der Esch, 'Main Issues of Community Law Governing Access to Air transport and Member States Control of Fares', Slot and Dagtoglou, op. cit., p. 337.

22. Frederik Sørensen (EC Commission), address to an aviation law conference, Brussels, 26 May 1989. He cited the precedent of Scandinavian Airlines (SAS) which is owned jointly by Sweden, Norway and Denmark. The most interesting aspect is the fact that two of the partners (Sweden and Norway) are not EC states but members of the European Free Trade Association (EFTA) while the third (Denmark) is a EC member which makes their airline part of the Community framework.

23. As outlined by Paul Channon, then Secretary of State for Transport, to the Scottish Conservative Party, 12 May 1989.

24. P.D. Sutherland, 'Civil Aviation: Where Do We Go From Here?', foreword in Slot and Dagtoglou, op. cit.

25. Randolph Gherson, address to a Conference on EC Air Transport Policy and Regulation, McGill University Institute of Air and Space Law, Montreal, September 1989.

26. Statement by J. Klinkenborg, vice-chairman of the Committee of Transport of the European Parliament, 13th triennial session of ECAC, Strasbourg, 1988. Doc. ECAC/13, p. 119.

27. J. Erdmenger, former Director for Transport of the European Commission, 'A New Dimension to Civil Aviation Through European Economic Integration', in *International Air Transport in the Eighties*, op. cit., p. 38.

28. ICAO Doc. AT-WP/1580 prepared for the 27th session of the ICAO Assembly, 1989. The EC Commissioner for Transport, Karel Van Miert, sounded a hopeful note when he addressed that session of the

Assembly. He said the Commission would work closely with ICAO on these issues.

29. John H. Cushman Jr, 'Open U.S. Air Market Is Proposed', *The New York Times*, 6 October 1989.
30. Dr Detlef Winter, address to the International Aviation Club, Washington, DC, 12 April 1988.
31. *Air Transport in a Competitive Market*, Economist Intelligence Unit, Report No. 3, 1986, p. 139.
32. Wolfgang Weinert, corporate strategist for Lufthansa, address to the Airline Business Conference, London, 28 March 1988.
33. As reported to the 13th triennial session of ECAC, June 1988.
34. A flag-carrier is often given a dominant voice in the airport body which allocates take-off and landing slots.
35. As quoted in *Financial Times*, 26 September 1989.
36. Wolfgang Philipp as quoted in *Aviation Daily*, 26 September 1989. The project aims to develop standard requirements for operations, communications, navigation, traffic flow management, airspace organisation, training and possibly equipment.
37. Trevor French, 'The New Europeans', *Airline Business*, February 1989. One such grouping is Trans European Airways based in Belgium. It already owns ten aircraft and hopes to acquire 15 more to be used by a group of charter companies.
38. In France, for instance, where the postal administration has a monopoly on deliveries, mail is still defined according to an 1844 statute. Lucien Rapp, 'Les sociétés de services express et le monopole postal', *ITA Magazine*, no. 35, May 1986. The situation will change when the EC Commission lays down rules for cargo and express services.

12: FLYING THE FLAG IN THE GLOBAL MARKET

1. See Michael Levine, 'Deregulation: Evidence from Eight Years of Experience', *ITA Magazine*, no. 48, March/April 1988.
2. Louis Gialloreto, *Strategic Airline Management: the Global War Begins* (London: Pitman, 1988) p. 187.
3. Ibid., pp. 152–87.
4. Daniel Kasper (former Director of International Aviation for the US Civil Aeronautics Board), 'Toward Open Skies World-wide', *Wall Street Journal*, 3 August 1987.
5. Knut Hammarskjöld, 'Deregulation: Idealism, Ideology or Power Politics?', *Annals of Air and Space Law*, 12, 1987, (Montreal: McGill University), p. 75.
6. Mancur Olson Jr, *The Logic of Collective Action* (Cambridge, Mass.: Harvard University Press, 1965) p. 37.
7. As cited by Hammarskjöld, op. cit., pp. 74–5.
8. Interview with the author.

9. Airlines Business Conference, London, 28 March 1988. British Airways sends an altogether different message in its advertising campaign on the theme 'The World's Favourite Airline'.

10. See Chris Lyle, 'Computer-Age Vulnerability in the International Airline Industry', *Journal of Air Law and Commerce*, 54 (1), 1988; Vladimir Zubkov, 'The Development of Computer Reservation Systems: The ICAO View Point', *ITA Magazine*, no. 42, March/April 1987. As an ICAO report pointed out, there are important differences among the various CRSs in existence. While advanced systems contain a common database for a number of airlines (such as the Sabre and Apollo), some others consist essentially of the internal reservation system of a single airline. New developments are taking place at a rapid pace. For example, conglomerate 'megasystems' are being developed jointly by various groupings of carriers. European carriers have two such systems – Amadeus and Galileo – while in Asia, a number of carriers have joined to create Abacus. (*Report by the Council on Study of Computer Reservation Systems*, ICAO Doc. A27-WP/50, 30 June, 1989.)

11. Zubkov, 'The Development of Computer Reservation Systems'.

12. See Barry Humphreys (UK Civil Aviation Authority), 'Different Approaches to a Common Problem', *ITA Magazine* no. 53 (January/February 1989); 'Towards Worldwide CRS Regulation', *Avmark Aviation Economist*, August 1988; *Deregulation and Airline Competition* (Paris; OECD, 1988) p. 25.

13. 'Connecting the Empire', *Avmark Aviation Economist*, October 1987.

14. Ibid.

15. Robert C. Booth, *Airline Business*, December 1989, p. 54.

16. 'International Lease Places $1 billion of Jets', *Wall Street Journal*, 12 June 1989.

17. A précis of the Court's decision (Case 66/86) was published in the *Times of London Law Report*, 13 April 1989.

18. See J.R. Chesen, *Canadian–American Air Service Negotiations: Ending the Gridlock* (Washington, J.R. Associates, 1989).

19. Jeffrey Shane (Deputy Assistant Secretary for Transportation Affairs, Department of State), address to The Wings Club, New York, 24 February 1988. See also Jacqueline Gallacher, 'Bilateral Dogfights', *Airline Business*, June 1989 and Joan Feldman, 'US Could be forced to change negotiating stance', *Air Transport World*, May 1988.

20. John H. Cushman Jr., 'US Official Warns Airlines on International Route Sales', *The New York Times*, 13 June 1989.

21. 'Finance and Leasing report', *Air Transport World*, November 1988.

22. H.A. Wassenbergh, 'The Turn of the Tide? 1978–1993', *ITA Magazine*, no. 49, May/June 1988.

23. ICAO Doc. A16-WP/7 EX/1. Sweden noted that the ambiguous draft of Article 7 reflected the difficulty of the Chicago Conference to deal with cabotage after the collapse of the multilateral framework.

24. Krasner, *Structural Conflict: The Third World Against Global Liberalism* (Berkeley: University of California Press, 1985) p. 207.

25. It has been suggested without evidence that a global airline operated

in the public interest would have avoided all the ills which have
plagued the industry with the net result of a cheaper air transport for
all. Allan McKnight, 'Functionalism and the Specialised Agencies', in
A.J.R. Groom and Paul Taylor (eds), *Theory and Practice in International Relations* (London: University of London Press, 1975) p. 170.

26. Wassenbergh, *The Turn of the Tide?.*
27. Jacqueline Gallacher, 'Going for GATT', *Airline Business*, October
    1988.
28. R.C. Van Der Maaten, 'International Air Transport and GATT', *ITA
    Magazine* no. 54 (March/April 1989).
29. Resolution of the ICC Commission on Air Transport adopted on 20
    November 1989. See Wassenbergh, 'New aspects of aviation policies
    and the future of international air transport regulation', *Air Law*,
    XIII (1), 1988.
30. The analysis of GATT principles is based on a preliminary report by
    ICAO (Doc. AT/WP 1591) prepared for the 27th session of the ICAO
    Assembly, and a GATT document MTN.GNS/W/60 (restricted), 4
    July 1989, prepared for the Group of Negotiations on Services which
    examined the applicability of GATT rules in air transport in August
    1989.
31. GATT Doc. MTN.GNS/W/60, p. 12.
32. Ibid. p. 13.
33. Kasper, *Deregulation and Globalization: Liberalizing International
    Trade in Air Services* (Cambridge, Mass.: Ballinger, 1989) Chapter 6.
34. Ibid., pp. 117–18.
35. Van Der Maaten, article cited.
36. It should come as no surprise that the developing countries steadfastly
    resisted including trade in services in the Uruguay Round of Nego-
    tiations, so much so that for a period of about one year the GATT
    Secretariat was prohibited from gathering data on the subject. Gilbert
    R. Winham, 'The Prenegotiation Phase of the Uruguay Round', *Inter-
    national Journal*, XLIV (2), spring 1989, p. 291.
37. GATT encourages the settlement of disputes through bilateral consul-
    tations. If the parties involved cannot reach a negotiated settlement,
    the dispute is referred to a conciliation panel. Only if the panel's
    recommendations are not acceptable, can the plaintiff request per-
    mission to retaliate.
38. It certainly would not be an improvement if states bypassed the
    GATT dispute settlement mechanism to retaliate on their own against
    alleged unfair trading practices. The US which threatened to do so
    against Japan, Brazil and India came under virtually unanimous criti-
    cism of the GATT's Council. Burton Bollag, 'US Target of Criticism
    of GATT', *The New York Times*, 22 June 1989.
39. Wassenbergh, 'New aspects of aviation policies'.
40. There are still eleven countries party to this Agreement.

Appendix 1

FREEDOMS OF THE AIR

First Freedom
: The privilege to fly, and carry traffic,* non-stop over the territory of the grantor state.

Second Freedom
: The privilege to fly, and carry traffic, over the territory of the grantor state and to land for non-traffic purposes.

Third Freedom
: The privilege to fly into the territory of the grantor state and discharge traffic from the flag state of the carrier.

Fourth Freedom
: The privilege to fly into the territory of the grantor state and carry back traffic destined for the flag state of the carrier.

Fifth Freedom
: The privilege to fly into the territory of the grantor state for the purpose of picking up, or putting down, traffic destined for, or coming from, third states.

Sixth Freedom
: The so-called Sixth Freedom consists of the privilege to fly into the territory of the grantor state and pick up traffic destined for, or put down traffic coming from, a third state – this traffic having been carried via the flag-state of the carrier. (This Freedom is essentially a combination of Third and Fourth Freedom rights over two sectors, the flag-state of the carrier being in the middle.)

Cabotage Rights
: Right to carry traffic between two points in the territory of the same state, usually reserved for the carriers of that state.

* traffic = passengers, freight and mail.

Appendix 2
Convention on
International Civil Aviation
(Chicago, 1944)

PREAMBLE

WHEREAS the future development of international civil aviation can greatly help to create and preserve friendship and understanding among the nations and peoples of the world, yet its abuse can become a threat to the general security; and

WHEREAS it is desirable to avoid friction and to promote that cooperation between nations and peoples upon which the peace of the world depends;

THEREFORE, the undersigned governments having agreed on certain principles and arrangements in order that international civil aviation may be developed in a safe and orderly manner and that international air transport services may be established on the basis of equality of opportunity and operated soundly and economically;

Article 1

Sovereignty
The contracting States recognize that every State has complete and exclusive sovereignty over the airspace above its territory.

Article 2

Territory
For the purposes of this Convention the territory of a State shall be deemed to be the land areas and territorial waters adjacent thereto under the sovereignty, suzerainty, protection or mandate of such State.

Article 3

Civil and state aircraft
(a) This Convention shall be applicable only to civil aircraft, and shall not be applicable to state aircraft.
(b) Aircraft used in military, customs and police services shall be deemed to be state aircraft.
(c) No state aircraft of a contracting State shall fly over the territory of

another State or land thereon without authorization by special agreement or otherwise, and in accordance with the terms thereof.

(*d*) The contracting States undertake, when issuing regulations for their state aircraft, that they will have due regard for the safety of navigation of civil aircraft.

Article 3 *bis**

(a) The contracting States recognize that every State must refrain from resorting to the use of weapons against civil aircraft in flight and that, in case of interception, the lives of persons on board and the safety of aircraft must not be endangered. This provision shall not be interpreted as modifying in any way the rights and obligations of States set forth in the Charter of the United Nations.

(b) The contracting States recognize that every State, in the exercise of its sovereignty, is entitled to require the landing at some designated airport of a civil aircraft flying above its territory without authority or if there are reasonable grounds to conclude that it is being used for any purpose inconsistent with the aims of this Convention; it may also give such aircraft any other instructions to put an end to such violations. For this purpose, the contracting States may resort to any appropriate means consistent with relevant rules of international law, including the relevant provisions of this Convention, specifically paragraph (a) of this Article. Each contracting State agrees to publish its regulations in force regarding the interception of civil aircraft.

(c) Every civil aircraft shall comply with an order given in conformity with paragraph (b) of this Article. To this end each contracting State shall establish all necessary provisions in its national laws or regulations to make such compliance mandatory for any civil aircraft registered in that State or operated by an operator who has his principal place of business or permanent residence in that State. Each contracting State shall make any violation of such applicable laws or regulations punishable by severe penalties and shall submit the case to its competent authorities in accordance with its laws or regulations.

(d) Each contracting State shall take appropriate measures to prohibit the deliberate use of any civil aircraft registered in that State or operated by an operator who has his principal place of business or permanent residence in that State for any purpose inconsistent with the aims of this Convention. This provision shall not affect paragraph (a) or derogate from paragraphs (b) and (c) of this Article.

Article 6

Scheduled air services

No scheduled international air service may be operated over or into the territory of a contracting State, except with the special permission or other

---

* adopted on 10 May 1984. This amendment will enter into force when ratified by 102 states.

authorization of that State, and in accordance with the terms of such permission or authorization.

Article 7

Cabotage

Each contracting State shall have the right to refuse permission to the aircraft of other contracting States to take on in its territory passengers, mail and cargo carried for remuneration or hire and destined for another point within its territory. Each contracting State undertakes not to enter into any arrangements which specifically grant any such privilege on an exclusive basis to any other State or an airline of any other State, and not to obtain any such exclusive privilege from any other State.

Article 9

Prohibited areas

(*a*) Each contracting State may, for reasons of military necessity or public safety, restrict or prohibit uniformly the aircraft of other States from flying over certain areas of its territory, provided that no distinction in this respect is made between the aircraft of the State whose territory is involved, engaged in international scheduled airline services, and the aircraft of the other contracting States likewise engaged. Such prohibited areas shall be of reasonable extent and location so as not to interfere unnecessarily with air navigation. Descriptions of such prohibited areas in the territory of a contracting State, as well as any subsequent alterations therein, shall be communicated as soon as possible to the other contracting States and to the International Civil Aviation Organization.

(*b*) Each contracting State reserves also the right, in exceptional circumstances or during a period of emergency, or in the interest of public safety, and with immediate effect, temporarily to restrict or prohibit flying over the whole or any part of its territory, on condition that such restriction or prohibition shall be applicable without distinction of nationality to aircraft of all other States.

Article 37

Adoption of international standards and procedures

Each contracting State undertakes to collaborate in securing the highest practicable degree of uniformity in regulations, standards, procedures, and organization in relation to aircraft, personnel, airways and auxiliary services in all matters in which such uniformity will facilitate and improve air navigation.

Article 38

Departures from international standards and procedures
Any State which finds it impracticable to comply in all respects with any such international standard or procedure, or to bring its own regulations or practices into full accord with any international standard or procedure after amendment of the latter, or which deems it necessary to adopt regulations or practices differing in any particular respect from those established by an international standard, shall give immediate notification to the International Civil Aviation Organization of the differences between its own practice and that established by the international standard. In the case of amendments to international standards, any State which does not make the appropriate amendments to its own regulations or practices shall give notice to the Council within sixty days of the adoption of the amendment to the international standard, or indicate the action which it proposes to take. In any such case, the Council shall make immediate notification to all other states of the difference which exists between one or more features of an international standard and the corresponding national practice of that State.

Article 44

Objectives
The aims and objectives of the Organization are to develop the principles and techniques of international air navigation and to foster the planning and development of international air transport so as to:

(*a*) Insure the safe and orderly growth of international civil aviation throughout the world;

(*b*) Encourage the arts of aircraft design and operation for peaceful purposes;

(*c*) Encourage the development of airways, airports, and air navigation facilities for international civil aviation;

(*d*) Meet the needs of the peoples of the world for safe, regular, efficient and economical air transport;

(*e*) Prevent economic waste caused by unreasonable competition;

(*f*) Insure that the rights of contracting States are fully respected and that every contracting State has a fair opportunity to operate international airlines;

(*g*) Avoid discrimination between contracting States;

(*h*) Promote safety of flight in international air navigation;

(*i*) Promote generally the development of all aspects of international civil aeronautics.

Article 54

Mandatory functions of Council
The Council shall:

(*a*) Submit annual reports to the Assembly;

(*b*) Carry out the directions of the Assembly and discharge the duties and obligations which are laid on it by this Convention;

(*c*) Determine its organization and rules of procedure;

(*d*) Appoint and define the duties of an Air Transport Committee, which shall be chosen from among the representatives of the members of the Council, and which shall be responsible to it;

(*e*) Establish an Air Navigation Commission, in accordance with the provisions of Chapter X;

(*f*) Administer the finances of the Organization in accordance with the provisions of Chapters XII and XV;

(*g*) Determine the emoluments of the President of the Council;

(*h*) Appoint a chief executive officer who shall be called the Secretary General, and make provision for the appointment of such other personnel as may be necessary, in accordance with the provisions of Chapter XI;

(*i*) Request, collect, examine and publish information relating to the advancement of air navigation and the operation of international air services, including information about the costs of operation and particulars of subsidies paid to airlines from public funds;

(*j*) Report to contracting States any infraction of this Convention, as well as any failure to carry out recommendations or determinations of the Council;

(*k*) Report to the Assembly any infraction of this Convention where a contracting State has failed to take appropriate action within a reasonable time after notice of the infraction;

(*l*) Adopt, in accordance with the provisions of Chapter VI of this Convention, international standards and recommended practices; for convenience, designate them as Annexes to this Convention; and notify all contracting States of the action taken;

(*m*) Consider recommendations of the Air Navigation Commission for amendment of the Annexes and take action in accordance with the provisions of Chapter XX;

(*n*) Consider any matter relating to the Convention which any contracting State refers to it.

Article 62

Suspension of voting power

The Assembly may suspend the voting power in the Assembly and in the Council of any contracting State that fails to discharge within a reasonable period its financial obligations to the Organization.

CHAPTER XVI JOINT OPERATING ORGANIZATIONS AND POOLED SERVICES

Article 77

Joint operating organizations permitted
Nothing in this Convention shall prevent two or more contracting States from constituting joint air transport operating organizations or international operating agencies and from pooling their air services on any routes or in any regions, but such organizations or agencies and such pooled services shall be subject to all the provisions of this Convention, including those relating to the registration of agreements with the Council. The Council shall determine in what manner the provisions of this Convention relating to nationality of aircraft shall apply to aircraft operated by international operating agencies.

Article 79

Participation in operating organizations
A State may participate in joint operating organizations or in pooling arrangements, either through its government or through an airline company or companies designated by its government. The companies may, at the sole discretion of the State concerned, be state-owned or partly state-owned or privately owned.

CHAPTER XVIII DISPUTES AND DEFAULT

Article 84

Settlement of disputes
If any disagreement between two or more contracting States relating to the interpretation or application of this Convention and its Annexes cannot be settled by negotiation, it shall, on the application of any State concerned in the disagreement, be decided by the Council. No member of the Council shall vote in the consideration by the Council of any dispute to which it is a party. Any contracting State may, subject to Article 85, appeal from the decision of the Council to an *ad hoc* arbitral tribunal agreed upon with the other parties to the dispute or to the Permanent Court of International Justice. Any such appeal shall be notified to the Council within sixty days of receipt of notification of the decision of the Council.

Article 85

Arbitration procedure
If any contracting State party to a dispute in which the decision of the Council is under appeal has not accepted the Statute of the Permanent

Court of International Justice and the contracting States parties to the dispute cannot agree on the choice of the arbitral tribunal, each of the contracting States parties to the dispute shall name a single arbitrator who shall name an umpire.

CHAPTER XIX   WAR

Article 89

War and emergency conditions
In case of war, the provisions of this Convention shall not affect the freedom of action of any of the contracting States affected, whether as belligerents or as neutrals. The same principle shall apply in the case of any contracting State which declares a state of national emergency and notifies the fact to the Council.

Article 93

Admission of other States
States other than those provided for in Articles 91 and 92 (*a*) may, subject to approval by any general international organization set up by the nations of the world to preserve peace, be admitted to participation in this Convention by means of a four-fifths vote of the Assembly and on such conditions as the Assembly may prescribe: provided that in each case the assent of any State invaded or attacked during the present war by the State seeking admission shall be necessary.

Article 93 *bis*

(*a*) Notwithstanding the provisions of Articles 91, 92 and 93 above:
(1) A State whose government the General Assembly of the United Nations has recommended be debarred from membership in international agencies established by or brought into relationship with the United Nations shall automatically cease to be a member of the International Civil Aviation Organization;
(2) A State which has been expelled from membership in the United Nations shall automatically cease to be a member of the International Civil Aviation Organization unless the General Assembly of the United Nations attaches to its act of expulsion a recommendation to the contrary.
(*b*) A State which ceases to be a member of the International Civil Aviation Organization as a result of the provisions of paragraph (*a*) above may, after approval by the General Assembly of the United Nations, be readmitted to the International Civil Aviation Organization upon application and upon approval by a majority of the Council.
(*c*) Members of the Organization which are suspended from the exercise

of the rights and privileges of membership in the United Nations shall, upon the request of the latter, be suspended from the rights and privileges of membership in this Organization.

Article 94

Amendment of Convention

(*a*) Any proposed amendment to this Convention must be approved by a two-thirds vote of the Assembly and shall then come into force in respect of States which have ratified such amendment when ratified by the number of contracting States specified by the Assembly. The number so specified shall not be less than two-thirds of the total number of contracting States.

(*b*) If in its opinion the amendment is of such a nature as to justify this course, the Assembly in its resolution recommending adoption may provide that any State which has not ratified within a specified period after the amendment has come into force shall thereupon cease to be a member of the Organization and a party to the Convention.

Appendix 3
ICAO Conventions Dealing With Unlawful Interference With International Civil Aviation

The Convention of Offences and Certain Other Acts Committed on Board Aircraft, signed at Tokyo on 14 September 1963, imposes upon states certain obligations concerning the return of a hijacked aircraft and its cargo and the release of the passengers and crew. *The Convention for the Suppression of Unlawful Seizure of Aircraft*, signed at The Hague on 16 December 1970, obliges states to make such offences punishable by severe penalties (Article 2). Article 7 obliges the state party in the territory of which the alleged offender is found, either to extradite or submit the case 'without exception whatsoever' to its competent authorities for the purpose of prosecution. The system of extradition established by the Convention is dealt with in Article 8, which states that the unlawful seizure of aircraft is 'deemed to be included' in any extradition treaty existing between states and which also obliges states to include the offence as an extraditable offence in every extradition treaty to be concluded between them. Last, the Convention contains provisions obliging state parties to afford one another judicial assistance in any criminal proceedings brought in respect of the offence (Article 10) and to report to the Council of ICAO any relevant information in their possession (Article 11). *The Convention for the Suppression of Unlawful Acts Against the Safety of Civil Aviation*, signed at Montreal on 23 September 1971, establishes a system of suppression that in outline is the same as that laid down in the 1970 Hague Convention. It covers a series of acts, mostly committed on the ground, which are likely to cause the destruction of the aircraft or otherwise endanger the safety of aircraft in flight. Finally, a protocol to the Montreal Convention extending the jurisdiction of states over attacks committed at international airports was adopted in 1988. It is in the process of ratification.

Appendix 4
ICAO Assembly Sessions

Interim Assembly	Montreal, 21 May–7 June 1946
First Session	Montreal, 6–27 May 1947
Second Session	Geneva, 1–21 June 1948
Third Session	Montreal, 7–20 June 1949
Fourth Session	Montreal, 30 May–20 June 1950
Fifth Session	Montreal, 5–18 June 1951
Sixth Session	Montreal, 27 May–12 June 1952
Seventh Session	Brighton, 16 June–6 July 1953
Eighth Session	Montreal, 1–14 June 1954
Ninth Session	Montreal, 31 May–13 June 1955
Tenth Session	Caracas, 19 June–16 July 1956
Eleventh Session	Montreal, 20 May–2 June 1958
Twelfth Session	San Diego, 16 June–9 July 1959
Thirteenth Session (*extraordinary*)	Montreal, 19–21 June 1961
Fourteenth Session	Rome, 21 August–15 September 1962
Fifteenth Session	Montreal, 22 June–16 July 1965
Sixteenth Session	Buenos Aires, 3–26 September 1968
Seventeenth Session (*extraordinary*)	Montreal, 16–30 June 1970
Seventeenth Session A (*extraordinary*)	New York, 11–12 March 1971
Eighteenth Session	Vienna, 15 June–7 July 1971
Nineteenth Session (*extraordinary*)	New York, 27 February–2 March 1973
Twentieth Session (*extraordinary*)	Rome, 28 August–21 September 1973
Twenty-first Session	Montreal, 24 September–15 October 1974
Twenty-second Session	Montreal, 13 September–4 October 1977
Twenty-third Session	Montreal, 16 September–7 October 1980
Twenty-fourth Session	Montreal, 20 September–10 October 1983
Twenty-fifth Session (*extraordinary*)	Montreal, 24 April–10 May 1984
Twenty-sixth Session	Montreal, 23 September–10 October 1986
Twenty-seventh Session	Montreal, 19 September–6 October 1989

Source Material

ICAO source material used in this study consists of documents (DOC) and Working Papers (WP). Each document has a serial number and a reference symbol which identifies its originating organ (that is A for Assembly followed by the session: C for Council, ANC for Air Navigation Commission, AT for Air Transport Committee, LC for Legal Committee and UI for Unlawful Interference Committee. Most of these documents are available only in the ICAO Library. Some resource documents can be purchased, such as Assembly records including resolutions and recommendations, reports and minutes of the various sessions and commissions, Council records, including proceedings and actions, reports of Council Committees and Council publications. These documents as well as others related to the activities of the Organisation, air transport studies, statistics and miscellaneous publications of a general nature are listed periodically in a catalogue which can be obtained from the ICAO Documents Sales Unit.

There are dozens of specialised aviation publications covering all aspects of the industry, the most important being *Aviation Week & Space Technology*. Other publications which are indispensable for serious research are *Air Transport World*; *ITA Magazine*, published by the Air Transport Institute in Paris, and *Avmark Aviation Economist*.

Select Bibliography

It would be practically impossible to provide a comprehensive bibliographical listing on international aviation. I have compiled the articles and books, mostly from the scholarly literature, which could be useful for further study of the various issues discussed in this book.

Akweenda, S., 'Prevention of Unlawful Interference with Aircraft: A Study of Standards and Recommended Practices', *International and Comparative Law Quarterly*, 35 (2), 1986.

Alexander, Y., et al., *Terrorism: Theory and Practice* (Boulder, Colo.: Westview Press, 1979).

Alexander, Y., and E. Sochor (eds), *Aerial Piracy and Aviation Security* (Dordrecht: Martinus Nyhoff) in preparation.

Ameri, H., *Politics and Process in the Specialized Agencies of the UN* (Aldershot: Gower, 1982).

Bertrand, M., *Some Reflections on Reform of the United Nations* (UN Doc. JIU/REP/85/9) 1985.

Brierly, J.L., *The Law of Nations* (Oxford: Clarendon Press, 1955).

Buergenthal, T., *Lawmaking in the International Civil Aviation Organization* (Syracuse: Syracuse University Press, 1969).

Button, K., and D. Swann, 'European Community Airlines: Deregulation and Its Problems', *Journal of Common Market Studies*, XXVII, no. 4, 1989.

Caporaso, J., *Functionalism and Regional Integration* (Beverly Hills: Sage Publications, 1972).

Cheng, B., *The Law of International Air Transport* (London: Stevens, 1962).

Claude, I., *The Changing United Nations* (New York: Random House, 1967).

Corbett, D., *Politics and the Airlines* (London: Allen & Unwin, 1965).

Cox, R., H. Jacobson, et al., *The Anatomy of Influence: Decision-making in International Organization* (New Haven: Yale University Press, 1973).

Dempsey, P.S., 'The Role of ICAO on Deregulation, Discrimination and Dispute Resolution', *Journal of International Law and Commerce*, 52, 1987.

Doganis, R., *Flying Off-Course: The Economics of International Airlines* (London: Allen & Unwin, 1985).

Dutheil de la Rochère, J., *La politique des Etats-Unis en matière d'aviation civile internationale* (Paris: Librairie générale de droit et de jurisprudence, 1971).

Eban, A., *The New Diplomacy* (New York: Random House, 1983).

Elmandjra, M., *The United Nations System: an analysis* (London: Faber & Faber, 1973).

Evans, A.E., and J. Murphy (eds), *Legal Aspects of International Terrorism* (Lexington, Mass.: Lexington Books, 1978).

FitzGerald, G.F., *The International Civil Aviation Organization – A Case Study in the Law and Practice of International Organization* (The 1986–7 revision of unpublished lectures at the Institute of Air and Space Law, McGill University).

FitzGerald, F.G., 'The International Civil Aviation Organization: A Case Study in the Implementation of Decisions of a Functional Organization', in S.M. Schwebel (ed.), *The Effectiveness of International Decisions* (Dobbs Ferry: Oceana Publications, 1971).

Folliot, M., *Le transport aérien international* (Paris: Librairie générale de droit et de jurisprudence, 1977).

Franck, T.F., *Nation against Nation* (New York: Oxford University Press, 1985).

Frankel, J., *National Interest* (New York: Praeger, 1970).

Gal-Or, N., *International Cooperation to Suppress Terrorism* (New York: St. Martin's Press, 1985).

Gialloreto, L., *Strategic Airline Management: The Global War Begins* (London: Pitman, 1988).

Gidwitz, B., *The Politics of International Air Transport* (Lexington, Mass.: D.C. Heath, 1980).

Goodrich, L.M., and D.A. Kay (eds), *International Organization: Politics and Process* (Madison: University of Wisconsin Press, 1973).

Gordenker, L. (ed.), *The United Nations in International Politics* (Princeton: Princeton University Press, 1971).

Haanappel, P.P.C., 'The external aviation relations of the EEC and of EEC Member States', *Air Law*, XIV (1 and 2) 1989.

Haas, E., 'Regime Decay: Conflict Management and International Organizations, 1945–1981', *International Organization*, 37(2), 1983.

Hammarskjöld, K., 'Deregulation – Idealism, Ideology or Power Politics', *Annals of Air & Space Law*, 12, 1987.

Harari, D., and J.G. Bouza, *Permanence and Innovation: the Nature of United Nations Bureaucracy* (London: Croom Helm, 1986).

Jacobson, H.K., *Networks of Interdependence: International Organizations and the Global Political System* (New York: Knopf, 1979).

Jönsson, C., 'Sphere of Flying: The Politics of International Aviation', *International Organization*, 35 (2), 1981.

Jönsson, C., *International Aviation and the Politics of Regime Change* (London: Frances Pinter, 1987).

Kasper, D., *Deregulation and Globalization: Liberalizing International Trade in Air Services* (Cambridge, Mass.: Ballinger, 1989).

Keohane, R.O., *After Hegemony: Cooperation and Discord in the World Political Economy* (Princeton: Princeton University Press, 1984).

Keohane, R.O., 'Reciprocity in International Relations', *International Organization*, 40 (1), 1986.

Keohane, R.O., and J.S. Nye, *Power and Interdependence* (Boston: Little, Brown, 1977).

Kratochwil, F., 'On the Notion of Interest in International Relations', *International Organization*, 36(1), 1982.

Krasner, S.D., *Structural Conflict: the Third World against Global Liberalism* (Berkeley: University of California Press, 1985).

Krasner, S.D., *Defending the National Interest: a Statist Approach* (Princeton: Princeton University Press, 1978).

Lahogue, R., *l'Organisation de l'aviation civile internationale (OACI) et les états du Tiers Monde*, doctoral thesis, University of Paris (Pantheon), 1976.

Lissitzyn, O.J., *International Air Transport and National Policy* (New York: Council on Foreign Relations, 1942).

Lissitzyn, O.J., 'The Treatment of Aerial Intruders in Recent Practice and International Law', *American Journal of International Law*, 47, 1953.

Lowenfeld, A.F., 'A New Take-Off for International Transport', *Foreign Affairs*, 54, October 1975.

Lowenfeld, A.F., *Aviation Law*, second edition (New York: Matthew Bender, 1981).

Luard, E., *International Agencies: the Emerging Framework of Interdependence* (Dobbs Ferry, NY: Oceana Publications, 1977).

McWhinney, E., *Aerial Piracy and International Terrorism*, second revised edition (Dordrecht: Martinus Nyhoff, 1987).

McWhinney, E., and M.A. Bradley (eds), *The Freedom of the Air* (Dobbs Ferry, NY: Oceana Publications, 1968).

Milde, M., 'Dispute Settlement in the Framework of the International Civil Aviation Organization' in *Studies in Air & Space Law* (Koln: Carl Heymanns, 1979).

Milde, M., 'The Chicago Convention after 40 Years', *Annals of Air & Space Law*, 9, 1984.

Milde, M., 'Interception of Civil Aircraft vs Misuse of Civil Aviation', *Annals of Air & Space Law*, 11, 1986.

Milde, M., 'Legal Aspects of Future Air Navigation Systems', *Annals of Air & Space Law*, 12, 1987.

Miller, J.A., *Air Diplomacy: The Chicago Civil Aviation Conference of 1944*, doctoral thesis, Yale University, 1971.

Morgenthau, H.J., *Politics among Nations*, fifth edition (New York: Knopf, 1973).

Morgenthau, H.J., *Dilemmas of Politics* (Chicago: Chicago University Press, 1958).

Nashat, M., *National Interests and Bureaucracy versus Development Aid* (Geneva: Tribune Editions, 1978).

O'Connor, W.E.O., *Economic Regulation of the World's Airlines: a Political Analysis* (New York: Praeger, 1971).

Phelps III, J.T., 'Aerial Intrusions by Civil and Military Aircraft in Times of Peace', *Military Law Review*, 17 (1), 1985.

Pillai, K.G.J., *The Air Net* (New York: Grossman, 1969).

Pitt, D., and T.G. Weiss (eds), *The Nature of United Nations Bureaucracies* (London: Croom Helm, 1986).

Prebisch, R., *Towards a New Trade Policy for Development* (New York: United Nations, 1964).

Rosenau, J., *Interdependence and Transnational Relations* (New York: Nichols, 1980).

Sampson, A., *Empires of the Sky: the Politics, Contests and Cartels of World Airlines* (London: Hodder & Stoughton, 1984).

Schanes, S.E., *International Cooperation in Civil Aviation 1945–47*, doctoral thesis, Cornell University, 1949.

Schenkman, J., *International Civil Aviation Organization* (Geneva: H. Studer, 1955).

Slot, P.J., and P.D. Dagtoglou (eds), *Towards a Community Air Transport Policy* (Deventer: Kluwer, 1989).

Sochor, E., 'Terrorism in the Sky: the Rhetoric and Realities of Sanctions', *Terrorism: an International Journal*, 10 (4), 1987.

Sochor, E., 'Civil and Military Aviation: Who Rules the Rulemaker?', *Comparative Strategy*, 7 (3), 1988.

Sochor, E., 'International Civil Aviation and the Third World', *Third World Quarterly*, 10 (3), 1988.

Sochor, E., 'L'OACI au sein de l'ONU: le fonctionnalisme et ses applications', *Études Internationales*, 19 (2), 1988.

Sochor, E., 'Deregulation Dilemma: Where is the Flag in the mega-carrier', *World Competition: Law and Economics Review*, 12 (2), 1988.

Sochor, E., 'ICAO and armed attacks against civil aviation', *International Journal*, 44 (1), 1989.

Sochor, E., 'Conflicts in International Aviation', *Conflict*, 8 (2), 1988.

Sochor, E., 'Decision-making in the International Civil Aviation Organization', *International Review of Administrative Sciences*, 44 (2), 1989.

Sochor, E., 'From the DC-3 to Hypersonic Flight: ICAO in a Changing Environment', *Journal of Air Law and Commerce*, 55 (2), 1989.

Sorauf, F.J., 'The Public Interest: the Conceptual Muddle', in C.J. Friedrich (ed.), *The Public Interest* (New York: Atherton Press, 1962).

Straszheim, M.R., *The International Airline Industry* (Washington, DC: Brookings Institution, 1969).

Taneja, N.K., *The International Airline Industry: Trends, Issues and Challenges* (Lexington, Mass.: Lexington Books, 1988).

Taylor, P., and A.J.R. Groom (eds), *International Organization* (London: Frances Pinter, 1978).

Thayer Jr, F.C., *Air Transport Policy and National Security* (Chapel Hill: University of North Carolina Press, 1965).

Thornton, R.L., *International Airlines and Politics: a Study in Adaptation to Change* (Ann Arbor: Michigan International Business Studies no. 13, 1970).

Thornton, R.L., 'Governments and Airlines', in R.O. Keohane and J.S. Nye (eds), *Transnational Relations and World Politics* (Cambridge, Mass.: Harvard University Press, 1971).

Verploeg, E.A.G., *The Road Towards a European Common Air Market – Civil Aviation and European Integration*, doctoral thesis, University of Utrecht, 1963.

Wardlaw, G., *Political Terrorism: Theory, Tactics and Counter Measures* (Cambridge: Cambridge University Press, 1986).

Wassenbergh, H.A., *Post-War International Civil Aviation Policy and the Law of the Air*, second edition (The Hague: Martinus Nyhoff, 1962).

Wheatcroft, S., *Air Transport Policy* (London: Michael Joseph, 1964).

Wheatcroft, S., *The Economics of European Air Transport* (Manchester: Manchester University Press, 1956).

Williams, D., *The Specialized Agencies and the United Nations: the System in Crisis* (New York: St. Martin's Press, 1987).

Index